CUSTOMER EXPERIENCE MANAGEMENT

Nihat Tavşan, Ph.D.
Can Erdem, Ph.D.

Customer Experience Management:
How to Design, Integrate Measure and Lead

ISBN 13: 978-1-934690-95-6

Tasora Books
5120 Cedar Lake Road
Minneapolis, MN 55416
United States of America

Per aspera ad astra

Foreword

Michael R. Solomon, Ph.D.

Every marketing student learns that the Holy Grail for an organization's initiatives is ROI: Return on Investment. However, in today's attention economy we also need to focus on another kind of ROI: Return on Involvement. Success comes to marketers who realize the customer experience isn't just everything; it's the only thing. The greatest ad campaign, the most artfully designed product, or the most finely honed supply chain mean nothing to a disappointed consumer. As Peppers and Rogers put it, "Brands have been untouchable, immutable and inflexible parts of the twentieth-century mass marketing era. But in the interactive era of the twenty-first century, enterprises are instead strategizing how to gain competitive advantage from 'brands' that create the best customer experience…"

Customer experience (CX) describes your customers' perceptions – both conscious and subconscious – of their relationship with your brand resulting from all their interactions with it over time. This book presents much of what you need to know to craft that experience. It reflects a recognition that the key to marketing success is to become consumer-centric; to appreciate what your buyer's world looks like from his or her point of view rather than yours. It also acknowledges that the organization should maintain an ongoing relationship with the customer that starts well before the point of purchase and (ideally) continues long after. Thus learning about the customer journey is like filming a movie about the buyer's life, rather than just a snapshot you take at the moment he or she makes a transaction. In other words: Don't solve the problem you have. Solve the problem your customer has.

The dawning CX era in Marketing coincides with an explosion of interest in "design thinking." The leading practitioner <u>IDEO says</u> that, "Design thinking utilizes elements from the designer's toolkit like empathy and experimentation to arrive at innovative solutions. By using design thinking, you make decisions based on what future customers really want instead of relying only on historical data or making risky bets based on instinct instead of evidence." IDEO lists the four phases of design thinking as:

1. Gather Inspiration: Inspire new thinking by discovering what people really need.
2. Generate Ideas: Push past obvious solutions to get to breakthrough ideas.
3. Make Ideas Tangible: Build rough prototypes to learn how to make ideas better
4. Share Your Story: Craft a human story to inspire others toward action

The customer journey this book describes is like an offspring of these two movements. It spans a variety of touchpoints by which the customer moves from awareness to engagement and purchase. Successful brands focus on developing a seamless experience that ensures each touchpoint interconnects and contributes to the overall takeaway – hopefully one that will keep him or her coming back for more of the "secret sauce."

Customer experience. Design thinking. Consumer journeys. All in the family, and all about consumer-centric marketing. Enjoy the journey.

www.michaelrsolomon.com
February 2018

Introduction

The goal of most businesses is to satisfy their customers. In exchange, they expect to make a profit or to receive a comparable benefit. They are aware that if they fail at this task, they will not survive long in the sea of competition. The methods that businesses use to achieve customer satisfaction have evolved significantly throughout the centuries, as you will discover in this book. Moreover, in today's digital environment, customers themselves now have a heavy hand in redefining what it takes to make them happy enough with a product or service to buy it, and then to keep coming back as loyal customers.

Too many businesses flounder because they either didn't know how to give their customers a satisfying customer experience, or else they hang onto the mistaken assumption that seeing things from the customer's viewpoint isn't all that critical to the future of their company. Businesses obviously want as many customers as possible to buy their company's offering, but it is also critical that these customers come away from the customer experience with an eagerness to purchase that brand again.

The cog in the wheel is that planning out the "ideal" customer experience is complex: Not every customer appreciates the same experience, and a brand's description of the "ideal" customer may not fit most actual customers. The reason is that a customer base is usually a mixed demographic that has a wide range of interests and priorities that make determining their psychographic and experiential preferences a nightmare. On top of that, businesses have to take into consideration what their brand offers, the size of their company, the economy, who their competitors are (and what they are doing), and the company's own marketing goals and budget.

As a result, without clear data to track customer preferences, there is little chance that businesses can even guestimate their customers projected feelings and behaviors in relation to a new product. Moreover, if companies are pulling their data from the wrong models, any "guestimate" they make could be wildly off target.

Most companies understand that what customers experience in relation to their product is THE key factor in whether or not customers will buy from them or switch to a competitor. The Oracle Customer Experience Impact Report noted that "89 percent of consumers began doing business with a competitor following a poor customer experience." [1] This shocking statistic should put every company on notice. The "customer experience" is far more than simply customer service. It covers potential customers from their very first exposure to the offering, via an ad or social media, for example, to "boundary spanners" (the sales team, in-store sales representatives and customer service), coupons and specials, and follow-up, to name a few touchpoints. Businesses have to ensure that their total experience is positive and will not send prospects running to a competitor.

But the true secret to reaching and retaining customers is to create an absolutely mesmerizing customer experience that solves their problems, answers their questions, leaves them longing to own the product or use the service, and launches them toward brand loyalty. This is Customer Experience Management and the heart of this book. Customer Experience Management is not something that a company can simply tack onto their marketing and expect it to work. Rather, it is a proactive mindset that addresses each psychological and emotional need of a potential customer as it relates to the product. If this sounds complicated or almost impossible to get right, it is—but with this book as a guide, business owners and marketers alike will discover how to achieve effective, high-impact Customer Experience.

Authors' Note to Fellow Researchers:

Our research explores a variety of perspectives on what makes customers behave the ways that they do when they come into contact with a brand offering. The applicable concepts and models we present each focus on key factors that help to explain why customers respond well to some brand-related stimuli and not to others. One of our aims is to provide academicians and researchers who specialize in marketing with a wealth of experiential data models with which to further explore the field.

Authors' Note to All Businesses:

As this book's researchers, you can trust that we have an in-depth understanding of which factors go into creating incredible brand experiences for customers. We hope to inspire businesses like yours to consider your customers' perspectives and emotions first when designing customer touchpoints for your products or services.

We can show you how to feed into their perspectives, satisfy their desire to know everything about your product that relates to them, calm their fears of being taking advantage of, and prompt them to "take the plunge" and become loyal to your brand.

This process should not be left only to your marketing or sales departments, or even to customer service. We believe that the "customer experience" should be seen as an "organizational mindset" that engages every department in your company. It should be embraced by every executive and employee and seen as a high priority.

Thus, in order to deliver tremendous customer experience, every single touchpoint that the customer interacts with across the consumption journey should be carefully thought through and designed. Delivering exceptional customer experiences needs the contribution of your entire organization— from operations to sales, finance, human resources, aftersales and so on.

Small or big, whether a service or product provider, any company can use our methodology to raise their customer experience to hold a distinctive position in the minds of customers. As a result, over time, that business will reap the benefits of customer loyalty, profitability and sustainability.

A successful "customer experience" program, like any project, starts with a vision. Its vision statement more or less resembles a typical company statement, covering the essence of positioning of the company in the eyes of the potential customer. But a "customer experience" vision statement goes much further than this: It clearly defines **what the company wants customers to feel, think and do as the result of their interaction with the brand, as compared to competing brands**, Customer experience programs have often failed because the company insists on keeping their "ego-centric" approach while simultaneously trying to adopt an "outside-in" perspective. (In an "outside-in" perspective, the company puts the customer in the center and builds its value chain out from there.) Hence, these businesses failed because they were trying to take two opposing approaches at the same time. Moreover, these businesses did not bother to consider the effects their competition had on the customer as they developed their Customer Experience plan.

Today's customers are far bolder than in the past. They no longer consider the brand to be the expert. They do intensive comparative shopping on their own and force companies to prove that they are better than another brand.

Consequently, to ensure an accurate customer experience vision statement, a company must consider its target market, customer expectancies, competition and company capabilities. When starting your CE management program, experiential research such as experiential segmentation, customer journey mapping, etc., should be performed. This is because what customers experience in the consumption stages is revealed through this type of analysis.

After completing the experiential analysis, companies can now see their market through the eyes of the experiential expectancies of the various customer segments. Hence, they can pinpoint which customer expectations they are not meeting and which their competitors are meeting. When customer experience management is done correctly, the company finds its "blue ocean"—in other words, gains actionable knowledge which shows them which options will get a specific customer segment away from the competition.

In the Customer Experience Management Initiative chapter, there is a clear walkthrough of CEM that explains how to reveal the experiential needs of customers, how to design the experiential offering to meet those needs, how to communicate the offering in an experiential way, how to lead your organization in implementing the CEM, and how to measure and monitor customer experience. We hope that this chapter will equip you with a new perspective and an arsenal of practical tools so that you can effectively enhance your customer experience.

The aim of this book is to expound upon customer experiences in a way that couldn't be explained sufficiently by early customer-experience researchers. For example, in 2003, Bernd Schmitt offered a new customer research paradigm, but, because it was such a new concept, he couldn't fully describe it, or explain how to do it or why a new research approach was needed. Since terms such as "experiential positioning" and "segmentation" had not even been coined yet, businesses that sought more effective marketing tools were left with a hint that there was a better way to engage customers, but the research didn't help them know how.

The transformative attitude that a growing number of companies today exhibit towards customer experience resembles the early steps of brand management in the 1930s. Brand management was born in those years as a response to mass production and became a key component of business success. Times changed and the market evolved. Branding had fulfilled its mission; Customer Experience is definitely the upcoming wave.

But before any company can start managing customer experiences, having a broad definition of the customer experience concept would be useful. That is where this book starts....

The models and data sources as well as the precise CEM framework that we have designed are crucial for **enabling businesses and managers to see inside their customers' heart and mind**—and consequently, to be able to better predict their customers' behavior in response to the product experiences they offer.

We know that it can be time-consuming and often frustrating to try to take an abstract concept and apply it to your company. That is why you will see boxes sprinkled throughout this book. These are "Takeaway Boxes." In them are tips for implementing the concepts and models that we have just explained. By taking the actions suggested in the Takeaway Boxes, you will be able to integrate what you have learned into your company's marketing strategy.

takeaway!

Use the suggestions in these boxes to gain practical guidelines for designing amazing Customer Experiences that will both engage your customers and position your company.

Another helpful feature of this book is its supplementary webpage, www.theCEMbook.com, which demonstrates how other companies have implemented many of the concepts described in this book. Feel free to check out the page.

If you want your business to succeed in today's fast-paced, competitive environment, you need to do more than simply glance through this book.

You need to make it your "Marketing-for-Success" Manual.

Commit yourself to enhancing the Customer Experience.

Nihat Tavşan, Ph.D.
Can Erdem, Ph.D.

What is Customer Experience?

Chapter 1

HOW DID THE CUSTOMER EXPERIENCE CONCEPT EMERGE?

C ustomer Experience has emerged during the past two decades as a distinct concept. Ensuring that the customer is satisfied has been a priority of successful businesses for centuries. Today, however, satisfying one's customer has been crystalized into a methodology, turned into a system that can be taught and duplicated. This was a necessary development because so many companies now operate on a global scale. They felt compelled to start "Customer Experience" programs in order to gain an edge over their competition. So they formed new departments to oversee their company's efforts to give their customers a positive experience, created new positions, and even recruited C-suite executives to handle "The Customer Experience." Consequently, today Customer Experience Management (CEM) is recognized as a distinct profession, complete with its own associations and certification programs.

According to a global study by Ernst and Young, customer experience is the "Number One" requisite for a brand to exist and grow.[1] A study by Accenture found that top managers of leading global companies see customer experience as their top priority.[2] Surprisingly, the Accenture research revealed that these managers also consider customer experience to be more important than both growth and profitability. A Deloitte report states that customer experience is the key to foster differentiation.[3] In a highly competitive and crowded marketplace, it is hard for companies to distinguish themselves in the minds of customers without offering outstanding experiences. These findings leave no doubt that today's businesses are in the midst of a widespread Customer Experience Movement. As a result of its 2011-2013 and 2014-2016 releases, the Marketing Science Institute suggested that customer experience is the topic of TOP PRIORITY for marketers research[4, 5] and that there is still so much more to explore about the subject. This new emerging "customer experience" concept has the business world bubbling with excitement over the ramifications.

The Evolution of Customer Interaction Eras

In order to truly understand what has triggered the paradigm shift that is expressing itself today, it is necessary to look back into the ancient social interactions of man. Early history suggests that interest in satisfying customers began after humans switched from being hunters to farming the land. Crops offered a tangible way to obtain needed foods and supplies. By trading, both parties were satisfied and over time developed a relationship. As artisan crafts and merchant businesses emerged, such as weaving and dying cloth, metallurgy and carpentry, customer satisfaction became a natural part of life as people bartered amicably for what they needed. The concept of Customer Experience was a natural outgrowth of need.

Man's understanding of "Customer" was radically altered in the 19th century by the First Industrial Revolution, which is generally noted for its steam-powered engines. This new source of power transformed product-making. The Second Industrial Revolution, marked by Ford's mass production factories, boosted human civilization forward by making product parts standardized, interchangeable and able to be manufactured faster. Henry Ford's moving assembly line was the first mass production factory in history. The Model-T automobile was first launched with several color options; it was then reduced to a single color—black. Ford had savvy reasons for doing this. The black paint was less expensive and dried faster than the other colors.[6] This reduced the cycle time and increased the total units-per-day production. The Model-T was produced at a phenomenal average of 9,500 cars per day. By 1925, more than half of the cars in the entire world were Model T's, an amazing 15 million vehicles. Mass production also positively affected the price of the car. When Ford's Model-T was first released, it cost $825. By 1927, thanks to mass production and standardization of parts, the price of a brand new Ford Model-T had dropped to $360.[7]

As more companies realized the benefits of mass production, they started establishing factories in cities. The sudden demand for labor caused a migration of workers from rural areas to the cities. Whether blue or white-collar employees, they brought their patterns of living with them. Urban living, however, severely limited the ability of these employees live the way they were used to. Factory work days averaged 10-12 hours a day plus travel time, drastically cutting into time for baking their own bread or sewing clothes. Limited space in tiny, crowded apartments made storing extra food and supplies another challenge for these new city residents. Consequently, they had to buy food and other items more frequently. This boosted the demand for goods. Soon producing and providing as many products as possible became the "success factor" for businesses. This was a "win-win" for everyone because now, with automation, products could be mass produced inexpensively and were cheap enough to be afforded by the masses. The **Production Era** was in full swing.

Companies in a variety of industries also became efficient at producing large quantities of goods at lower prices. During those years, the United States took production capacity leadership away from the UK; but producing lots of duplicate products, it turned out, was causing the buying public to become dissatisfied. Businesses soon found that customers didn't want to "have a car painted any color they want as long as it's black," as Henry Ford is often quoted as saying. Customers seriously wanted the color they wanted. Thus, the **Product Era** began. The main concern of businesses shifted from cost-leadership to product attributes in order to attract more customers. Companies began creating existing products with new attributes, such as colors, durability and style. Soon a car was not simply a means of transportation anymore, rather, it was becoming a symbol of status or personal expression for many. So, companies used marketing to showcase these attributes in order to stand apart from their competitors.

During the 1920s, companies began adopting a "Father Knows Best" approach to marketing. They saw themselves as the "father" who "knows best" when it came to their products. They knew all the features. They knew why their product was the best of its kind on the market, and they certainly did not feel that they needed to ask the customers ("the children") what they thought about the product. (Coincidentally, in the 1950s there actually was an American TV sit-com called, "Father Knows Best." In the show, no matter what scrapes the children in the TV family got into, the father had the right answers to settle the issue.[8]) During the Product Era, the company dictated the product, the benefits to the customer and the price.

Unfortunately, differentiation based on attributes was not a permanent solution to increase the demand for brands in markets, especially where there was already an excess supply and the excess supply mostly consisted of "me, too" products—in other words, copycat products. So, companies began pushing their brands via a variety of channels, such as newspaper ads, radio, billboards and direct marketing. Their main goal was to sell that brand, but during this **Sales Era**, companies were still not making what customers wanted; what they were trying to do was sell what they were already making by using intensive marketing.

There was a reason for this: During World War II, product inventory in the US dropped drastically due to severe rationing. Consequently, companies sought to convince customers to buy the products that were already in stock or those the companies could still produce under wartime guidelines. Slogans became the norm for promoting products—the catchier and more memorable the jingle, the better. Advertisers linked the products they did sell to patriotic pride and the war effort. Automobile manufacturing ceased altogether in 1942 because the raw materials were needed to produce guns, ammunition, tanks and planes. So, in order to sell the Oldsmobile sitting on their lots, General Motors used the slogan, "Firepower is our business," urging customers to identify with the troops and buy the car. An ad for Buick proclaimed, "Buick Powers the Liberator," and touted, "As of Sept. 1, 1944, Buick has built more than 55,000 Pratt & Whitney aircraft engines." Desperation to make sales soon evolved into the hard sell. [9]

By the 1950s, though, there was a definite shift away from high-pressure selling. Companies had started realizing that they were losing customers because of this practice. Some forward-thinking marketers decided that their brands should focus on satisfying the needs of customers instead of satisfying production efficiency Key Performance Indicators (KPIs). Consequently, customer marketing research took off and became as important as operations research. Quality was soon considered as critical as Quantity. This was the dawn of the **Marketing Era**.

This era lasted only a few decades. While most companies adopted a Marketing Era mindset and tried to put their customers at the center of all their marketing efforts, the competition was brutal. Moreover, it was extremely difficult during this period to acquire new customers, since almost all their prospective customers had already become customers. Once companies realized that their bread and butter was obtaining loyal customers, the Marketing Era dissolved into a new era that revolved around loyalty—the Relationship Era.

During the **Relationship Era**, which lasted from 1980-2000, marketers recognized that the various drivers of marketing needed to work together in order for marketing to be effective, given the current consumer mindset. This meant that businesses needed to integrate all aspects of the marketing/

sales process, find ways to support their employees, and start building relationships with customers. Hence, this new approach formed the hub of marketing research and implementation

The Marketing and Relationship Eras contributed a number of tools to modern businesses. The concepts of brand management, positioning, customer relationship management, etc., are the products of these latter eras. However, like sand being washed away by the ocean, these concepts are quickly becoming obsolete—one by one—as the result of today's fast-changing world.

What has survived these changes is "Customer Experience," which is the essence of today's **Experience Era**. Now businesses must be aware of and anticipate how the customer will interact with their marketing, with the product, and with the company's representatives (sales and customer service, etc.). Even more critical to a product or service's viability is how the customer feels about it, starting from the very first exposure and throughout the entire process.

Customer perceptions about products and services are now the driving factor. No longer can companies use their marketing to dictate how customers should feel. Rather, many potential customers have already made up their minds early in the marketing process because they have access through the Internet to staggering amounts of information related to that product. They rely on their own research and the opinions of prior purchasers to determine if that product is right for them. Businesses must either follow a customer-centric approach or be left behind in this Experience Era. Marketing must start where the customer is and branch out from there.

Markets are more saturated than ever before. Everything has become a brand. Being a brand, however, is not simply a privilege anymore, but a "must" to survive in today's fast-paced world. In the past, entities could capture and hold market share by developing relevant brands and by supplying standardized offerings. But in today's crowded marketplace, capturing and holding market share, requires a more aggressive strategy. Brands shouldn't rely on their personality or equity, since a new competitor may come along with better customer experiences and pulverize the incumbent, regardless of the name-recognition of the brand.

In nearly every industry, it is possible to count dozens of brands. One brand may be obviously distinct from another, but distinction is not a guarantee of customer fascination with the product or their intent to purchase. On the other hand, with today's cutthroat competition, customer experiences literally have distinction-capability. Branding is everywhere, so it is next to impossible to create differentiation through traditional approaches. This is because the customer is being assaulted every day with thousands of brands. Unlike in the past, when an advertisement was rare enough to be a novelty, today most marketing platforms are flooded with "me-too" promotions. This means that companies must think "out of the box" in order to survive and thrive—even if their "box" is among the top-tier brands on the market. Rather than using traditional marketing or "tried and true" branding methods, companies should adapt to the new set of rules and focus on Customer Experiences—because "The Age of Customer Experience" has arrived, and from the looks of things, will be around for a long while.

Shifts of Focus in Marketing

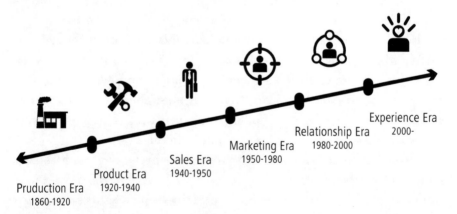

Chapter 2

WHAT EXACTLY IS CUSTOMER EXPERIENCE?

A touring circus always brings an elephant when it comes to town. In one particular village, according to legend, six blind men, who had never encountered an elephant before, try to describe it to the others by examining it with their hands. The blind man who grabs its leg says that an elephant is like a pillar. The one who gropes the trunk disputes him, insisting that the elephant is like a tree branch. The third one feels the tail and says the elephant is like a rope. The fourth one inspects its belly and says the elephant is like a wall, while the fifth one examines the tusk and says the elephant is like a solid pipe. The last one, who grabs the ear, says the elephant is like a hand-fan. The blind men keep arguing among themselves, each insisting that he is right and his friends are wrong. A passer-by witnesses this unusual discussion and decides to explain to them what an elephant really looks like. He says, "Believe it or not, all of you are right. The reason you don't agree is because each of you touched a different part of the elephant. That's why you each picture the animal differently. The truth is that the elephant has every one of those features."

Like this well-known elephant fable, a surprising number of explanations, definitions, walkthroughs, concepts, terms and models have been offered up to describe the Customer Experience concept. Unfortunately, instead of providing a clearer picture of it, this bombardment has caused misunderstandings and misconceptions. For such a young concept, wide variations like these are normal. Typically, as time passes and other competent scholars contribute their research, the concept tightens up and becomes more workable. Therefore, before discussing how to design, manage and measure customer experience, it is wise to deeply and omni-dimensionally explore what customer experience really is.

The customer experience concept involves two separate entities, each with distinct functions and needs: They are the "customer" and the "brand" (or company). Experiences are encoded by brands and decoded by customers. In the encoding phase, companies develop products or services, brand them and launch them into the market. Companies, however, are not the sole encoders, or builders, of their own brands. Their formation efforts have limitations since they do not possess total control over the image of their offerings. A company may design the logo, the colors, the product or service, delivery and other elements of the brand; but once it is launched, the customer plays a significant role in shaping its image. When customers consume a product or service, they share their experiences through online platforms or in close environments, and thus act as encoders as well as decoders. Sometimes customers contribute to the encoding phase by just consuming, instead of by commenting about a consumption experience. Consider Harley Davidson. This brand is popular among a specific group of people who have values such as freedom, adventure, discovery, and so forth; however, the brand wasn't designed to be affiliated with such a group of customers when it was first launched in 1903. William S. Harley and Arthur Davidson actually designed the bike to be a racer.[1] As time passed, a specific group of people with similar interests and values became the largest group of customers for the bike. Hence, the codes of Harley Davidson have evolved by the contribution of the customers of the brand. Not surprisingly, today's motorcycle customers don't perceive the bike at all as a racer.

Customer Experience Process

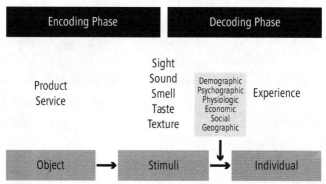

Customers, in the case of decoding, stand on the opposite side of the transmitting process when they experience any kind of offering-related stimuli, such logo color, quality, online comments, customer service calls, and so forth. They decode the brand related to the stimuli and form experiences. The mind of the customer stores this experiential knowledge and retrieves it when needed, such as at the call-to-action touchpoint. The frequency, relevancy, strength and tone of brand-related stimuli determine how long it will be stored in a customer's mind. Marketers should be aware that stimuli without sufficient supporting experiences can lose their vividness and after a while disappear from the conscious mind. Customer experience is about the set of interactions between the brand and the customer at every touchpoint. Since each encounter with the brand creates impressions and judgments, it shapes the attitudes and behavior of that customer. The final outcome of this behavior and attitude is what businesses are most interested in—since it demonstrates either loyalty or disloyalty. The customer's experience is the determinant of loyalty. If the experiences of a customer are positive, then the customer has great potential to repurchase the offering. On the contrary, if the experiences provided by the brand are negative then the customer will most likely avoid repurchasing. In other words, there is a strong positive correlation between customer experience and loyalty. Due to this relationship—especially for brands that compete in highly saturated markets—companies should focus on delivering an enhanced customer experience since it is the trigger for both attitudinal and behavioral loyalty.

Experiences are non-physical phenomena, so they shouldn't be evaluated as though they were physical; on the other hand, it is true that experiences stem from the physical world. Man perceives the world through five senses—sight, smell, taste, touch and hearing—and these senses can detect only physical things. When you look at a hot dog, you see bread, sausage and the condiments. You get it into your hand and feel the soft bread. You smell the tantalizing aroma and experience the delicious taste when you bite in. If you eat hot dogs from a street vendor in New York City every day for lunch, it could lose its meaning, but if you eat a hot dog in a stadium while watching the Yankees and Red Socks ballgame, you most probably will have a different experience due to the context. Context can also be time-related. For example, people are encouraged to read the classics three times during their lifetime—youth, middle age and old age, —because each reading will create different impressions. At each stage of life, the individual is a different person as a result of his (or her) accumulated experiences. The way he thinks will evolve and even sometimes conflict with his own past self.

Hierarchy of Offerings

Basically, the offerings of brands fall into four different categories, depending on the characteristics they possess and the value they provide. It is important to note that not all offerings require the same level of detail when demonstrating "added value." On the other hand, the proportion that companies gain as profit is highly correlated with the proportion of value provided to the customers. According to this classification system, the four categories are: Commodities, Products, Services and Experiences.

Commodities are undifferentiable offerings that are produced in nature and harvested by various means: such as, oil off wells, wheat off lands or wool off sheep. Commodities have known physical qualities, so understanding them doesn't require massive cognitive elaboration. As such, they are easily standardized. Consider oil. There are several types of oil: Grade 3 Oil, 6 Fuel-Oil, OPEC Oil, etc., and they are distinctive. API Gravity, for example, is easily distinguishable from Brent Oil or West Texas Intermediate Oil. On the other hand, a barrel of Brent Oil can't be differentiated from another barrel of Brent Oil. The price of Brent Oil is standardized globally regardless of whether that barrel was provided by ExxonMobil, Chevron or Royal Dutch Shell. Customers understand this, so, when they hear the term, "Brent Oil," it is recognizable and they don't confuse it with other oil brands despite its source.

The majority of **Products** are manufactured from commodities. Tires, for example, are made from oil. Tires, unlike most commodities, have distinctive features which separate them from other tires. They may be winter, summer or all-season tires. Their treads may be symmetrical, asymmetrical or directional, determining under which road and weather conditions that particular tire functions best. These concrete features cause customers to need more cognitive elaboration than commodities like oil do before they are satisfied that they know enough to make an informed decision about purchasing. Since the original commodity from which the product was made is standardized, that standardization carries down into the product as well, making prospective customers trust the product. This is because the products still have the raw material's determinant characteristics, such as fixed Avogadro numbers and the same number of electrons, etc., which dictate how the product functions. But it is through differences in the concrete features that customers come to trust specific brands like Michelin, Pirelli, Good Year or Bridgestone and are willing to pay different prices for the characteristics they desire.

Services, as opposed to products, are intangible offerings that are delivered on demand through a benefit proposal. Services such as dry cleaning, car repair, haircuts, etc., require much more customization than products and, hence, need more cognitive elaboration. Human beings are the resource of services. Unfortunately—or fortunately (whichever your perspective)—man is not "standardized" like products. Products have fixed qualities with minor deviations, but man by nature varies across a wide spectrum, and this diversity makes the standardization of services much harder than standardization of products. This is because man as an "input" of services is a non-determinant. Since man's characteristics as a customer cannot be standardized, there is no way to insert him as a single variable into a set marketing formula. Consider the customer who seeks legal advice. That customer will intensively explore all the options based on his own knowledge, needs and past experiences. This means that the touchpoints that the company offers must somehow consider all these possible variables in order to be effective.

Experiences, as products of the five senses, can't be imposed by an outside source but are perceived by customers. A company may develop and market its offerings in order to have a consistent but unique image in the customer's mind, but consistency doesn't guarantee solidarity. When decoding brand-related-stimuli, customers, because of their individual experiences, assign subjective and therefore different meanings to the same stimuli. Those meanings are influenced by their age, gender, income level, etc., so that experiences are unique and specific to the individual. Thus, standardizing experiences is a challenge. For example, it is impossible to invoke exactly the same experiential meaning in everyone who visits a theme park like Disneyland, but a well-designed experiential setting provides consistency to the brand experience. Due to their complexity, experiences require an intensive cognitive elaboration. In comparison to the qualities of commodities, the features of products and the benefits of services, experiences are designed to meet values, which are much less subjective than experiences.[2]

What Makes an Experience Memorable?

The intention of this next section is to explain what memory is, so that readers will be able understand what is meant by "memorable" as a major element of any concept attached to experience. Although a psychological issue, it is one of the most important concepts in understanding how experiences interact with memories and how memories are gained, stored and retrieved both long and short term.

The modus operandi that renders experiences more memorable compared to commodities, products and services, relies on man's memory mechanism. The human brain stores and retrieves long-term knowledge in either procedural or declarative memory.[3] "Procedural memory" is a type of implicit memory that aids customers in performing tasks that don't require conscious awareness.[4, 5] It frees them from massive cognitive elaboration. Adding salt into soup is performed from procedural memory. Most people, if they notice that their soup needs more salt, would just grab the salt shaker that is sitting on the table. They would not ask for a specific brand of salt—since salt is salt, and it is nothing more than a commodity. In most cases, commodities are treated with either procedural, or else semantic, memory. "Semantic memory" stores the knowledge that is associated with the meaning of an object.[6] Consider coffee. Semantic memory stores the qualities of coffee, such as: it is a liquid, it is made from beans, in most cases very hot, may be a blend of coffee types, and that Nescafe, Jacobs, Folger and Douwe Egberts are brands that offer this food. Products usually fall into this area of memory since they answer the basic question of, "What is this?"

Semantic memory, when combined with "episodic memory," constitutes "declarative memory",[7] which is the conscious part of the memory system".[8] Unlike semantic memory, episodic memory stores the knowledge that is associated with the specific events based on the contexts of who, when, where, why, etc.. [9, 10] Episodic memory is not about knowing coffee as a general concept, but about remembering a coffee drinking session, such as the time you drank coffee (last Saturday, this morning), the people you drank it with (friend, colleague, spouse), the way you sensed the coffee (vanilla aroma, dark, hot), the name of the place where you drank it (Starbucks, Costa Coffee, Caffe Nero) etc. Due to its knowledge diversity, intensity and relatively higher degree of involvement, episodic memory has a better ability than semantic memory to differentiate the phenomena.[11] Moreover, as far as surpassing a threshold,[12] it has great potential to form strong brand associations.[13] This is something companies should keep in mind when designing customer experiences. Services, on the other hand, are stored in memory through their episodic quality. This is because services are delivered over a time period and are not instantaneous. Broadly, semantic memory and episodic memory interact during the experience and when retrieving knowledge.[14, 15, 16, 17]

Content of Offerings

	Commodities	Products	Services	Experiences
Origin	Nature	Materials	People	Senses
Nature	Indifferentiable	Tangible	Intangible	Relative
Arousal	Production	Manufactory	Delivery	Perception
Proposal	Qualities	Features	Benefits	Values
Cognitive Elaboration	Minimal	Low	Moderate	Extensive
Standardization	Quite Common	Common	Hard	Very Hard
Memorability	Procedural	Semantic	Episodic	Chronesthesic
Specificity	Global	Cultural	Ritual	Personal

Episodic memory however, is the most fragile type of memory.[18] In some cases, episodic memories fade immediately after feeding into a person's semantic memory. Previous studies show that individuals may remember specific information but may not remember where they learned it.[19] You may know that Coke is a drink, Tide is a detergent or Gillette is a razor, but may not remember when you learned these facts.[20] Similarly, there are cases where customers remember the advertisement of an offering but don't remember the brand. Even worse, sometimes they attribute the advertisement to a competing brand.[21] Services that can't reach into the experiential level and can't gain enough distinction in the mind of customers, are doomed to semantic or procedural memory as a consequence of episodic memory decay.

Episodic and semantic memories have different assurance levels in terms of the knowledge they offer.[22] Semantic memory is all about knowing, whereas episodic memory is more about remembering. "Knowing" is more assertive than "remembering." It involves certainty at an emotional level that remembering doesn't have. The reason for this difference might be due to the deductive nature of semantic memory and the inductive nature of episodic memory. Despite this, both types of memories contribute to the formation of autobiographical memories, which is [an ego-centric] recollection of events, people, personal experiences, and general facts about the world.[23]

The autobiographical memory is about self; it contains knowledge regarding the past, present and prospective self.[24] The event-specific knowledge function of autobiographical memory bears vividly detailed information about specific events in the form of sensory-perceptual features or visual images.[25, 26] The details of this knowledge are subject to fading quickly; however, certain memories that affect the distance between the self and the goals, values and beliefs of an individual, resist memory decay and last longer.[27] Repetition of the experiences generates a broader frame of general event knowledge in autobiographical memory.[28] A customer, who had the first date of his life at Starbucks, will store it as event-specific knowledge, whereas a customer who had been to Starbucks multiple times will store it as one of many Starbucks experiences under general-event knowledge.

Customer experiences are mostly stored as episodic memories and some, that surpass a threshold, transpose into autobiographical memories,[29] but this does not limit the contribution of episodic memories to the procedural or the semantic memories. Thus, memories that are products of intense experiences have deeper and stronger positions in customer's mind compared to the services, products or commodities themselves.

Products and commodities are stuck with the three spatial dimensions of height, width and depth. A customer can see a mobile phone or feel the texture of wool because they have physical attributes, whereas services and experiences don't just rely on tangible qualities. We can't consider the width of a laundry service or depth of a ferry ride, thus spatial dimensions are not sole factors of services and experiences but are inputs into their formation. The featured dimension of services and experiences is "time," as the fourth dimension of the perceived world,[30] because without time flow it is impossible to talk about motion.

The relationship between time and motion had been a fundamental concern since ancient Greece. The arrow paradox of Zeno of Elea [31] seems to be the first genuine attempt to explain it. The paradox sets forth that motion is an illusion that occurs due to the summation of succeeding time pieces. When a customer parties in a club with friends, gets on a cruise line for vacation or sees the doctor for complaints, he or she spends time during the experience or service. Experiences and services are both enabled by time, but how they are stored in memory differs. Services perish immediately after their consumption; they are not saved or stored. [32, 33, 34] Experiences, on the other hand, are saved and stored as knowledge and are resistant to memory decay.[35] This memory continuity enables the person to mentally relive each part of the experience in sequence. Hence, episodic memories and autobiographical memories have the potential to provide mental time travel to man.[36]

When strong and persistent experiences are retrieved from memory, the individual enters into the same cognition mood that he experienced when going through the original event.[37] But mental time travel is not associated with semantic memory. It doesn't happen when remembering a chemical formula or one's mother's maiden name. An individual may know lots of things, such as the features of a product or the menu of a restaurant without mental time travel, but can't remember events or anticipate the future without it.[38] The mental time travel phenomenon is known as "chronesthesia" in literature.[39]

"Chronesthesia" updates the knowledge of an individual, helps him thrive and deal with changes, provides temporal and emotional dimensions to his experiences, and feeds semantic memories through the attachment of personal stories.[40, 41, 42] Thus, mental time travel possesses a meta-time trait. Besides that, it is both the source and consequence of experiences,[43] as the fox discovers in the story, "The Little Prince" of Saint-Exupéry (1943):

"…..you are still nothing more than a little boy who is just like a hundred thousand other little boys. And I have no need of you. And you, on your part, have no need of me. To you, I am nothing more than a fox like a hundred thousand other foxes. But if you tame me, then we shall need each other. To me, you will be unique in the entire world. To you, I shall be unique in the entire world…"

"…My life is very monotonous," the fox said. "I hunt chickens; men hunt me. All the chickens are just alike, and all the men are just alike. And as a consequence, I am a little bored. But if you tame me, it will be as if the sun came to shine on my life. I shall know the sound of a step that will be different from all the others. Other steps send me hurrying back underneath the ground. Yours will call me, like music, out of my burrow. And then look: you see the grain-fields down yonder? I do not eat bread. Wheat is no use to me. The wheat fields have nothing to say to me. And that is sad. But you have hair that is the color of gold. Think how wonderful that will be when you have tamed me! The grain, which is also golden, will bring me back the thought of you. And I shall love to listen to the wind in the wheat . . ." [44]

Why Are Customer Experiences Considered Subjective?

A number of years ago, Colgate launched a new toothpaste brand into the French market. The company decided to challenge the competition with a charming brand name. They decided on "Cue"; it was intriguing, easy to spell and simple. They believed that with a great typography it would quickly gain success in the market. The brand was launched, but the product didn't move from the shelves as expected. This was because Colgate didn't do its homework. When a company launches a brand, they need to study what kinds of experiences the brand name invokes in the minds of customers. Although in French the word "cue" has the same meaning as in English, Colgate neglected find out if there were other products on the market with the same name. There actually was another product named "Cue" that was well known in certain circles. In fact, brand awareness for that brand was quite impressive, but not in a positive way. Unfortunately for Colgate, that brand name belonged to a hardcore porn magazine. Consequently, when the French people saw Colgate's toothpaste brand "Cue," they immediately connected it with any experiences they had had with the magazine—even just knowing it existed—and refused to buy the toothpaste. At the end of the day, Colgate realized its mistake and pulled the "Cue" brand toothpaste from the shelves. Failure to adequately research the market—including word associations and connotations—doomed the brand. Ironically, if Colgate had launched the brand name "Cue" into the Danish, Finnish, Brazilian, Canadian or Bulgarian market, there would have been no such association between hard porn and the word, "Cue." Therefore, it should be kept in mind that the cultural context in different environments has a direct impact on the way the experiences are perceived and treated.

The French consumers absolutely refused to buy Colgate's new toothpaste due to this reason. It had nothing to do with how well the product cleaned teeth or the colors of the logo. Rather, the word, "Cue" had such a strong association with pornography that the customers could not re-associate the same name with a toothpaste product. The approach explains the failure of many brand extensions. Think of Colgate again. Apparently, its marketing department never learned its lesson from the Cue debacle. The Company decided to extend its brand—this time getting into the ready-meal market. They saw that this niche was growing exponentially and felt that Colgate could get its stake by using the power of its reputable toothpaste brand. They jumped into the project with two feet, developing recipes, designing their product line and soon launched "Colgate Kitchen Entrées." The company considered itself a multi-product entity, so adding this new product line made sense from the executive perspective. The idea was that customers would eat Colgate food at dinner and after dinner they would brush their teeth with Colgate toothpaste. Not surprisingly, the idea didn't work. The Colgate name had such a strong association with toothpaste that customers couldn't divorce themselves from it. That association made the Colgate food line unappetizing. In other words, Concept C (food) conflicted with Concept B (toothpaste) which was already strongly associated with Concept A (the Colgate brand name). Unable to disregard Colgate's toothpaste image, when customers ate the food, it made them feel as if they were chewing and ingesting toothpaste.

There is no way to avoid the fact that customer experiences are subjective. They vary from person to person, time to time and context to context. The goal of any brand should be to make the subjective experience a pleasant, positive and memorable one for as many customers as possible despite the factor of subjectivity.

Subjectivity is not limited just to brand names. Several dimensions affect the way that the customer experiences brand-related stimuli, such as online comments, interaction with the brand's employees, colors, store designs, slogans, customer service and so on. A word, symbol or other stimulus might have a very specific effect on one individual while having a totally different effect on someone else. Consider a woman who attends a funeral wearing a white dress. American and Chinese mourners would have completely different experiences if they were to observe an individual dressed all in white attending the funeral. In America it is considered disrespectful or at least poor etiquette to wear white to a funeral ceremony because death is symbolized by the color black, whereas in China, since white is the color of death, it is the perfect color to wear.

The difference in reactions between these two peoples is due to knowledge that they gained throughout their lives—a shared tradition passed down either intentionally or unintentionally to the next generation. But how did they gain this knowledge? According to Einstein, the only source of knowledge is experiences. By the way, Einstein was not first scholar to articulate this. The truth is, he is in a great company of thinkers and scholars throughout man's history who supported the idea of "tabula rasa," that the mind starts out as a blank slate.[45] Aristoteles, Avicenna, Locke, Hobbes, Berkeley and many more all shared this perspective.

Perspective...

According to this prevailing view, man builds his knowledge thanks to experiences, and, not surprisingly, the source of experiences is the five senses. People perceive the world around them through these senses, with at least one needing to be stimulated in order to trigger an experience. When encountering any situation, the stimulation of one or more senses leads to knowledge-building about that situation. The same holds true for a brand, product, service, event, person, place, and so on. However, individuals don't perceive the world exactly as it is. Rather they perceive it through filters that may alter or distort their experience, and these filters are their cultural background, gender, age, values, the region they live in, past experiences, and so forth.

As the number, intensity, frequency, content, valence and relevancy of sensory stimuli change, the nature of the experiences that the product, service or brand provides changes accordingly. A customer experience does not occur in a vacuum — it is related to all the other experiences in the life of the customer. In other words, experiences achieve valence (positive or negative) relative to the person's other experiences. Hence, the factor that makes an experience distinctive is other experiences—not the experience itself.

Competition has effects on the experiencing process of customers, since in assigning meaning to the experiential stimuli, man uses the methods of combining, comparing and relating. Thus, the experiences are processed in relation to the competition when they are converted into knowledge. Consider Singapore Airlines. This company distinguishes itself by being the youngest fleet in airline industry. It is famous for providing newly launched models from plane manufacturers for its customers. This company is also known as a trend-setter that pioneers many make-sense novelties. For instance, they introduced the first free headsets, a meal choice and free drinks in economy class in the 1970s. They also pioneered the first in-flight telephone in 1991 and the first in-flight Internet connection in 2001, to name a few of their innovations. What makes Singapore Airlines "Singapore Airlines" is not Singapore Airlines itself, but the airline companies that are not Singapore Airlines. When a customer judges Singapore Airlines, he doesn't judge it and assign value to it simply on its own merit. Rather, the customer compares his previous experiences with other airlines when experiencing a Singapore Airline flight. The experiential attributes give Singapore Airlines a competitive experiential distinction in the mind of the customer. On the other hand, low-cost flight companies like RyanAir distinguish themselves from most other airlines by delivering limited service and limited positive customer experiences at a low price. Their approach is, "you get what you pay for." It works for them because there are enough customers who are willing to have fewer amenities if they can fly from Point A to Point B for less money than what other airlines charge. Their value is based on budget rather than amenities.

Traditionally, when babies are born, boys are wrapped in blue and girls are wrapped in pink. The nursery is usually decorated in the corresponding colors as well. Tradition in many cultures dictates that the colors blue, navy and indigo are colors for boys and men, while pink, red and purple are associated with girls and women. A study by Joe Hallock,[46] which was conducted in 22 countries, shows that 35% of female participants stated purple as their favorite color whereas none of the male participants identified that color as their favorite one. Additionally, 2% of the male participants expressed red as their least favorite color; not surprisingly, none of the female participants picked red as their least favorite preference. Blue ranked as the favorite color of men at 57%. So how might companies benefit from these results? The real question is, "What is the relation between customer experience and color preferences?" Consider a company operating a pure click online retail business. If that company were to design two separate customer interfaces with different colors, one with colors that women prefer and another with colors that men prefer, do you think this would enhance the customer experience of visitors to their site? Probably.

Think of the effect of geographical factors such as regions, climate differences etc., on customer experiences. Consider a couple that enjoys spending holidays in the Caribbean. The hotel they stay in sends them free complimentary welcome drinks. Should the hotel send up hot chocolate or a cool drink? Which one would produce a more positive customer experience? Most probably the latter one. If, on the other hand, if they were spending their holiday in a mountain resort in winter, hot cocoa would be a better complimentary tool to raise positive customer experience.

Conscious versus Subconscious Customer Experiences

Attention is a limited, divided and selective brain function that helps an individual process data received through his (or her) senses. It is limited because the individual can't simultaneously pay attention to every single stimulus surrounding him. If he is reading this book, for example, he will have difficulty trying to order lunch or paint a picture at the same time without losing track of what he is reading. Attention is divided because the average person has five senses and has to split his focus among the five receptors.

When he talks on the phone, he allocates more resources to listening skills, whereas tasting a wine would cause him to shift his attention to his sense of taste. It is necessary to select which sense is critical at that moment. Attention is also selective because people tend to pay attention to stimuli that are relevant to them, such as, when they hear their name spoken, they focus on that conversation. Advertising capitalizes on this natural tendency. Its priority is to grab the customer's attention. In fact, this may be the first and perhaps the most important part of communication to transmit the message of the brand.

An Illustration of Conscious and Subconscious Mind

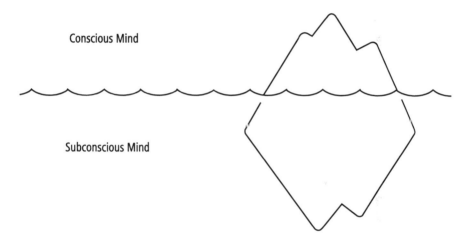

On the other hand, if a customer isn't paying close attention to brand-related stimuli, this doesn't mean that he isn't processing the sensory input. The limitations of attention may limit conscious cognition but don't totally extinguish subconscious cognition. The stimuli that the customer is exposed to—even if he is not paying close attention—are stored in his subconscious He will probably not even be aware that his mind has recorded the information. You may have heard about subliminal messaging. Hotly debated, this ethically-questionable practice inserts split-second messages into movies to promote a brand or to urge the customer to feel a particular way without him being aware of it. His conscious mind cannot pick up the message fast enough, but it is recorded in his subconscious mind and he responds positively to it nevertheless.

This method works because people can receive input faster than they can pay conscious attention to it. Normally, responding to brand-related stimuli requires consciously receiving, processing and storing brand-related knowledge, but knowledge-building is not limited to attention. Individuals receive, process and store "to be-processed-later" information from stimuli around them all day long. They are just not conscious of it all; the information that they can't pay attention to is processed at the subconscious level.

How Do Customers Become Involved with Experiences?

Customers process experiences at certain involvement levels. Some experiences require the customer to develop a high involvement level, whereas others require a low involvement level. During an experience, a customer will show a certain degree of cognitive involvement and a certain degree of physical involvement. Cognitive involvement refers to cognitive efforts such as thinking or feeling in response to the experience. Physical involvement refers to being a physical participant in an experience. As a result of there being both cognitive and physical involvement when customer experiences brand-related stimuli, a definite experiential pattern emerges.

There are four different kinds of experiences, each with a specific blend of cognitive and physical involvement. Mellowing experiences grab a low level of cognitive and a low level of physical involvement in a customer. The experience is described as "mellowing" because that experience is not the primary focus of the customer at that moment; rather, the customer sees the experience as complimentary to the experiential picture that the customer wants to be a part of. Consider a customer who is on a "chill-out" vacation in the Caribbean. The customer just wants to relax and get rid of stress. He lies on the chaise lounge, enjoys a cocktail and watches the sunset. He is "mellowing out," soaking in the experience, and expending as little mental and physical energy as possible.

Conductive experiences require customers to engage in action and be a part of the experience arousal. This experiential pattern attracts customers who seek physical involvement without much cognitive involvement. Do-it-yourself (DIY) products that don't require much cognitive effort provide this kind of experiences to customers. A customer who purchased unassembled furniture from IKEA and starts assembling it at home is having a conductive experience. By following simple assembly instructions, the customer expends little cognitive effort, but a relatively massive amount of physical effort.

Customer Experience Involvement Matrix

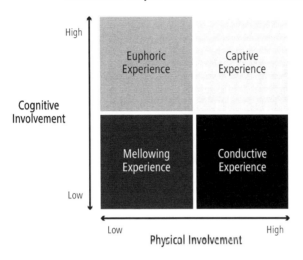

Euphoric experiences are the products of cognitive efforts, but they don't require physical involvement. Usually euphoric experiences focus on knowledge, thoughts and feelings, or challenge the customer to figure out a pattern or a puzzle. Consider a customer who watches a TV documentary about the universe. It requires a reasonable amount of cognitive effort to absorb the information and react emotionally to the beauty of a nebula or the unfathomable force of a black hole, for example; however, watching TV demands very little physical effort. Euphoric customer experiences that provide customers with cognitive satisfaction get a big slice of attention and perception from the customer. Consequently, if the cognitive level is high enough, time and place become irrelevant concepts as the customer goes through the experience.

Customers who have captive experiences surrender themselves totally to them. Their physical and cognitive involvements increase in intensity simultaneously. Because they are so focused on both levels, it is hard to break their concentration and get them to engage in unrelated behaviors, such as carrying on a conversation. This is because their complete attention and behavior is entwined with the experience. A customer who plays a video game on the computer or with an Xbox on TV, for example, will often have captive experiences because he has to allocate nearly all his behavioral and cognitive resources to the game in order to win. If companies can create this kind of synergy in their customer experiences, the customer will most likely to become loyal to the brand.

Direct and Indirect Customer Experiences

Customers may gain experience with a brand in two ways: either directly or indirectly. Direct experiences occur when a customer is in physical contact with the offering itself, whereas any interactions that are second-hand or through an intermediary, such as an advertisement, are labeled indirect. Suppose that a bank wants to promote its services. If a potential customer watches a TV commercial about the services, reads comments about the bank on social media, or happens to see a friend take that bank's debit card out of his wallet, these all are indirect experiences. They are indirect because the experiences only give the customer clues about what the offering is like; they don't give him the opportunity to judge the offering for himself. However, when that customer goes to one of the bank's branches or banks online, the customer has direct experiences, because then the customer starts to form his own judgments and feelings towards the offering through direct interaction. Similarly, seeing an advertisement for a car would be an indirect experience, but going to the showroom and seeing, touching, feeling and driving the car creates a direct experience.

All of the factors that have been discussed so far in this chapter are leading us to an understanding of what Customer Experience is. So now we have a workable definition for "Customer Experience":

Customer Experience (CE) is the sum of subjective ideas regarding a product or service that occurred at a conscious or subconscious level due to direct or indirect interaction of a customer with brand-related stimuli.

What Customer Experience ISN'T

Customer Experience focuses on all kinds of customer-related issues and corresponds to the entire experience of the customer with a brand. Customer Experience, however, as a predictor of loyalty, should not be confused with other loyalty predictors such as Customer Satisfaction or Customer Relationship Management.

Customer Satisfaction, due to its results-oriented nature, leans on the features or benefits of a specific brand. In contrast, Customer Experience provides process-oriented satisfaction outputs. The process-oriented framework of Customer Experience also should not be evaluated as part of Customer Relations Management. This is because Customer Experience goes far beyond building strong connections by analyzing recorded linear transactions. Customer Experience cannot be "freeze-dried" into single transactions. Rather, it accepts the fact that customers are subjective and respond to brand stimuli on multiple levels. In fact, it capitalizes on it.

Customer Experience Management (CEM) differs from Customer Relations Management (CRM) in several crucial ways: CRM focuses on analytics and tries to explain the customer through quantitative models. Most CRM input tracks what the customer does. In contrast, CEM scrutinizes the customer through qualities as well as quantities; in other words, it tracks and measures what customers think and feel, as well as what they do. Consequently, CEM is able to build a broader framework that is supported by measurable quantities.

All too often employees are urged to "go the extra mile" in the name of customer experience. Going the extra mile may provide a positive experience for a few customers, but delivering customer experience is not about sporadically acting heroically to make sure that one customer is satisfied, where dozens of others suffer due to the same concern. It is about consistently providing satisfying experiences and making that priority a fundamental company policy.

A common misconception is that customer experience is something that relates more to delivering great customer service. Look again at the definition of Customer Experience. Customer Experience may include customer service, but it is much broader and deeper because it deals with more than making sure that a customer is happy with the product or service. CE is interactive, reaching deep into the customer's emotions, memories and perspective on life. It requires the customer to respond on multiple levels.

Another mistaken belief is that effective Customer Experience can only be accomplished by companies that evoke extreme emotions and enthusiasm, such as theme parks, theme hotels and theme restaurants. Disneyland, Caesars Casino, Rain Forest Café and others are touted as the epitome of companies offering terrific customer experience. The truth is that every company has the potential to provide terrific customer experience. They just have to learn how. Even a small shoe store or a business supply shop can provide extraordinary customer experience through proper design and consistency. So, marketers should never assume that their business can't possibly create powerful customer experiences to boost growth and build loyalty. Any company can grow base of loyal customers through a carefully designed customer experience that integrates both qualities and quantities.

takeaway!

Never assume that customer experience is something specific only to specialized industries or big businesses. The choice before you is this: Continue with the status quo or move in the direction of truly becoming "customer-centric." If you continue relying only on Customer Satisfaction and Customer Relations Management metrics, your company or brand will be left behind. As mentioned earlier in this book, today's customers no longer blindly trust the brand. They no longer consider the company to be the expert. They have already done their homework and have researched and comparison shopped. It is your responsibility to prove that yours is the right brand to meet their needs. You need to prove that your brand is better than the competition at understanding what they really want. This is why the Customer Experience you offer has to personally connect with your potential customers—mentally, physically and emotionally. Customer Experience needs to always be relevant to their needs and values.

Why is Customer Experience that Important?

So far throughout this book we have proposed and supported, a critical concept that managing customer experience properly is the most reliable way to build loyal relationships with customers. The next question should be why is loyalty so important?

When a new market emerges, in most cases it starts as a niche with few customers. If the offering is alluring enough, the number of customers increases exponentially. At some point, the growth speed of the market decelerates and the market hits a stationary phase, which means that almost every potential customer in the market has already been converted into an existing customer, and there are not many prospects entering into the market. So the company struggles to keep their existing customer base, because the cake does not get any larger, The Market Growth Phases chart below shows how the stationary phase occurs when the market is saturated. The second graph portays this phenomenon with real life data from the global mobile communication niche.which exemplified with global mobile communication market.

Market Growth Phases

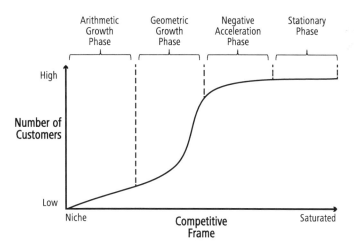

During the stationary phase, a percentage of companies panic and retreat from the battleground like leaves falling in autumn. This defoliation benefits the remaining competitors that are willing to hang on during the tough times. Consequently, those remaining get to enjoy bigger shares leading to financial growth in the short run. This flush of profit, however, may be only short-lived. As competition infensifes among the remaining companies, the profit margins get lower and retaining customers become more of a challange. In other words, some customers may prefer not to remain loyal at all.

Number of Mobile (Cellular) Subscriptions Worldwide [47] from 1993 to 2017 (in million)

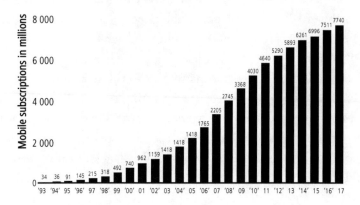

Companies invest capital to acquire customers and incur costs to retain them; however the customers may not be content with the received value and may ask for more. Mean while the competition is already offering more to persuade the customers to quit the brand. At that point, the company has to make a decision whether to do more to keep those customers or to just let them go to the competition.

Customer Lifetime Value Curve

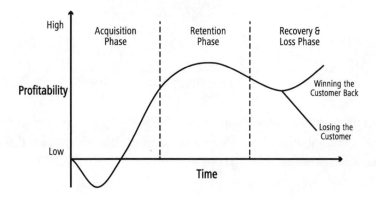

The companies, in such cases, decide on recovering the relationship or breaking it. They do it not by relying on their gut-feelings, but by relying on cost-benefit ratios, These cost-benefit ratios however, are not based on a single transaction but on both past and prospective transactions that a customer may do in his entire lifetime. In business this is called "Customer Lifetime Value" (CLV). CLV is a prediction of the face value of net profit expected from the entire relationship with a customer. The CLV is calculated through various methods and formulas, but conceptually the basic formula CLV calculation is:

$$\begin{matrix} \text{Customer} \\ \text{Lifetime} \\ \text{Value} \end{matrix} = \begin{matrix} \text{Total Revenue} \\ \text{Received From} \\ \text{Customer} \end{matrix} - \begin{matrix} \text{Customer} \\ \text{Acquisition} \\ \text{Cost} \end{matrix} - \begin{matrix} \text{Customer} \\ \text{Retention} \\ \text{Cost} \end{matrix}$$

The aim of companies is the capture the lifetime value of customers by building long-term relationships with them and strengthening the loyalty bond as long as the CLV results positively in favor of the company. In order to achieve this customer experiences they provide must be handled in a conscious manner.

How Customer Experience Paves Way to Loyalty, Growth and Profitability?

Nearly every book and article written about Customer Experience focuses on how creating great customer experience yields more profits, enhances customer loyalty and spurs financial growth. Unfortunately, how customer experience can help a company achieve these benefits has not yet been laid out in terms of economics. Companies need to know this.

In other words, we need to see how Customer Experience relates to the Science of Economics, or more specifically, to Microeconomics, which is the study of the decisions people make within specific settings. This is "Customer Experience Economics"—to coin a phrase.

To explore this, Drs. Tavşan and Erdem developed a theory to link the two. They also support and demonstrate it on a practical level with a few restaurant studies.

In Customer Experience, pleasure is frequently cited as a determining factor in customer response.   In fact, "providing pleasure" is central to the customer experience concept (Holbrook and Hirschman 1982).[48] The logic behind this concept is straightforward: People tend to seek what delivers pleasure and avoid what delivers pain, as Aristotle noted nearly two and a half millennia ago.[49] That's why defining which pain points to eliminate and pleasure points to add or sustain is the first axiom of Customer Experience Management.

On the other hand, in economics there is a concept known as "consumer surplus." Perloff defines it as follows: "The monetary difference between what a consumer is willing to pay for the quantity of the good purchased and what the good actually costs is called <u>consumer surplus</u> (CS). Consumer surplus is a dollar-value measure of the extra pleasure the consumer receives from the transaction beyond its price." [50]

Notice a key word in Perloff's definition: PLEASURE! This is the same word used to explain the focus of customer experience. The definition implicitly proffers that if the pleasure delivered to customers increases, then— Voila! The consumer surplus margin will widen consequently. Actually, this is one of the long-term objectives of all companies.

When discussing economy, it is assumed that the increase in demand causes an increase in consumer surplus margins. However, as the examples below show, demand doesn't cause an increase or decrease in consumer surplus, but rather, consumer surplus affects demand. Thus, by focusing on Customer Experience, companies can gain the capability to widen consumer surplus margins and, as a result, boost demand for their products. This is the second axiom.

And now it's time to scrutinize the above theory in terms of the practical evidence. How does delivering more pleasure and, hence, widening consumer surplus; through carefully designed experiences help companies achieve financial growth?

Strohmetz et. al. (2002) conducted a research study in a restaurant with the idea of providing small "gifts," such candy at the end of the dining experience. Their hypothesis was that offering a gift would increase the pleasure that customers perceive from that experience; this unexpected gift would have a positive impact on customers' moods, and consequently, the size of tips would increase.

According to the research design, before giving a check to a table, the waiter would pick a card from a deck and then would follow its instructions. In one scenario, the waiter would bring a tray of candies along with the check to the table and would offer each customer his or her choice of one piece of candy, and then, after each customer had picked one, just as the server was about to leave, he or she would stop and offer each customer a second piece of candy from the tray. In the control scenario, the waiter would deliver the final dining check as usual without offering any candy. The results in the "candy" scenario were exciting: Customers left 21% higher tips compared to the "no-candy" scenario. By providing added pleasure, without incurring much cost to the company, there was an average 21% increase in customer surplus.[51]

In another study conducted by Rind and Strohmetz (1999), the restaurant even didn't need any gift to get more consumer surplus margin. According to the research design, there were again two different scenarios—a "control" scenario and the "manipulation" scenario. Before delivering the check to customers, the waiter selected an instruction card as in the previous study. If the word "Message" was written on the card, then the waiter was to write the following words on the back of the check before delivering it: "We have a special dinner on (specified date). The menu will feature delicious seafood. Why not give it a try? It's great!" If the server picked a card with "No Message" written on it, then he or she was to deliver the check with no note written on it. The result was as exciting as in the aforementioned study. Something as simple as a note written on the back of a check enhanced customer experience sufficiently to increase tips. In the "message" scenario, the tips were on average 17% higher compared to the "no-message" scenario.[52]

Sometimes even a note is not needed to enhance the customer experience and boost growth; just a few words can be enough, as in the following example:

Seiter (2007) conducted an experiment in a restaurant to explore whether just a few spoken words would be enough to increase financial performance. In the study, six coins were placed in the pockets of the participating waiters—three coins were marked with ink and the other three had no mark. Before approaching a table to get orders, each waiter was to randomly select a coin from his or her pocket. If the coin was not marked, the waiter was to treat the customers no differently than normally. But if the coin was marked, then the waiter was to compliment the guests right after they gave their orders. The waiter would say something to the effect of, "Excellent choice!" If there were other customers sitting at the table, the waiter would compliment them on their choices as well. The results showed that there was a significant difference between the "compliment" and "no-compliment" scenarios. The waiters who complimented their customers triggered a 15% of increase in tips.[53]

As supported by these examples, designing and managing customer experience in a worthy and relevant way enables a company to widen their consumer surplus margin. As we have seen, in the restaurant business, this phenomenon exhibits itself through larger tips. Today, many restaurants are aware of this and incorporate this secret metric. In other words, they follow the tips! They measure the ratio of tips to total revenue, and calculate it table by table, shift by shift, and day by day. By the end of the month they have tracked their best-performing waiters, shifts and strategies by relying on this ratio. If the ratio between tips and revenue increases and maintains its higher position for a few months, then they can safely conclude that their customers feel that they are getting more pleasure in exchange for what they are paying.

These restaurants then use this metric to make important decisions, such as promoting employees, offering specials and determining the right time to raise prices.

Adding pleasure to the dining experience has been confirmed to increase tips. Assuming that higher prices also increase the amount of those tips, it follows that doing both increases the consumer surplus margin even more. Hence, restaurants can glean additional consumer surplus by slightly raising prices without leaving any money on the table—no pun intended.

1.   *The region 1 shows the current demand for an offering of Company X*

2.   *Through delivering great experience and fostering more pleasure, the company extends its consumer surplus margin (Shift 2)*

3.   *As a consequence of increases in customer experience and enhanced consumer surplus, the demand for the offerings of Company X increases (Shift 3)*

4.   *Company X responds to this increased demand either by increasing pric-*

es (Conquers Region 4A) or by delivering more quantity (Conquers Region 4B)
and achieves an increase in profitability, financial growth and loyalty

Economic Statement of Customer Experience

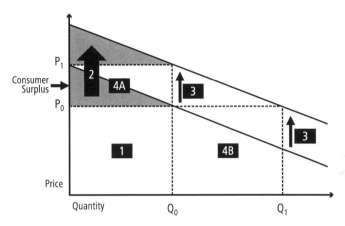

Although tipping needs to considered in a cultural context, the tip metric, compared to attitude-measuring metrics such as NPS, CSAT and so
forth, is quite different and in most cases more reliable. Because this metric
doesn't measure what people think, but rather what they actually do, it is the
"real" thing, whereas NPS®, CSAT and the others are merely projections,
and less reliable.

As supported by the restaurant examples, it can be argued that a company is capable of increasing demand to its offerings or raising price without sacrificing much demand when it delivers relevant and worthy enough
experiences. The facts drawn from this can be summed up in the following
Economy-Integrated Model:

takeaway!

Delivering an added element of pleasure in your Customer Experience effectively widens the margin of consumer surplus and enables you to: 1) increase demand for your offerings 2) increase the price level of your offerings, and 3) build a loyal customer base due to the enhanced pleasure derived from your offerings. Done strategically, this helps you achieve financial growth, profitability and customer loyalty. Another important point to remember: In the Customer Surplus diagram, although the letters P_1 and P_2 stand for "price function," you should not think of price as having only monetary value. In this case, price stands for what customers pay in exchange for an offering, so it has monetary value, but may also include the value of the experience to them. People will often pay extra for quality and for the pleasure they receive from a product or service. Moreover, customers pay to have a choice, which has worth beyond its monetary value.

Chapter 3

FACETS OF CUSTOMER EXPERIENCE

Recent literature has sparked many postulations about the "Customer Experience" concept. These postulations mainly try to define the facets. Some of them have actually hit the bull's eye, whereas others have definitely missed the mark. To help sort through the confusion, this chapter will spell out the fundamental facets of customer experience and offer some practical insights to guide customer experience enthusiasts for when they design their own customer experience program.

The facets of customer experience are: Brand, Product, Shopping, User, Price, Delivery, Consumption and Disposal. These facets may seem to overlap somewhat; and one facet may appear to intersect with another. The reason for this is that experiences cannot be divided into distinct parts or broken down into convenient components. In reality, the facets of experience themselves are neither mutually exclusive nor collectively exhaustive, but this doesn't change the fact that customer experience is a holistic concept consisting of all of these facets of experience.

Brand Experience

"Brand experience" refers to sensations, feelings, cognitions and behavioral responses evoked by brand-related stimuli.[1] There is some confusion in marketing literature about the concept of "brand experience"; it is often confused with "customer experience." Some of the literature even suggests the terms be used interchangeably, but they are not the same concept, so they cannot be used interchangeably. That is because brand experience is actually a component of customer experience.

Brand experience is the static component of customer experience. Brand experience includes design, identity, packaging, communications and environments. It does not cover processes like delivery, interactions with employees in the store, customer service or word-of-mouth testimonials by customers. Brand experience is totally under the control of the company and the company can design the logo, colors, uniforms for their salespeople, the website, a welcome message for customer service, or create the store atmosphere; but when it comes to employee and customer interactions, word-of-mouth, or an experience that a predetermined process yields, etc., the company has relatively less control. Hence, these activities are not considered to be under the umbrella of "brand experience." Brand experience can be copied; in contrast, the dynamic part of consumer experience cannot be copied.[2] The components of brand experience, such as intellectual equity, corporate culture and the customer retention know-how of the company, are embedded throughout the organization. If we consider a restaurant chain, the logo, signs and jingle might be copied or imitated by the competition, however, qualities such as customer interactions with employees and processes of delivery cannot be easily copied. The JSB Company, one of the largest entities in Japan to operate in the payment solution industry, launched a credit card for woman that has a long-lasting scent.[3] The competition can copy it and launch an aromatic card. Their card may even have a similar scent to JSB's. Having a credit card with a scent is all about brand experience. Putting legal and possible fraud issues aside, both companies are using their scented-brand experience to try to form a total customer experience. If JSB performs well above the competition, even though the competition was able to copy the card scent, this indicates that the competing brand was not also able to copy the level of customer experience that JSB had achieved. This is because, customer experience is the reflection of the attitude that a company possesses rather than the physical traits of a scented credit card or, for instance, relaxing music that treats the customer's ears while they shop. In order to gain sustainable distinctive competitive advantage, companies should support their brand experience with hard-to-copy components as part of a holistic system of customer experience.

When designing an effective brand experience, companies can take advice from semiotics. This branch of science studies how signs and symbols function as elements of communicative behavior. Hence, semiotics provides unique opportunities for companies to deliver outstanding brand experiences. In order to build a distinctive experiential brand, a company should dig into semiotics to formulate a natural-born competitive brand. Edward Barneys, nephew of Sigmund Freud who was highly involved with semiotics in collective unconsciousness studies, used semiotics to target women with his PR campaign for smoking.[4] The growth in woman smoker market attracted cigarette corporates. Philip Morris was among those, when the company first launched Marlboro brand, the target audience was woman. The filter on the cigarettes was wrapped with a dark red band and advertised to disguise any lipstick stains that might occur when woman smoked. The filter on the cigarettes was wrapped with a dark red band and advertised to disguise any lip-stick stains that might occur when woman smoked. This would have worked expect for one problem: Marlboro cigarette promised mild taste for woman, but the product failed to meet that performance benchmark; the taste was simply too strong. So the company went back to semiotics research. Which indicated that there was an experiential gap in the market: The tough, ma-cho American man was a better fit for the strong taste of Marlboro.[5] In order to fill this gap, the company switched to cues that customers naturally iden-tified as masculine, strong and tough, and soon the symbol of the "Marlboro Man" was born. Repositioning the cigarette created a positive brand experi-ence for customers, catapulting Marlboro into the ranks of the top cigarette companies.

Currently the brand experience concept is widely used in product pack-aging design. When customers shop at a store, they see similar symbols in each category—regardless of the brand. These are called "category conven-tions." All the brands in a particular category share similar cues or symbols. When designing brand experiences, companies usually make sure that their brand possesses the cues that belong to the relevant category. Otherwise customers may be confused as to which category the product belongs in and may even avoid purchasing it. For example, the dairy products category has certain cues. One of them is the color white, which is the most prominent color for this category, because it is associated with milk. Other colors in this category are blue and green. Blue suggests the sensation of cold and is a sym-bol that the product has been kept cold and is fresh, whereas green connotes nature and reminds customers that the product originated on a farm. This means that if a company decides to use all-black packaging for their dairy product, it probably won't deliver great brand experiences because that color is far outside the conventional cues for dairy. Some brands may be limited in showcasing their distinctions because of these conventions. In such cases, the company should compensate by emphasizing other elements of the cus-tomer experience. Insisting on delivering distinctive brand experiences that don't fit into category conventions runs the risk of ruining the total customer experience and consequently failing as a brand. So it is wise to pursue de-signing distinctive brand experiences that don't sacrifice customer relevancy. Building brand experiences that are relevant to customers and distinct from the competition—without sacrificing category conventions—should be the motto in designing brand elements.

Another important fact to know about brand experience is that delivering outstanding brand experience is not a guarantee of delivering outstanding customer experience. A company may deliver an amazing brand experience, but fail to deliver positive customer experience and lose customers to the competition. Here is a personal experience that illustrates this: "It was mid-spring, a few years ago. The air had become mild, the rains were almost gone and there were more bright sunny days. This reminded me that it was time to switch from winter to summer tires. I telephoned the tire service to get appointment and I was told to come in on Saturday afternoon at 1:30. The tire service I regularly go to offers their customers a special deal: They will store your winter tires in summer and your summer tires in winter. Customers just needed to call for an appointment to get their tires switched. I arrived on time, but my tires were not there. Apparently, they were still in the storage warehouse, which was about five minutes away. I was not upset about this. Given how many people were in line ahead of me, I was sure the tires would be here by the time it was my turn. I walked into the waiting lounge and was impressed. The facility had every amenity, creating an incredible brand experience. There were tables with colorful signs promoting their tires and services, corporate-colored chairs, complimentary snacks, drinks in cups with the brand logo, a billiard table, a ping pong table, a TV with a wide range of channel options, and much more. It was clear that the brand experience had been carefully designed. I sat down and enjoyed my coffee. Forty minutes later, I was still there, waiting patiently, but I noticed that the employee in charge of my car was missing. A bit worried, I asked around and discovered that he had left to go to the warehouse. Ten minutes later, the employee showed up with my summer tires. I thought the delay was because there had been a mix-up at the warehouse, but that was not the case. By asking why it took so long to get my tires, I unintentionally activated the detonator, and the gloomy man began to unburden himself. He complained that the factory warehouse had just sent over a truckload of tires and he had to help unload it, which was why I had to wait so long. Then I asked him why the warehouse sends the truck out on Saturday, since everyone knows that most people go shopping and do errands on the weekends. The man sighed and answered that his service department had contacted company headquarters several times and asked them not to make tire deliveries on the weekends, but the factory warehouse continued to do so at the cost of sacrificing customer experience. I asked, "Don't you think delays like this negatively impact customer satisfaction?" The guy shrugged and said, "Sure, but what can we do?" As soon as he posed this rhetorical question, a fellow employee interrupted and said to him, "How can you be so calm about this? Customers who experience delays are definitely not as calm as you are. I hear how frustrated and angry they get—and they have a right to be! We feel bad for them. On the other hand, management is oblivious because they don't deal directly with customers. We deal with them. We're the ones whose hands are on the tires and ears are on the customers." The employee was right. The company may have delivered absolutely outstanding brand experience, but they failed miserably at delivering positive customer experience. All they had to do was schedule deliveries of their tires at a time that would not hold up customers whose only chance to get their tires switched was on the weekends. After this incident, I had to shake my head at the irony when I heard that this 'market leader' tire company announced in 2015 that they had started a 'customer experience' program."

Product Experience

Product experience is the result of an encounter between a customer and a product. Customers expect meaningful experiences from products. Anything less than that could create a negative perception of the product and the company as well. These encounters, as noted earlier, can occur either directly or indirectly. In the direct form, consumers interact physically with the product itself; in the indirect form, customers do not physically interact with the product, but rather gain experiences through advertisements or word-of-mouth. Indirect experiences often act as a teaser which convinces the customer to seek direct interaction with the product. Often after indirectly experiencing a product in an advertisement, by word of mouth or on the Internet, the potential customer may visit the website or the store to gain direct experiences before possibly purchasing. This marketing phenomenon is known as "showrooming." The test-drive service that car brands provide is one of the older ways of providing direct product experience to customers. The judgments, preferences and behaviors of customers are formed by a blend of direct and indirect experiences with a product. Companies struggle to provide exceptional product experiences for their customers, since these types of experiences are a major instrument for enabling companies to differentiate themselves from competitors.

In order to enhance the product experience, companies should fulfill the needs of the customer in an unconventional way. One Japanese company, Yanko Design, won the coveted Red Dot Design Award for creating a butter pack with a knife-shaped cap. To further enhance the experience, they embedded one of four delicious aromas in the cap itself: honey, chocolate, strawberry or peanut. When customers opened the pack, they instantly owned a scented butter knife for spreading and enjoying their butter.[6]

Similarly, BMW is one of the savvy brands that focuses on delivering outstanding product experience—and, by this, ensures a total customer experience. BMW takes the experiential expectancies of the target audience into account when designing their cars. Since sound is one of the key variables that affect product experience when a customer is planning to purchase a car, the car companies should fine-tune the experience based on the expectations of the customer. For example, in their Mini, they try to create an exciting and playful experience; consequently, the exhaust sound of the car is designed to create an impulsive and sporty product experience. In contrast, BMW's 7-series is designed to be absolutely quiet because a 7-series driver wants to own an exclusive environment that is totally controlled by him or her. For that reason, the sound isolation of the 7-series is designed to be at maximum level. Similarly, the door-closing sound of BMW is an outcome of careful research and design and was not left to chance. BMW, knowing the impact that the door-closing sound has on the buying decisions of customers, carefully designed that sound to impress prospective customers in the showroom atmosphere.[7] The seatbelt warning sound is another aspect of the product experience that BMW pondered on. Instead of the aggressive, persistent dinging used by Nissan or other brands, BMW has installed gentler tones to remind riders to fasten their seatbelts, replacing an annoying experience with a more pleasant one. BMW has taken the product experience even a step further, recognizing that what customers smell is as important as what they hear. The scent of leather upholstery was selected out of hundreds of upholstery options to provide a more outstanding product experience for customers.

Several product traits give customers cues about a product and thus play a role in the formation of their product experience. One of these cues is the material of the product. If a laptop is made of metal as opposed to plastic, it will influence a customer's opinion as to the quality and durability of the computer itself. This perception is separate from the fact that, inside, both computers are exactly the same. Nevertheless, a metal case has a significantly more positive effect on quality and performance perceptions in customers. Apparently, customer response has had a reciprocal effect on the manufacture of these products, since the majority of computers are now made to look like metal, but are, in reality, plastic.

Another smart example of product experience is Firebox's unique concept for getting kids to enjoy washing their hands and taking baths. The company created several vegan soap bars that looked like the actual Game Boy and SNES cartridges that children insert into their video game players. Soon after, the company also introduced soaps that were perfect replicas of PS3 & 4, NES and SNES, Sega, and Xbox game controllers.[8] By using them while washing hands, children can pretend that they are playing the game. The product experiences with these soaps thrilled the children and convinced them to wash their hands willingly. Meanwhile, their parents enjoyed not having to remind them to wash.

There is a fairly new phenomenon known as "product unboxing." It is a "product experience" sharing activity that has grown out of the social media mindset. It is one step up from fans taking a selfie while holding their newest digital gadget to prove to their friends that they now own one. With product unboxing, customers purchase a product, videotape their experience unpacking it, and then post it to YouTube or another online video platform. The anticipation and excitement of getting, for example, the newest Apple phone or tablet after waiting in line for six hours to purchase it, in their minds, should be shared with the world—just as they freely share other precious moments in their lives.

Ease of use is another aspect of the product experience that companies need to keep in mind. Hard-to-use products indeed have the potential to create frustrated customers. This is especially true for non-tech-savvy customers. If a product is complicated to operate, a percentage of customers will opt to switch to a brand that is simpler to use. Similarly, hard-to-open thick plastic packaging that is designed to prevent theft in stores is immensely frustrating to customers. Customers usually want to conveniently open what they buy. They don't want to struggle for several minutes to get the package open. This type of packaging creates a negative product experience that has nothing to do with the product itself. When designing products, companies need to think about ease of opening, ease of installation, as well as application and storage for the products that they offer.

Product experiences can be strong determinants of behavior. In China, where air pollution in the large cities is a serious health hazard, customers are willing pay for access to fresh air. This is a case where the product and the experience are deeply intertwined. Vitality Air is a brand that provides bottled fresh air. As strange as it may seem, there is a growing market for air that comes in a can or bottle. The air is collected from two Canadian fresh-air sites: The town of Banff, which lies near the glacial peaks of the Canadian Rocky Mountains, and Lake Louise, an emerald lake "crowned by white-tipped mountains."[9] Vitality Air also sells oxygen, and to appeal to even more people, offers three flavored varieties: strawberry, grape and beer.[10] Thus, this example demonstrates that even air can be differentiated when providing relevant experiences.

Shopping Experience

Visiting a retail store or a mall affects the perceptions of customers and thus contributes to the formation of customer experience. Customers look forward to exciting experiences during shopping and any favorable shopping experiences they have result in behavioral responses, e.g. purchasing and sharing the purchasing experience; Both of these have the potential to increase revenue for retailers. Therefore, focusing on the enhancement of shopping experiences should be one of the priorities for companies. Many retail businesses understand that shopping experiences are also a great tool for enabling them to differentiate from their competition.

The first foot-falls of awareness about the shopping experience echoed in the early 1980s with the expansion of McCarthy's Marketing Mix 4 P's[11] to 7 P's. The experience-intensive focus by brands had caused marketers to re-evaluate the mix and increase the number of P's to seven. Called "The 7 P's of Service Marketing," they added People, Processes and Physical Evidence to the original Product, Price, Promotion, and Place, emphasizing that the shopping experience did not occur in a vacuum.[12]

Retailers today employ various methods to provide outstanding and distinctive retail experience to customers. The <u>Adidas</u> store in Champs-Élysées is one of the great examples of how to provide such a memorable shopping experience. The experience begins as the customer steps into the store. Resembling an R&D lab rather than a regular store, it is filled with "high tech" equipment. Customers can use touch screens to view the latest high-fashion Adidas shoes. Very hands-on, customers can opt to design their own personalized trainers. An Adidas employee accompanies each customer along their shoe-creation journey. Customers start by jogging on a rectangular platform behind a virtual jogger shown on the screen. While running on the platform, the characteristics of their feet are analyzed through sensors beneath the runway. After the jogging session is over, the customers head to an interactive screen, on which they design other characteristics such as color, tread, etc. This screen is not a touch screen; rather, the customers simply move their fingers in the air in front of the screen to trigger the shoe modifications. Following the design phase, the customers get to see their assembled personalized trainer on their foot through a "magic" mirror. At that moment, the customer has the option of ordering the trainers. [13]

Another great example of shopping experience is what HomePlus (HomePlus is an affiliate of Tesco) did in Korea. The company was tired of being the Number 2 store in the country. They realized that the key to becoming Number 1 was not to add more stores, but to change the customer's shopping experience. They sought a way to bring their store to where the people were, and chose the subways as the ideal location. Instead of opening new physical stores, they took pictures of the products on their shelves, made giant copies and mounted the pictures of their store shelves on the walls of the subway. Very busy Korean customers could now walk by and use their smart phones to take pictures of the products they wanted to buy. The products would be added to their virtual shopping cart. Once they paid, their purchases would be shipped immediately to their home. HomePlus had transformed the shopping experience by turning customer wait time at the subway station into shopping time. The brand gained a new reputation as the store that is the most convenient and most accommodating to the customer. Customers loved that they could do all their shopping while going to or from work and never have to take time out to go into a store. [14]

This maneuver by HomePlus, triggered HomePlus's greatest competitor, Emart, to retaliate with a sales-boosting move of its own. Emart (The Walmart of Korea) had noticed that sales at their 141 stores dropped drastically during the lunch hour. They came up with a novel idea to solve this recurring problem that would give their customers incentive to come to the stores during this lull. Since most of their customers had smart phones, Emart designed a giant outdoor 3D QR code that customers could scan using their phones. This QR code would only work during the lunch hour, between the hours of 12 noon and 1 pm, when the sun hit the device at the correct angle to cast shadows in the shape of the code. After scanning the code, customers would then go to the Sunny Sale mobile home page on their phone, receive a coupon and select the products they wanted to buy. Their purchases would be delivered to their residence. Sales during the lunch hour zoomed up 25%. Emart accomplished its mission—by making the shopping experience fun, exciting and very convenient. [15]

How a company sets up its customer shopping experience directly influences the feelings, cognitions and physiological responses of the customers. This affects their perceptions of the brand. Amazon is one brand that has rephrased its business model to capitalize on customer perception. The brand started operations as an online "click" brand more than a decade ago with incredible success. In 2016, Amazon decided to invest in a brick and mortar operation; it opened stores where customers can see the actual products, grab them off the shelves and leave the store without having to wait in line for the cashier to ring up the items. Called <u>Amazon Go</u>, it lets customers scan in the Amazon Go app on their smart phones as they walk into the store. Amazon's "Just Walk Out" technology uses sensor fusion and deep-learning algorithms to know when a customer takes a product from the shelf. The customer may either place it in a shopping bag or cart or carry it. The item is automatically added to the virtual shopping cart on the app. If the customer happens to change his mind and puts the product back on the shelf, then the product is removed from the virtual cart. There are no cashiers or cash registers. The customer just selects the items and goes. As the customer leaves the store with the products he decided to purchase, Amazon automatically charges the customer's Amazon account and the total shows up on the customer's smart phone app. [16] By combining the latest technology and keeping an ear to the heart of the customer, Amazon has already gained an extraordinarily large base of loyal customers and consequently boosted profits.

Creating outstanding shopping experience, though, is not always about big companies with big budgets: it is about having a visionary outlook. For example, Pike Place Fish Market in Seattle, WA, is one of those small entities that has built outstanding customer experience and attracts thousands of customers from across the US.

Watch out for low flying fish! Being at Pike Place Fish Market is a fun experience because the employees themselves are having fun while doing their jobs. It is lively and noisy with laughter and employees enthusiastically calling out to each other. Once an employee helps a customer select a fish, he tosses it across the room to the person who will weigh it, wrap it and complete the sale. They involve customers in the action as well, like catching fish thrown at them or touching a 6 ft. octopus. This empowering attitude rubs off on the customers who leave there not just with fish, but with a happy, memorable experience. This little market still operates locally in Seattle, but by embracing what a true "shopping experience" is, it has engaged customers worldwide. [17]

User Experience

User Experience mainly focuses on the experiences that arise as the result of the virtual interactions between the customer and the offering. The popularity of user experiences has been growing exponentially among designers, as noted by Shedroff[18] and Garrett[19]; today, most companies create user experience for virtual offerings, such as online stores, websites, online libraries, applications and mobile phones.

The user experience initially sprouted its shoots in the early 80's, with the inception of devices with customer interfaces. The most influential model for user experience had been the Technology Acceptance Model (TAM), postulated by Davis in 1989. This model was applicable when companies promoted a new technology. It showed how perceived ease of use and perceived usefulness play a significant role in convincing customers to adopt the offering.[20] This early model, however, proposed a very utilitarian approach and totally disregarded the hedonic needs of customers. In other words, it ignored the role that seeking pleasure plays in the user's decision-making process. Later, both the hedonic aspects and the utilitarian aspects, (such as colors, text font, icons, navigation aesthetic, etc.,) were considered in user experience literature and practice.

In order to deliver outstanding Customer Experience, the User Experience facet must address usability, content, information architecture, visual design and interaction design. User experience, due to its technological nature, provides relatively easier solutions for collecting data from customers. Tools such as Click-Through-Rates, Heat Maps, A/B Design Comparison, etc., provide companies with abundant opportunities to measure and enhance the user experience they provide. User experience, however, is not the whole story for brands when it comes to delivering gorgeous total customer experience. The following anecdote is a perfect illustration of how user experience is only part of the process. One of this book's authors was at a meeting with a C-suite member of one of the leading online retailers who shared his own user experience. The executive's wedding anniversary was right around the corner and he decided to buy his wife a dress. In order to kill two birds with one stone, the executive decided to get the dress from a major competitor. That way, he could both get a present for his wife and gain some insight into how his competitor created their user experience. He entered the website, filled out the registration form with a fake name and looked for a dress. Here is what he said: "When I went for the search results on the first page, I was quite impressed. The page numbers I surfed were relevant and the relevancy dropped gradually. It was quite obvious that the algorithms working behind the interface were great. They traced my electronic footprint and offered me products that I didn't even know I really needed. The site navigation worked impeccably. With a few clicks I handled the purchase—a size "S" blue dress with a bargain price—all was great. Two days later, the product was delivered within the estimated delivery time. I opened the box to repack the dress into a velvet box for my wife. I quickly checked the quality of the product and it was exactly as described on the website. As I was folding it into the velvet box, though, I noticed a serious problem: the size. Instead of a small, they had sent me an "XL." It felt like some kind of joke. I could return the item and ask for a refund or a replacement, but tomorrow I had to give a gift to my wife! In any case, the company that provided me with such outstanding user experience had failed to deliver a positive customer experience. Later I searched on the Internet for comments about the company. Yes, there were multiple reviews about their delivery failures. At first glance, the competition had appeared to be a step ahead of us on delivering excellent user experience, but it seemed to fall behind in the race of delivering total customer experience." This story doesn't have a happy ending either for the husband, who has to explain things to his wife, or for the competitor, since the user experience they provided didn't result in an outstanding customer experience.

A well-designed user experience creates solid trust in the company; however, if there is a break in the chain from marketing to delivery, the company risks losing that customer. Companies need to verify that every silo is actually functioning in harmony if they want their user experience to create customer loyalty.

Price Experience

Price experience refers to the contribution of the price variable to the total consumption experience that a customer passes through. Price is a great but a seldom considered tool when providing experiences; it actually provides opportunities for brands to distinguish themselves from their competition. The price of an offering communicates cues about its nature. For example, an extremely low price may cause customers to feel negative about a brand, since a low price often has the connotation of low quality even if the quality of the product is high; on the contrary, high price is more often associated with high quality. It should be noted, however, that enhancing the experience that the customer passes through is not solely about regulating the price level of the offering. Rather, in some cases an anticipatory approach might be needed to achieve it.

Customers are quite familiar with special discounts, giveaways and the advantages that product bundles offer, so that conventional pricing strategies are far from effective in forming differentiated price experiences. Rather, companies should adopt an experiential pricing strategy that provides exceptional pricing experiences for customers.

Stock-exchange type pubs are a great example of how to design outstanding pricing experiences. Reserve Bar Stock Exchange is this type of pub. Located in London, it is famous for providing "Unique Price Experience" to its customers.[21] The pub is situated in Europe's biggest financial district. What makes this pub different from other pubs is its unique and distinctive pricing experience. Drinks in this pub do not have fixed prices; instead, the demand for the drinks determines the prices on a real-time basis—just the way it happens in stocks. "Effectively, if someone buys three beers, then the price of that beer will rise and the price of others will decrease. The more popular a drink is, the more expensive it will be—it's market economics."[22] Also there is a bell, just like at the real stock exchange. Customers start purchasing drinks at the sound of the bell, and the drinking period continues until the closing bell. In the case of a price crash, sirens are sounded like the real thing, but, unlike the stock exchange, these sirens indicate good news, since they mean that the price of a drink has seen the bottom. Customers follow the sliding stocks monitors that show the price of each drink and the price trends. If a patron prefers a particular drink, it is worth keeping an eye on it because, if demand is low, he might be able to buy it for as little as half off. [23]

There are places all across Europe like this pub. In these businesses, customer demand determines the price; in other words, customers are contributors and determinants of the pricing function. This resembles an auction pricing strategy, but due to the fun this model provides, customers return back to their homes with memorable and relevant experiences.

When designing products, companies too often neglect the experiential facet of the pricing function. The price in fact is not counted as a component of the customer experience in most organizations, but is seen as a sole and separate economic function. However, with the rise of customer experience, the classical utilitarian approach to price should be supported by a more hedonic view. This way companies can increase their potential to deliver outstanding customer experience.

Delivery Experience

Delivery experience plays a significant role in the formation of total customer experience. Delivery experience, like price experience, tends to be neglected by companies. The raison d'etre offered by bussinesses is that they can only be profitable if they genarete revenue; consequently, these companies tend to focus on the earlier stages of consumption—the ones that bring in revenue—and may not pay enough attention to the delivery of their offerings. However, delivering what is promised in the promised condition and on time is vital to enhancing the customer experience and gaining loyal customers. Companies should avoid a solely revenue-generation focus. For example, when a customer orders a product from an online store, the retailer should deliver the product on time and in the condition promised. In order to enhance customer experience, the company may give out a tracking number so that the customer can know when to expect the delivery, or send a SMS to notify the customer and make him feel relaxed and confident about his purchase and its delivery. These steps go far to spur customer loyalty and, in fact, have become industry standards—especially for online retailers.

If a company wants to be ahead of the competition, it should find distinctive ways to enhance the delivery experience the way Amazon does. This brand has started offering an amazing delivery experience through drones. When a customer needs a product urgently, he can opt for Amazon Prime Air delivery service. The product that the customer purchased is delivered to the home of the customer by a drone in thirty minutes or less. This delivery system is being tested in countries such as the U.K., the U.S., Australia and Israel with packages that weigh up to five pounds, and the geographical scope is being expanded daily.[24]

Amazon ensures that its reputation for excellent delivery service is maintained with this new innovation; the delivery is trackable the entire way and displayed on customers' smart phones or tablets. It can be tracked down to the very second.[25] Thus the anxiety of wondering when it will arrive is lifted from their shoulders. Amazon Prime Air really is "out-of-the-box" thinking—no pun intended. Companies that use such experiential delivery systems are not limited to Amazon. In New Zealand, Domino's Pizza is testing pizza delivery by drones. China's Internet retailer JD.com also has a fleet of drones for its deliveries.[26]

Different segments of customers expect different delivery experiences. Some customers want to be a proactive part of the value stream. Tracking the package and eagerly waiting for the delivery is part of the excitement of purchasing. Others are not concerned that the delivery experience be effortless. As a matter of fact, they want to participate in the delivery process. Do-it-Yourself products mainly address this segment and IKEA, as an iconic Do-it-Yourself brand, provides such a delivery experience. In Ikea stores, customers choose the product they want to buy, note the storage location code and get the box off the shelf themselves. Later, at home they unpack it and assemble it, becoming the final part of the delivery. Outstanding customer experience is even stronger when it has a well-designed delivery experience.

takeaway!

Suppose that you have called your friends over to play a game of Taboo. Your friends have all arrived, but you realize that you had forgotten to buy the game. No problem. Just order it through Amazon Prime Air. The product will be in your hands within 30 minutes. Sounds fantastic, doesn't it? This service can also be a life-saver for companies that run out of critical supplies during a seminar or a repair shop that needs a specific product for a customer. If Amazon has it in stock at one of its Prime Air fulfillment centers, it can be delivered quickly by drone.

Consumption Experience

Consumption experience refers for the experiences that arise as a result of using, applying or having an offering. A customer who takes a taxi from point A to point B consumes the travel service from catching the cab at point A until getting out of the cab at point B. That constitutes the consumption experience with the taxi. Similarly, when a customer decides to eat a frozen dinner at home, from the moment he gets it out of freezer and pops it into the microwave until he finishes eating, he gets a consumption experience.

Consumption experiences, like other facets of customer experience, contain both utilitarian and hedonic elements. At a restaurant, for example, the consumption experience has utilitarian outcomes, such as nourishment, gaining energy to operate one's body, gaining vitamins to support one's immune system and so forth. The same consumption experience has hedonic outcomes as well, such as the aroma, taste and appearance of the food, the recognition cues perceived from the waiter, lively conversation with friends or colleagues, etc. In fact, whether one eats a birthday cake or sole bread, Kobe beef or lentil soup, Pule cheese or Cheddar cheese, the body reads all of these as fats, carbohydrates or proteins. In functionality, there is little utilitarian difference between Pule cheese and Cheddar cheese, since both have similar nutrition. However, a pound of the first one costs $600, but the same size piece of the latter one is only $4. Despite the utilitarian similarity, there are people who prefer eating Pule cheese rather than Cheddar. The impetus lying behind the irrational consumption of such an expensive cheese is emotions. By the way, although irrationality sounds negative, it is not negative at all. It is de facto—a matter of fact. It is a fact that people behave both rationally and irrationally. They are both utilitarian and hedonic. Do people marry for just utilitarian reasons or have children simply for government benefits? Is having children and allocating resources to them in return for love something rational? Even if it sounds irrational, many people have children and nearly all do it for hedonic reasons. Consequently, rational thinking is not the sole driver that gives direction to human behavior. There will always be customers who are willing to pay premium for unique and exceptional consumption experiences, and they do it to meet their hedonic experiential expectancies.

Benihana is one of those companies that deliver outstanding consumption experience to their customers. This restaurant chain serves customers in Japanese style at over 70 restaurants across the globe. The restaurant is known for reflecting the teppanyaki cuisine culture of Japan. Teppanyaki is a traditional Japanese cooking device that consists of a large earthenware pan, which is heated to high temperatures. Today's modern teppanyaki is a large rectangular stainless-steel cooking surface attached to a long table. Guests sit with their plates around the table leaving one side free for the chef to cook. The chef, after welcoming his customers, starts cooking while performing amazing tricks. He rapidly juggles and twirls knives, and tosses a raw egg into the air with the flat side of his knife, catching it behind his back—never breaking it. Or he might flip the egg into a basket, into his pocket or even catch it in his hat—all effortlessly. He might build and burn a volcano made of onion rings, all while preparing the various meats and vegetables for the guests' meals and expertly placing them on their plates. During the dazzling performance, the chef spontaneously interacts with the guests. He might even toss a piece of meat at them to catch in their mouth. Each experience is unique and memorable.[27]   A few years ago a dear friend of the authors was visiting from Austria. While they were making plans for dinner, he insisted they should go to a Benihana restaurant, adding, "I always go to Benihana if there is one in the city I'm traveling in." It was clear that the consumption experience that Benihana provides had generated a loyal brand tribe member. Delivering outstanding consumption experience is a vital facet of delivering outstanding customer experience and, as in this case, fosters loyal customers for the brand.

Disposal Experience

In general, a customer passes through three major stages when interacting with a product or service: buy, use and dispose. Most companies focus mainly on the "buy" and "use" stages and tend to disregard the "disposal" stage. However, the disposal experience is an important facet of the total customer experience. A related misconception shared by many businesses is that products are disposed of but services are not, due to their intangible nature. Believe it or not, services are disposed of, but in a different way than products. To picture product disposal, imagine drinking a beer and disposing of the glass into the recycle bin, or using up Eau de Toilette and putting the container into the garbage. Surprisingly, the disposal experience of a product actually contributes to the shaping of the total customer experience. Think of it this way: The disposal process prompts the customer to make a mental note to either replenish the supply of that product or, if dissatisfied with it, to look for another brand. In other words, the disposal experience is a precursor to further action—either to seek out another customer experience with that same brand or to hunt for a replacement.

How about services? How does one develop a disposal experience regarding a service? HangerPak, which was designed by Steve Haslip, is a great example of a service disposal experience. The pack is designed to be used by online clothing retailers. When a customer buys a shirt, blouse or tee-shirt, for example, the retailer ships the product in a HangerPak. When the customer unpacks the HangerPak, he instantly owns a durable paper hanger and can use it in his closet. Normally, when a customer receives the article of clothing he purchased, he disposes of the packaging it was delivered in because he has no use for it. In contrast, the HangerPak transforms the Disposal Experience into a meaningful and memorable one. The customer saves the hanger, but gets more than simply a hanger. Every time he uses it, he is reminded of the brand and how thoughtful the company was to give him a free hanger to use over and over again. The hanger communicates the brand on a personal level because it is occupying a spot in the most private place in the house—the bedroom. Hence, it becomes a personalized message from the brand to the customer. HangerPak has transformed a product experience into a service experience and even in the disposal phase creates meaning for the customer.[28] Both service and product businesses can take a lesson from this innovative company and focus on all three stages of the customer experience to gain competitive advantage for their brand.

Capri-Sun is another brand that popularized the disposal experience. In the 1990s, one of its commercials showed a little boy at a concert who wants to see a popular singer in his private room, but he can't get past the bodyguards. The boy then drinks a Capri-Sun that he has taken out of his backpack. He blows into the empty container to inflate it and then stomps on it, creating a loud blast to get attention. The star's bodyguard is startled and confused by the noise, long enough for the boy to sneak into the star's room. The disposal experience shown in the commercial boosted sales almost immediately. People bought packs of Capri-Sun, enjoyed the drink and then exploded the juice packs. It became the rave and even grabbed the attention of newspaper columnists, some of whom wrote articles about the phenomenon and the ensuing "sound" pollution.[29]

The disposal experience does not always have to be a way to discard the used product. Rather, especially with the modern customer being concerned about protecting the environment, disposal could mean transformation. Previous studies have shown that some customers prefer to recycle either the used product, the packaging it came in, or both. Thus, companies should take reuse experiences into consideration when developing products.[30] Turning an empty food can into a flowerpot or repurposing wine bottles into vases are great examples of upcycling. Customers who recycle tend to be imaginative. They might look at the large empty box that their dishwasher came in and cut square holes in it and decorate it up to make a playhouse for their children. The recent trend of upcycling, which means reusing disposable material in creative and functional ways, seems to be an offshoot of the recycling concept.[31] This trend signals that the contemporary customers pursue meaningful disposal experiences and, through providing it, companies have potential to outperform their competition.

takeaway!

If your touchpoints are not relevant to your customer, he or she might assume that your offering is not relevant either. How you approach your customer, the value that you provide and your offerings' relevancy will either reinforce what you are trying to say or cancel it out.

How to
Manage
Customer
Experience

Chapter 4

THE CUSTOMER EXPERIENCE MANAGEMENT MODEL

When companies try to manage their Customer Experience one piece at a time, it becomes a daunting task. This is because there are so many moving parts to keep track of. While the CE team is focusing on one aspect, others tend to get out of control. Moreover, many CE components are interrelated and don't function well by themselves. So, unless there is a dynamic overview of the entire process, or a solid management program in place, brands risk being less than successful in designing an exceptional customer experience.

The best way to elevate and enhance a brand's customer experience is to implement "Customer Experience Management" (CEM). This refers to designing, tracking and optimizing the processes and interactions that a company provides to meet the experiential needs of customers, all while aiming to generate sustainable business value. The ultimate goal of CEM (sometimes referred to as CXM) is to transform the company into an agile customer-focused organization—thus reaping the fruits of loyalty. [1, 2, 3] In order to achieve this goal, a company should develop a strategy that puts the customer in the center and takes customer brand interactions into consideration at every step of the plan.

Customer Experience Management is a holistic system that includes all the components shared in the two previous chapters and respects the intrinsic value of each one. At the center of it all is the customer. Being customer-centric is the only way to create experiences that take into account the customer's perspective, immediate response and potential behavior toward a brand's product or service. As mentioned earlier, most marketing used to be ego-centric, where the business boasted its brand and tried to arm-twist customers into buying and loving what they purchased. Today's customer would rebel against that kind of treatment. Instead, a company should develop a CEM strategy that puts the customer in the center and builds out from there. The objective should be to meet the needs and exceed the expectations of the customer at each touchpoint. Customer Experience Management is effective because it allows the customer to be subjective within the framework of each direct and indirect touchpoint. By being sensitive to the customer, the management program will increase customer satisfaction, foster loyalty and encourage brand advocacy.

takeaway!

The following model, created by Dr. Can Erdem and Dr. Nihat Tavşan, shows how all the components of Customer Experience Management fit together. With it, you will be able to judge where your brand's strengths and weaknesses are. Even more importantly, it will help you target where you need to focus more energy and resources in order to make your customers' experiences with your product or service exceptional.

The Erdem-Tavşan CEM Model (below) shows how the key components of Customer Experience relate to one another; it also delineates how companies can tweak what they are doing now to improve effectiveness. The questions asked at each level of the model force CE leaders to think seriously about the specific objectives they are trying to achieve. Hence, they can easily see what changes they need to make so that their customers get a much better experience, thus fostering attitudinal and behavioral loyalty.

Customer Experience Management reaches beyond knowing how frequently customers buy an offering, which purchase channel they prefer, which media they follow, and so on. CEM makes a note of these quantitative metrics, but it goes even further. It seeks out qualitative metrics by capturing customer emotions and thereby is able to deliver offerings that are both relevant and valuable to them.

This Customer Experience Management Model consists of seven components distributed onto four hierarchical layers. **The Cognizance Level** is the first step. It is the starting point through which a company aims to understand which experiences customers pursue and why. If a brand ignores or is simply unaware of what is important to the customer they are trying to serve, they will never connect with the customer enough to convince that customer to start a relationship with the brand.

Cognizance has multiple meanings—all of which are relevant to what a company needs to find out about their customers before marketing their product or service. Cognizance means "awareness, realization, knowledge, notice, perception, observation and range or scope of knowledge." It also means taking heed, paying attention and scrutinizing. All of these variations of meaning involve taking conscious action to gain information. Observing, paying attention, noting key points, being aware of the little things and realizing their significance all increase the range or scope of knowledge that a company can collect about the customer's perspective and behavior. Cognizance then requires a degree of scrutinizing in order to ensure comprehension.

The Erdem - Tavşan Customer Experience Management Model

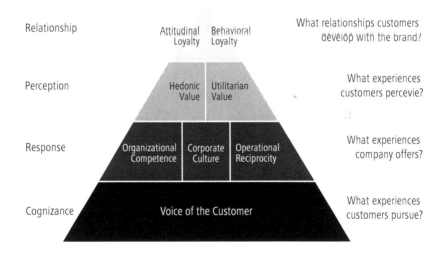

In the Erdem-Tavşan CEM model, the first level, "Cognizance," consists of the "Voice of the Customer." By listening to the Voice of the Customer, a company will get critical answers about what types of experiences potential customers pursue, how they feel about the offering and how they feel about the company, as well as the competition. There are several ways to gain access to the Voice of the Customer: Companies can use reviews, surveys, polls, focus groups, boundary spanners and online communities, etc. Businesses should not ignore the significance of the voice of even one customer. Customers use powerful avenues to express their opinions. They want to be heard by companies. They implicitly or explicitly are telling companies what is important to them when they plan to buy. The way to give customers a phenomenal experience is to listen to what they are saying and to incorporate that into the product or service touchpoints. Thus, in the context of Customer Experience Management, the "Voice of the Customer" start where the customers actually are—not at the point where the product is marketed.

The Response Level of the CEM Model stands for the capability of the company to close the experiential gap. The "experiential gap," refers to the "disconnect" between what companies assume about customers based on their own corporate perspective and what customers are actually feeling, thinking and doing. The touchpoints for any offering must integrate as much of the customer's viewpoint as possible.

In order to be able to provide a sound response to the voice of the customers, companies need to orchestrate three major functions that operate "behind the scenes" of the Customer Experience: Organizational Competence, Organizational Climate and Operational Reciprocity. Organizational Competence refers to existing skilled human capital that is responsible for delivering the intended experiences to the customers. This is the first component of the Response Level on the Model. If the needed skills are not immediately available within the company, HR can be called upon to bring in the right talent. Organizational Climate, as the second component of the Response level, refers to conditions or an atmosphere in the workplace that may encourage or discourage correct responses to the voice of the customers. Corporate culture is a strong determinant of the organizational climate; other factors such as industrial conventions, national culture and external economic conditions have indirect influence on organizational climate. Those in charge of Customer Experience Management need to honestly evaluate whether conditions exist within the company that are detrimental to achieving proactive and satisfying responses to the voice of customers. Operational Reciprocity refers to capabilities of production, operations, processes, suppliers and channels that the company will use delivering designed experiences to customers. All three of these "Response" elements need to be correlated in order to properly respond and engage the Voice of the Customer.

The Perception Level refers to how customers perceive the brand. Customers gain either utilitarian or hedonic values from experiences. As noted earlier, utilitarian values are about functionality, whereas hedonic values are about pleasure. Wine consumption, whether in a luxury restaurant or at home, provides the same utilitarian value, since in both places the nutrition facts of the wine do not vary. In contrast, the hedonic value gained during each consumption occasion does vary. Enjoying the thrill of tasting a new brand of wine in a cozy winery with close friends is different from drinking a glass of the same brand of wine in a kitchen by oneself. Utilitarian values are mostly about the results, whereas hedonic values are mainly based on experiencing the consumption journey through the process-oriented nature of pleasure-seeking.

Companies need to be aware of which kinds of values their product or service triggers in customers. Usually it is a blend of the utilitarian and hedonic, because it is logical to buy a product that meets a need, but customers cannot divorce themselves from their own emotions when they purchase. In fact, in most cases, the more hedonic values a product triggers, the more emotions are involved and the more likely customers will feel drawn to make the purchase.

The Relationship Level explains the nature of the bonds between the customers and the company. Depending on their consumption experience, customers start to develop a relationship with the product or service. That relationship may be triggered indirectly via advertisements, or by observing a friend, relative or online contact's experience with it. Or it may be triggered directly while the customer goes through the consumption. The bonds have four variables: content, strength, valence and frequency. Content is a measure of the caution or eagerness that the customer is displaying toward the product or service. It also measures the trust the customer has in the brand based on how trustworthy the company has demonstrated itself to be. Strength measures whether the relationship between the customer and the product is strengthening or weakening. Valence describes how attracted the customer is to the product. In other words, it stands for the degree of attachment or detachment. Frequency measures whether the customer seeks out experiences with this product over and over again or if his relationship pattern diminishes over time.

The bonds that develop between customers and products are interpreted by companies as proof of loyalty. Loyalty has two facets: Attitudinal and Behavioral. Attitude refers to sum of the ideas that a person has toward an object, whereas behavior is the outward or physical expression of that individual's attitude. The main distinction is that behaviors are explicit, which means they can be observed by others, while attitudes are implicit, meaning that they can't be observed by others but are only sensed by the individual himself. The concept of loyalty can be at both attitudinal and behavioral stages. <u>Attitudinal loyalty</u> refers to the state of mind that causes a customer to lean toward the repurchase of a product or service.[4] <u>Behavioral loyalty</u> refers to the act of repurchasing regardless the customer's attitude.[5] Behavioral loyalty can be observed and interpreted, whereas determining the presence of attitudinal loyalty is far more complex because is it not directly observable and can only be inferred.

Customers develop a state of loyalty or disloyalty as a sum of experiences obtained at the buying, using or disposing stages of the consumption process. This happens through a natural feedback process: Initially the consumer experiences an internal or external need. The arousal of need triggers stress.[6] Since stress causes the customer to be uncomfortable or agitated to some degree, it is a natural reaction to want to get rid of the stress, so he seeks a solution.[7] From then on, the customer directly or indirectly interacts with products or services that have possibility of satisfying his need. He may have already formed attitudinal loyalty toward a particular brand. This, however, does not guarantee behavioral loyalty for that same brand. For instance, a customer may be attitudinally loyal to Brand A, but due to budget constraints may not be behaviorally loyal to Brand A. He instead becomes behaviorally loyal to Brand B (i.e. repurchases) because of its more affordable price. Hence loyalty is a key factor to be considered when assessing a customer's relationship with a brand.

These four levels in the CEM Model are part of a process that goes from Cognizance to Relationship. Think of an arrow starting with the first level and pointing diagonally up the triangle to the fourth level. One cannot skip levels or start with, say, Perception because each level builds on the one below it. Recall at the beginning of this chapter the point that all the Customer Experience components from Chapter 2 are interrelated and cannot be activated individually. It is critical that any company wanting to implement this CEM model study the model carefully in order to understand where each part fits in.

In order to implement this model, companies need to start at the bottom—researching to discover the "Voice of the Customer" In other words, they need to find out what their potential customers are thinking. Then they can work their way up the triangle, answering the four Customer Experience questions shown to the right of each level.

At the **Cognizance Level**, the goal is to hear the "Voice of the Customer." This means coming to understand how they feel about the products and services being promoted to them. In order to answer the question, <u>"What experiences do customers pursue?"</u>, the CE Team must find ways to connect with the brand's customers. This starts with gathering experiential data about those customers.

takeaway!

Are you even on the same page as your customers? Have you taken time to find out what they enjoy experiencing? Listen to your customers on product websites and social media as they share what is important to them and how they feel about your offerings, your company and your competitors. Then close the "Experiential Gap." Connect what makes sense from a company perspective with what makes sense to your customers. Once your customers see that you are listening to them and actively providing experiences with your brand that fit their needs, they will become loyal customers.

Armed with experiential data as to what customers are saying and wanting in reference to the brand, it is time to move to the **Response Level** on the model and answer the question, <u>"What experiences company offers?"</u>

First take an honest look at how the company is proposing to respond to the Voice of the Customer. Do the touchpoints for the offering address what customers are actually looking for or do they only reflect the company's organizational perspective? How the company responds at this level determines whether or not that offering will be profitable. Focusing only on organizational competence, corporate culture and operational reciprocity instead of being whole-heartedly customer-centric risks leaving a large "experiential gap" between what is being promoted and the types of experiences customers want to have when shopping for this type of offering. If there seems to be a disconnect, take immediate action to close that gap.

Before starting to design touchpoints for an offering, dissect the **Perception Level** of this model. Here the question to ask is: "What experiences customers percevie?" The customer experience that a company creates for its potential customers cannot be either just rational or just emotional, but must be a delicate balance between the two. This is because all customers perceive the world around them through two sets of lenses—utilitarian and hedonic. Hence, they do not see the exact same things through each lens— almost like the red and blue 3D glasses worn at an IMAX Theater. Both values must be addressed or the brand will lose some prospects before they ever reach the Call to Action. Worse yet, if these customers cannot relate to the product, they will move on to a competitor.

Once the CE Team is certain that they have incorporated both utilitarian and hedonic values that are important to their customers into the consumption journey, they can focus on solidifying the customer's relationship with the brand offering. It is not enough to convince a customer to purchase once. The goal is loyalty, so that the customer will be eager to come back and purchase time and time again from the company. If each of the lower levels of this CEM Model has been faithfully executed, then the top level— the **Relationship Level**—will be a natural outgrowth of everything that was accomplished earlier. To answer the question, "What relationships do customers develop with the brand?", it will then be a matter of finding creative ways to enable customers to express their attitudinal and behavior loyalty to the brand. As customers' relationships deepen with the brand, they will more likely repurchase their favorite product and trust the company enough to purchase additional product/services.

takeaway!

Never assume that you know what relationships customers will develop with your brand—unless you have gone through the steps of this entire model with a fine-toothed comb. Unless you have honestly answered each question and adjusted your organization according to those answers, you could be far off the mark of achieving either attitudinal or behavioral loyalty from your customers. If, however, you have faithfully followed this model and have made appropriate adjustments along the way, you will succeed in creating an outstanding and memorable customer experience that will bring them back again and again.

Chapter 5

EXPERIENTIAL RESEARCH

A group of scientists traveled to the North Pole to conduct research. Caught by an unexpected storm, they lost their way. Cold like a cruel monster beat the scientists, and when they were within minutes of freezing to death, a native randomly came across them and graciously took them to his hut. Here he gave them something hot to drink and stoked the fire in a pot-bellied stove by adding wood. He told them that he would be right back with some food for them. As the native left the room, the stove, which was in the center of the room, grabbed the attention of the scientists. They noticed that the stove was not resting on the floor, but instead was on top of several rocks, about a foot off the ground. The scientists began to ponder as to why the stove was placed on the rocks instead of directly on the floor. The geologist suggested that since that area was tectonically active, the native must have put the stove on a rock base to reduce the risk of fire spreading throughout the hut should there be an earthquake. The physicist had a different idea. Observing the size and shape of the hut, he suggested that the native had used the rocks to raise the stove up so that it would not just be in the horizontal center, but also in the vertical center of the room. This positioning would speed up the convection loop and distribute the heat evenly throughout the space. The anthropologist shook her head and posed a totally different explanation. She posited that since the concept of fire was equated with life by indigenous peoples in that region, this native was demonstrating a subconscious worship behavior towards fire that he had inherited from his ancestors. While they argued among themselves, the native returned with a basket of fresh fish to present to his unexpected guests. As the native passed out the fish, one of the scientists asked the reason for putting the stove on the rocks. The native shrugged and answered, "I didn't have enough stovepipes to place the stove on the ground."

Like this anecdote, too often in business, what executives assume about customers and what the customers actually think are not always the same. In fact, they may not even be in the same ballpark. Judging from the number of failed brands over the decades, it appears that too many decisions have been made by company representatives—from C-suite to front-line employees—that were based on incorrect assumptions about what customers really want. Determining the experiential expectancy of customers at every point of interaction is vital to the success of any business. For example, when a customer shows up at the service department with a broken auto part, if the service associate immediately assumes that the customer wants it replaced, he may be mistaken. Suppose that it takes two weeks for the new factory part to arrive. The customer might not want to wait that long. He may prefer just to have it fixed, which may only take a day or two. For the customer, timeliness is a priority. If you ask the associate, he would tell you that he recommends that the customer replace the part with a new one. His reasoning is: Who wants a refurbished part when he can have a brand new one? Unless the service associate asks, or listens to the customer, he will jump the gun and assume the customer wants a replacement, not realizing that that might be a hardship on the customer. In order to understand what really matters to customers at all levels of customer interaction, companies continuously need to do proper research.

Exploration of Qualities

Companies usually turn to Big Data Analytics to quickly gather metrics that will help them understand how to market their product. This traditional source of quantitative knowledge is critical, but as we have seen, it only reveals part of the picture when it comes to understanding the customer.

Big Data Analytics is a fast way to extract knowledge from multiple sources, but that knowledge won't be reliable without finding out which qualities matter to customers. In research science, when postulating a finding, it should be based on some previous hypothesis; otherwise, it is not scientific research, but rather a kind of alchemy. For example, suppose that a commodities company has access to all the data in the world. They analyze it and discover that there is an almost perfect correlation between the growth rate of trees in Central Park, New York City, and the growth rate of the fuel market in Botswana. Despite such an amazing correlation, it really doesn't prove anything unless they have relationship. Finding a correlation doesn't prove a casualty or that the correlation is due to the same effect. In the case of the trees and the fuel market in two different countries, chances are that a relationship cannot be found. Hence, the correlation is moot.

So we see that research, in reality, is a scientific process and has certain requisites that must be satisfied—one of which is that the scientific structure of research doesn't permit it to rely solely on quantitative data. A scientific hypothesis is built through inductions, deductions and abductions. These are not strictly quantitative. Even if you repackage these concepts using the latest buzz words, such as "divergent thinking" (which is really induction and abduction) or "convergent thinking" (a fancy term for deduction), they still are essentially the same. Although data-gathering is a basic necessity in research, what you do with the data is what research is all about.

What this means for businesses is that they should pursue exploratory research to generate inductive ideas. At the early stages of the research, Big Data is not especially helpful by itself, although it can point the way to qualitative analysis. In contrast, experiential research seeks a balance between formulating a perspective based on how customers are behaving toward a brand and gathering quantitative data.

Tracing Digital Footprints

When performing experiential research, starting with secondary data is a good option. Secondary data is actually second-hand knowledge that can be collected by surfing in the Internet, reading comments about a brand's offering—how customers use it, why they buy it, for whom they buy it, where and when they buy it, how they buy it, how they pay for it, how they consume it and how they dispose of it, etc. These digital footprints are extremely revealing because they reflect the honest intents and behaviors of customers. There are countless questions that a company can ask to help them paint a picture of what customers feel, think and do with the offering, so it is okay to test to see which questions give you the answers you need. The value of this information is that it tends to be word-of-mouth by nature. Thus, by using this peripheral method of surfing to gather experiential data, a researcher can access opinions that a customer may be hesitate to give in a survey or other forms of direct research. Besides gathering key information related to the brand, the researcher can explore the competition as well. In later stages, these research findings, combined with Big Data, will give clues for painting a quantitative scientific picture of the market. Understanding what customers think, feel or do about substitutes for your brand is as important as understanding direct competition. For example, in the cola market, Coca-Cola doesn't only compete with Pepsi, but it also competes with bottled water, so understanding the relationships customers have with bottled water is important to enable Coca-Cola to follow the right market-ing strategy.

Observations and Boundary Spanners

As we articulated earlier, there is often a disconnect between what customers want and what executives think, but even more interestingly, there is also a gap between what customers say they want and what they really want. In order to get to the truth, customers may need to be observed throughout the actual purchase, consumption and disposal stages. How does a company gather this kind of information? It can be done with some creative thinking and a simple camera and microphone, or else the company can use state-of-the-art equipment, like face and emotion recognition systems, eye-tracking devices, and so forth.

Another way to observe customers in action is by using "boundary span-ners." A boundary spanner refers to any agent of a company who works on the frontline of the value chain. This means that he or she is the represen-tative of the brand that directly encounters the customer. Sales associates, service department workers, customer service representatives, call center agents and cashiers, etc., are all boundary spanners because they work with-in the framework of their positions to connect the brand with the customer. Boundary spanners are also outside sales reps, bank employees, concierges and the reception staff of a hotel, reservation personnel and flight attendants for an airline, and so on. These people interact directly with customers and hear both what satisfies them and what disappoints them, which experiences delight them and which experiences estrange them from the brand. Some-times frustrated customers provide key knowledge about the competition when bemoaning about a brand. This helps the company get information about trends in the market—and perhaps glimpses about where their own brand might be falling short.

takeaway!

One way to keep abreast of changes in customer satisfaction is to set up monthly meetings during which boundary spanners can pass what they have observed on to management. Another way to collect this critical experiential data is to put up an employee webpage where your boundary spanners can post what they have seen and heard. A third option is to have them fill out a weekly "Customer Response" questionnaire. The insights gathered from boundary spanners are incredibly valuable for helping a company excel in this customer-centric marketing environment.

Induction of Customer Expressions

Most often customers do not consciously memorize details about what they feel, think and do; so that, if someone were to ask them, they couldn't provide a full picture of their consumption experience. There is a way, however, to counteract this and make the subconscious details rise to the conscious level. In the process, companies can gain vivid experiential impressions from customers. An <u>Experiential Expression Session</u> (EES) is the perfect tool for getting customers to recall details about what they had experienced when coming in contact with a particular brand. For the session, the company researchers should recruit a group of customers and go over all the consumption stages for that product or service with them. This means reviewing the buying, using and disposing stages with the customer. An EES enables researchers to gather lots of insights from the participants. Consider a business that sells appliances. The company recruits customers ideally based on personas (more about personas in Chapter 6) and have them test out the product. Let's say that the product is a steam iron. Typically during an EES, customers are also urged to articulate their impressions with a running monologue, describing exactly how they feel about the features of the product. For example:

"I see that the iron is white. I like that; it makes me think of crisp, clean clothes, and the black lines on the back end add a fashionable look to the iron. The handle has small indentations that help me grip the iron comfortably and safely. The on-off button has a nice design and when it is on, it lights up. That's a great safety feature! I like to use steam when I iron, but I can't tell where to put the water in. I can't find it—Oh! Here it is.... I wish that it were easier to see where you pour the water in, but now that I know where it is, I won't need to search for it again. Maybe if the company were to put a pull-off tab or label to show where it is, that would help new customers. I noticed that the iron heats up quickly—wow! That's fantastic, especially...."

The Experiential Expression Session is extremely flexible and can be adapted to any product or service. The information gathered from these impromptu sessions is invaluable and will provide exceptional experiential data for planning out or revising touchpoints.

Mystery Shopping

An ancient Chinese saying that is often attributed to Confucius has relevancy to contemporary marketing, especially as it relates to branding and customer experiences: "I hear and I forget. I see and I remember. I do and I understand." [1] Customers are inundated with countless brand-related stimuli. Expecting them to vividly remember every detail is wishful thinking on the part of companies; in reality, it is not possible. That is why getting prospects to "do" something in response to the brand is a more effective way to get customers than merely having them hear about it or see it.

Most customers do not analytically diagnose what encourages and discourages them as they travel through the consumption stages of an offering. Thus, they cannot be relied on to provide a detailed evaluation of how effective these stages are. In order to get a better idea of how the brand's touchpoints are working, one or more members of the CE Team should personally walk the consumption journey. The only drawback to this approach is lack of objectivity. To ensure objectivity, the company should also recruit <u>Mystery Shoppers</u>. Have them go through the touchpoints and give a detailed report about their experiences. Mystery shoppers are effective for both on- and offline offerings. By having a series of targeted questions for them to answer afterwards, this can be a fruitful method for extracting experiential insights for analysis.

Mystery shopping functions like this: Companies hire individuals to visit their stores (or go on their website) and pretend to be an average customer. They give the mystery shoppers certain guidelines to follow. In a store, they might be required to interact with at least two salespeople and report back on how they were treated. For example, they would report if the salesperson took time to answer their questions or if the interaction was minimal or not particularly helpful. Afterwards, the mystery shoppers get online and fill out a questionnaire about their experience. Companies typically pay mystery shoppers certain amount of money or coupons per shopping experience. If, as part of the experience, they are required to make a purchase, they are reimbursed a percentage of what they spent.[2]

Compared to an Experiential Expression Session, which is anecdotal, sending out mystery shoppers is considered a legitimate field study that provides random field data. Hence, the benefit for companies is that this data can be graphed, compared and analyzed so that they can pinpoint any weaknesses in their touchpoints as well as confirm which parts of their value stream are engaging customers the best. Please note that mystery shopping should not be considered a substitute for the EES research tool, but rather a supplement to it. By combining, comparing and relating the results of both methods, companies will achieve balanced experiential research that reveals what customers are thinking, feeling and doing about their product or service. Results from research that is both random and persona-based can be considered reliable.

Online Communities

The Internet provides fantastic opportunities for businesses to mine customer insights. An online community is one of the platforms that both provides a wealth of information for companies and is a pleasure to participate in. Many online communities are set up by brands themselves in order to hear the "voice of the customer." Online communities create a casual atmosphere so that customers feel comfortable enough to express their true feelings about the products, services and consumption journeys provided by the company; on the company side, this is where it is possible to harvest new insights, collect reliable experiential information, and bring decision-makers and brand fans together to address issues. On this community platform, the company can take quick polls to track the sentiments and opinions of customers, glean data that will help them make specific decisions and improvements, and even engage customers in co-creating new offerings.

Associational Maps

Individuals understand the world by comparing, combining and relating the stimuli around them. Similarly, in research, whether quantitative or qualitative, researchers do the same thing. What makes a Ferrari "a Ferrari" is all the brands that are not Ferrari. If all cars were Ferraris, no one could talk about the meaning of Ferrari. When people compare, combine and relate their knowledge about cars, it yields the meaning of Ferrari in their minds.

In the human mind, car-related knowledge has a position relative to billions of other concepts. These concepts are linked to each other by connections called associations. These associations can be either strong or weak. The more they are repeated, the stronger they become—just as muscles grow stronger as they are exercised.

The term "associations" is as old as the Greek philosopher, Aristotle. According to the branch of psychology called Associationism, all concepts exist in a relational state. When man thinks a thought, he can't think it by itself. It is linked to other thoughts and cannot be divorced from them. Even though there are different types of associational thought relationships, they can be grouped under three distinct laws: the Law of Similarity, the Law of Contrast, and the Law of Contiguity.

The Law of Similarity

Remembering or thinking of one thing often triggers the thought of other similar things[3], such as when a person thinks of tea, he might also think of coffee. The human mind groups together things that are similar so that when a person needs to process or retrieve information, he can do it faster and more efficiently. Thus, remembering one's mother might immediately bring up memories of one's father because they share the similarity of being the parents. In the same way, when a customer buys, uses or disposes of a product or service, he might think of the competition as well. For example, when the customer thinks of a Mercedes-Benz, he might also picture a BMW or Lexus at the same time, since these brands have similar positioning as luxury cars. Companies need to realize that when their brand falls into the same category as competing brands, customers tend to group them all together in their minds as "similar." Consequently, these similar brands form an "inert set" because they hold the same or similar experiential position in the mind of the customer. The "similarity" associational relation type stands for a point of parity or equality among brands—even if there are other aspects of the brands that are dissimilar. The goal of a brand that is stuck in an inert set is to find a way to distinguish itself from the other brands in that set.

The Law of Contrast

The Law of Contrast occurs when thinking about one concept automatically triggers the recall of the opposite concept[4] such as: hot and cold, left and right, good and bad. Concepts that fall under this law may not all be exact opposites, but they are different enough and commonly associated enough to be contrasting. Because of the Law of Contrast, one concept helps to define its opposite: In order to say that something is good, one should also know about bad. When a customer thinks of a cup of iced tea, he might also think of hot tea, since cold is associated with and defined by the existence of hot. Pre-Socratic Heraclitus criticized other philosophers for not seeing the unity in experience. He felt that although opposites are necessary for life, they were unified in a system of balanced exchanges, so that they become one through an everlasting Word or Logos.[5] Later Hegel, as pioneer of German idealism, claimed that everything has its negation within itself.[6] Believe it or not, the philosophies of Heraclitus and Hegel can be applied to the customer experience. They seem to explain how both well-performing brands and poor-performing brands (contradictions) are needed to create the standards for the industry and the expectations of customers (unity).

The Law of Contiguity

Experiences that occur close to each other in terms of time and space get connected to each other in the customer's mind.[7] This happens because of the Law of Contiguity. Contiguity is "a series of things in continuous connection." When an individual thinks of salt, he often also thinks of pepper. This is because people are accustomed to using salt and pepper together when preparing meals and when eating at the dinner table. Time is another dimension of the Law of Contiguity. When thinking about an object or an event, the mind often also brings up the proceeding or succeeding objects or events. Thomas Hobbes calls this the "Train of Thoughts."[8] When a customer decides to go to the bank, he thinks of the vehicle he will take to get there, the line he has to wait in, the transaction he will make, the receipt he will receive, etc.

A practical way to picture all these associations is with a method called Mapping Associations. A company that is trying to sort through all the associations that customers have related to their brand can use this technique to envision how they all fit together. With an association map, businesses can picture the mental associations that their offering likely triggers. It also provides insight about which values the offering serves in depth, as well as enabling them to spot which values are being missed.

When constructing an offering's mapping associations, all three laws— Similarity, Contrast and Contiguity—have to be incorporated. Below is an association map that shows the kinds of mental associations that customers of the Volvo car brand might have. Over the years, Volvo has distinguished its brand by placing customer safety first and foremost in the minds of customers. In order to foster that strong position, it has announced that by 2020 the brand will launch "death-proof" cars into the consumer market.[9] Currently, "death-proof" cars are used only in the movie industry by stuntmen.

Association mapping has several formats. Companies may select which format best fits how they want to arrange their data. The Laddering Map, which is shown below, clearly shows not only the Similarity and Contrasting links, but also allows the observer to follow the progression of Contiguity connections—those that progress in time. To help position the brand, a laddering map can be set up to picture the marketing position of the brand as it relates to what customers think about the brand's competition, its substitutes and even the values the brand portrays. Besides the laddering map, there are other association mapping methods that can be used. Some incorporate statistics and can paint a picture of the brand as it relates statistically to the rest of the market. Hence, mapping associations is critical tool for all businesses because it can be used to help with both branding and positioning.

Sample Hierarchical Laddering Map: Volvo

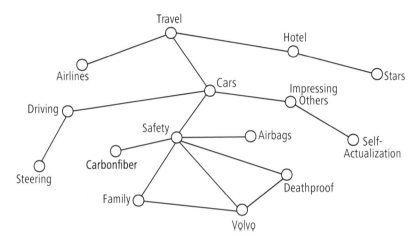

Value Extraction

It was a sunny summer afternoon. One of my colleagues came into my office with a box under his arm. As he set the box down on my desk, I realized from the label that it was a box of bitter almond cookies. He told me to open the box and help myself because he knew that I love bitter almond cookies. I opened the deluxe velvet box and took a cookie. It was okay, but not nearly as delicious as the cookies from our favorite bakery. I asked him why he chose a different bakery this time. He explained that he had planned to take cookies to a relative of his in another city, but due to unforeseen circumstances, the visit was cancelled. He couldn't return the cookies, so he thought he'd share them with me. He finally confessed that the real reason he had bought the less delicious cookies was that the other bakery has a great reputation, charming packaging and more pricing options. Personally, I would have chosen the cookies based on taste, but my colleague was extracting other values from the experience. He was not just buying cookies; he was buying a message from himself to his relative. He wanted to give a gift to his relative from a company that had a well-known reputation and an expensive-looking cookie box. If the taste of the cookies inside was not out-of-this-world, well, that was a worthwhile trade-off; he wanted to be recognized for giving a memorable gift. Customers do not buy products or services only to satisfy explicit hedonic or utilitarian needs. Very often, the consumption that a customer conducts has implicit goals as well—goals that serve a specific purpose for them. By getting customers to disclose their implicit objectives, and by sorting through their values, businesses will be able to get rid of myopia and focus on the desired end-state for their customers—in other words, try to satisfy the real goal of the customer.

Even though reaching a single desired goal is important to the customer, how that goal is reached matters just as much. For example, a customer may want to have a diamond wedding ring at an affordable price. If, however, the customer discovers that a child laborer died while extracting the diamond from a dangerous mine, most probably the customer will refuse to buy the ring—even if it had been the ring she had been dreaming of. The customer may not want the potential of a wonderfully pleasant experience if the cost is extreme loss to someone else. Yes, the desired end values are important, but the values an organization adopts when providing the satisfying values to customers is just as important. In other words, how an experience is delivered is as critical as delivering it. In order to ensure that these values are in place, the company should always take into account their customers' emotional frame of values as well as their rational frame of mind.

Scrutinization of Semiotics

Exploring semiotic clues helps companies to design the ideal experience for their customers. Semiotics, as mentioned earlier, is the science that studies signs and symbols as elements of communicative behavior. It doesn't only cover visual clues, but also other sensory signs. To employ semiotic analysis, the sensory stimuli that affect customers all along their journey should be broken into stage-based pieces. For example, during the purchase stage, an online retailer should capitalize on the visual and auditory senses. In contrast, a physical retailer has to think about how to incorporate the tactile and olfactory senses—even taste, if applicable. For instance, a garden supplier might introduce flower seed packets embedded with the scent of the flower that the seeds will grow into. These scented seed packets enhance the experience for the customers while expanding the semiotic presence of the retailer. Unraveling the experiential codes of the target audience and understanding how the subconscious plays a significant role in customer experience are part of semiotics. When performing semiotic analysis, remember to statistically validate the findings, otherwise the results will not be generalizable, representative and pervasively actionable. A side benefit of doing statistical semiotic analysis is that it frees the company in many cases from the obligation of expensive pre-tests before launch.

takeaway!

Remember Pike Place Fish Market in Seattle? As a prime example of what a great shopping experience is, this business has learned to capitalize on the semiotic cues that bring in customers. They toss fish across the store (visual), have loud enthusiastic conversations (auditory), encourage customers to touch the fish (tactile) and, of course, the aroma of fish (olfactory) is part of the experience. Engaging customers on so many levels has proven to be an effective marketing strategy for Pike Place Fish Market. What about your company? What about your brand offering? Are there semiotic cues that you can use to involve your customers at a deeper level? What are some changes that you can make to engage their senses?

Relevancy Diagnostics

When performing research, it is possible to encounter an experiential niche that the competition hasn't quite locked in on yet. This might seem like quite an opportunity for the company—but not so fast. Before leapfrogging into it and dedicated precious time and resources to this exciting new niche, it is critical to determine whether it is even relevant to the brand's customers.

takeaway!

It is smart to always be on the lookout for any untouched niche that is related to your brand. However, do your homework and research it before allocating resources to getting into it. A new product or service niche is only profitable if it is something your customers are genuinely curious about. You can't force them to be eager to consume an offering they are not interested in.

One company that made the mistake of going after a non-relevant niche was Pepsi. Always in intense competition against Coca-Cola, Pepsi was continually looking for ways to outshine the well-established Coke brand. In the 1980s, Pepsi tried to break into the breakfast beverage market. They saw an opening in the "soda-as-coffee-substitute" trend that had popped up. Called "Pepsi A.M.," its new product claimed that it had 28% more caffeine than regular Pepsi. Hoping to wake people up in the morning, it conveniently left out the metric that showed that it had 77% less caffeine than coffee. They hoped that customers would be so delighted at having an alternative to coffee, that they wouldn't notice that Pepsi A.M. didn't have the caffeine "kick" of regular coffee. Unfortunately for the brand, people did notice and after the novelty wore off, they stopped buying Pepsi A.M. Pepsi pulled it from the shelves in 1990.[10]

Quantitative Validation

When sketching out the dynamics of the market (both potential customers and the competition), it is important to remember that this data is qualitative, not quantitative, and needs to be quantitatively validated before applying it at the company level. If the results of the qualitative research cannot be scientifically validated, then the findings are no more than mere guesses. Avoiding statistical validation and depending on assumptions has the potential of getting a company into trouble.

Not everyone in marketing research trusts qualitative research. Those who still question the validity of qualitative studies may have a point: In the early years of qualitative research, too often techniques were used that were open to subjectivity in collection and interpretation. Moreover, standardized measures were applied after the fact to validate them. All qualitative inquiry must be held to "criteria and terminology that is used in mainstream science,"[11] so that its validity will be established and not questioned afterwards. Today's experiential researchers have taken this critique to heart and have devised a whole validation strategy to be used when doing qualitative research. In qualitative research, the aim is securing the **credibility, authenticity, transferability, and dependability** of the research findings. Focus groups, EES, and other qualitative research methods are now implemented with these protocols already in place so that the results and outcomes are valid. Specific validation strategies have been accepted by the scientific community as ways for qualitative researchers to increase the credibility of their research findings. These include: Reflexivity, Triangulation, Coding Checks, Member Checking, Peer Review and Negative Case Analysis. Each of these validation strategies helps to remove any bias on the part of the researcher by having the data re-checked and re-categorized by other researchers, compared with other data-collection methods, and even by finding cases that seem to disprove the findings. Results that survive these checks and balances are considered valid. Moreover, the qualitative validity mentioned above absolutely should be supported by quantitative studies to ensure their generalizability.

Big Data Integration

Big Data provides impressive opportunities for companies if it is executed wisely. At the initial stages of research, relying solely on Big Data has the potential to hurt a company or a brand. As previously mentioned, quantitative data may suggest some qualitative areas to explore, but a healthy marketing decision cannot be made based on quantities alone. The biggest objections to the CRM approach have come about because conclusions were made from quantitative data without any experiential context. In fact, the "Customer Experience Management" concept was born as a response to such CRM catastrophes. CRM used Big Data Analysis as its sole source of information, creating results that were skewed and causing many companies to be misguided in their marketing. This de facto situation, though, should not discourage businesses from benefiting from this kind of analysis. On the contrary, it should encourage them to challenge the status quo and find alternative ways to use Big Data wisely. Rather than beginning with Big Data, they need to start with isolating qualitative customer-brand experiences and paint a picture of what their customers really want as they relate to the brand. Then, Big Data can be used to examine their behavioral patterns and categorize customers to determine which customers are actually being served and which customers are being ignored or disenfranchised. After experiential research and Big Data have been integrated, then the company can opt to go deeper into the analysis.

Qualitative study is critical because it reveals details and critical facts about a brand's market and its competition. Big Data is limited because it only measures the customers who are consuming the brand—this, obviously, is not all the potential customers in the market. As a result, the external validity and external relational position of a company's current customers can only be partially investigated. Analyzing the whole population, other than with a census, is unrealistic for multiple reasons. In statistics, when performing analysis-over-samples, the designation "n-1" is used instead of "N" in formulas. Why? Because, regardless of the content of each statistical analysis at the sample level, a reference point is needed. Remember, the Big Data collected by a company represents the behavioral patterns of their customers—not all the customers in the entire market. Given this, instead of starting with Big Data, companies should start with the customers in the extended market, find the reciprocity in their data, and then go for further studies. This is how to conduct "outside-in" (customer-centric) research instead of "inside out" (ego-centric) research.

When applying Big Data Analytics, deterministic models are the ideal complement, since they provide reliable, validated knowledge to guide action. However, making it come true is not as easy as articulating it. When performing Big Data application of qualitative analysis, more than data science knowledge is needed. The company's business team, qualitative research team and quantitative analysis team should cooperate in the application phase of qualitative data collected on existing Big Data. Even a 1% change each day yields an incredible chasm between results. A quantitative analyst may miss it, since he sees the figures; but a qualitative analyst who played a role in the research would be able to catch it and diagnose the variation. Consider the difference between 1.01 and 0.99. They possess a change rate of just 1% from 1.00. But the compound change rate over 365 days yields an immense chasm:

$$1.01^{365} = 37.8$$
$$0.99^{365} = 0.03$$

Conclusion

In the mid-20th century, a space war between the Soviets and the Americans heated up. Both sides were in intense competition to raise the bar during the cold war. The first move came from the USSR. Yuri Gagarin became the first man to go into outer space. Soon after, the USA retaliated by landing the first man ever on the moon. Neil Armstrong and Edwin "Buzz" Aldrin made a small step for themselves but a big step in the name of human civ- ilization. It was discovered that the space program of both nations had a fundamental need: a way to write in a gravity-free environment. Both the American astronauts and the Russian cosmonauts had to write notes about measurements they made and the experiences they had, but the ink in the pens they were given did not function in a zero-gravity environment. The ink in the pens needed gravity to work; without it, the ink couldn't move down to the point of the pen. According to an urban myth, Paul C. Fisher, who was an US entrepreneur, saw the niche and invested millions of dollars to invent a pen that could write under zero-gravity conditions. After exten- sive research and experiments in the mid-1960s, Fisher got a patent for his Fisher Space Pen, which could write upside down, under water, over grease, and even in extreme temperatures ranging from 30°F to 250°F.[12] Finding a writing solution cost the USA a small fortune. On the other side, the USSR cosmonauts also needed something to write with, but the USSR's solution was different from the American's. They didn't incur the massive research costs that USA did. What the USSR did was just give their cosmonauts regular lead pencils to solve zero-gravity writing problem. The solution was so obvious, so simple and easy. We wonder why the Americans didn't think of it....

But not so fast—as we said, this is an urban myth that is often used in research training sessions to encourage critical thinking. The facts of history are quite different:

Originally, before the invention of space pens, both the USA astronauts and the USSR cosmonauts used pencils to make their notes. However, bro- ken pencil leads created a serious problem in the zero-gravity of the space capsules. The debris they created was dangerous in a space capsule that was full of electronic gadgets, since the loose bits of graphite in zero gravity could travel freely, get into the electronic circuits and possibly harm the devices. There was no choice. A solution had to be found—and quickly. So Fisher did develop the space pen and invested a small fortune. The pens were taken by astronauts on board the famous Apollo missions. Even the cosmonauts used these pens on some of their missions. Today, the Fisher Space Pen Company is still in operation, although the majority of their customers are, obviously, people on earth instead of people in space. Customers may pay $45 for a replica and as much as $700 to own an original pen used by an astronaut on a space mission.

When performing research on customer experiences, companies should first apply qualitative analysis, such as content analysis, in-depth interviews, focus groups, EES, association extraction methods, etc. Then they should integrate *quantitative* methods, such as regression, conjoint analysis, discriminant analysis, etc. The methods that are applied don't make the research proper or improper; rather, it is the company's objectives, mindset and philosophy while employing these methods that render research proper or improper.

takeaway!

The solution to a problem could be quite simple or it might be quite complex. Insisting that a solution has to be complex may prevent you from finding a simple solution, as in the case of the scientists at the North Pole. On the other hand, sometimes too simple can be dangerous, like using a pencil in zero gravity inside a space capsule. Lesson learned? Carefully evaluate your data and be sure that your conclusions fit within your qualitative framework.

Chapter 6

CUSTOMER EXPERIENCE JOURNEY MAPPING

More companies are adopting the "outside-in," "customer-first" perspective, but marketing obstacles such as economic crises, shrinkage or saturation of the markets, explosive competition and reduction in profitability leave little tolerance for businesses that fail to keep up. To combat this, companies invest vast amounts of money developing new products, creating new communication methods, and implementing new delivery channels. Unfortunately, too many companies make their decisions based on intuition rather than on smart Customer Experience focused strategies. At the same time, most are oblivious to the experiential expectancies of their customers. Consequently, each year approximately half of all new products fail after launch. Moreover, companies discover that they are bleeding loyal customers and they have no idea why. Even the consumption journey that customers take hides countless consumer insights because it is not analyzed properly. Businesses need to understand that the "Customer Experience Journey" is the key to success and that the only way to stay on top of that journey is with Customer Experience Management.

The Customer Experience Journey, due to its methodological framework, gives managers a practical way to diagnose failures and guides them in designing differentiated and memorable experiences. A Customer Journey Map (CJM) is a powerful tool that provides a visual representation across all the stages that customers pass through and records what they think, feel and do at each interaction with the brand.

Touchpoints refer to interactive points between the customer and the brand. TV commercials, web blogs, the showroom, the product itself and even transactions such as invoices, etc. are all touchpoints. Thanks to a journey map, the touchpoints of the customers can be clearly defined. Any touchpoints that are not managed (rather left to chance) can be diagnosed. The Customer Journey Map enables the company to design an outstanding experience for the customer.

The customer's journey may vary from one segment of customers to another, so that when creating a customer journey map, besides simply designing a generic map, additional journey maps should be developed for each targeted customer segment and scenario. To do this, each segment should be represented by a hypothetical "persona" which demonstrates the most prominent characteristic or tendency of the segment that the persona represents.

The following is an example of a hypothetical persona traveling through a consumption experience. Note the characteristics of the persona and the responses he makes to the brand's touchpoints:

John is a sales representative, who had started working for an insurance company a week ago; he is a 28-year old tech-savvy, organic- and green-conscious customer. Around 11:30 AM, John was in his office thinking about what to eat for lunch. It was raining outside, so he didn't want to leave the office, preferring to eat at his desk. He decided to ask his colleagues what they recommended for lunch options. They suggested a number of restaurants that made deliveries to their office. After getting advice and feedback from his friends, he quickly checked the nearby restaurants on his smart phone. Not wanting to waste time scrolling on his phone, he switched to his desktop computer and Googled the restaurants. He found some more options besides the ones his friends had recommended and read the comments about their service quality. Finally he decided to get an organic vegetable pizza and called the order line of a pizzeria at 11:45. John wanted to get the pizza as soon as possible, since he only had an hour's break for lunch. He figured that if the pizza arrived at 12:00, he could eat it and still have time left over to relax, check his social media accounts and so on. If, on the other hand the delivery ran late, then his plans for a relaxing lunch would fly out the window. While waiting and stressing about when the pizza would arrive, he became nervous and checked the pizzeria website to track his pizza. Finally the pizza boy showed up at the office. John wanted to pay his bill quickly so that he could enjoy his meal. He planned to pay with his credit card, but the delivery guy looked less than trustworthy, especially since John had heard from his colleagues that, last week, two of their credit cards had been copied. John tried to decide how to handle the payment, since he did not have enough cash on hand to cover it; he only had enough change for a tip. So he reluctantly offered his credit card. The pizza boy swiped the card. John entered his pin. The delivery boy handed John back his card, got the tip and left the room. John returned to his desk and started to enjoy the pizza. He was delighted to find that it was hot and delicious. He really liked it and felt that he was eating healthily because it was all organic. After eating his pizza, John was about to toss the pizza box into the recycle bin when he noticed that the box was made of non-recyclable Styrofoam. As a faithful green customer, John was disappointed in the packaging. He always felt a responsibility for the environment and it bothered him to have to dispose of it in the trash can. John then sat back in his chair and placed the free Italian pizza magnet that came with the pizza in his desk drawer. Just for fun, John had taken a "selfie" while he was having his lunch. It showed him holding up the pizza magnet with the pizza box in the background. He had even taken a minute to share the selfie along with a tagline: "My first office lunch in my new position!"

By creating specific personas like this for the brand's offering, it is possible to anticipate the responses of customers to the offering and to proactively design consumption stages that will be effective.

The Consumption Stages

Customers pass through three consumption stages: pre-purchase, purchase and post-purchase. In order to deliver outstanding holistic customer experience, which aims at fostering loyalty, each stage should be carefully examined. The stages can each be broken down into smaller actions or "micro-stages" for further scrutiny as shown on the chart below:

Pre-purchase	Purchase	Post-Purchase
Problem Arousal	Placement	Adaptation
Awareness	Payment	Extension
Recognition	Receipt / Delivery	Fixation
Exploration	Installation	Replacement
Evaluation	Division	Refund
Search	Consumption	Disposal
	Transaction	

Touchpoints

A touchpoint refers to any interaction point that a customer has with a brand. Social media, ads, the website, invoices, correspondence, sales or service representatives, delivery media, phone calls, the product's packaging, retail stores and memorabilia, etc., can all be touchpoints for a business. Each encounter between brand-related stimuli and the customer generates experiences. Consumption micro-stages, i.e. the touchpoints, should not only engage customers but also move them effortlessly forward in the consumption process. In the above example, hearing suggestions from his colleagues (word-of-mouth), searching his smart phone and the Internet, ordering on the order line, paying the delivery employee, consuming the pizza, disposing of the pizza box, and sharing pictures of the pizza and magnet on the Internet were all touchpoints for John.

takeaway!

Use the micro-stages from the above chart as a guide as you develop your own ad-hoc Customer Journey Map. The exact micro-stage terms are flexible. Adapt them to your particular brand. For example, the micro-stages that John passed through are as follows: Under Pre-purchase, Consider and Search; under Purchase, Order, Wait, Delivery/Pay, Consume; and under Post-purchase, Dispose and Share. John represents only one customer segment for the pizza brand. Review his persona (his description and tendencies) in the consumption experience example above. Being cognizant of the steps each segment of your customers takes in relation to your brand enables you to create several journey maps that accurately reflect the experiences of each segment.

Motivations of Customers

When a customer consumes a product or service, he consciously or subconsciously pursues goals at each micro-stage. The goal at each micro-stage both prompts the customer to complete that stage and guides him to next stage. By achieving the goal at each milestone, the customer eventually reaches his single desired end-goal. It is critical to note that the path to reaching that end-goal matters to customers; thus, the supplier brand should take into account all the micro-goals along the experience journey. In the example, John had different goals at each stage, which moved him towards achieving his final goal. John's ultimate goal in this consumption experience was to have a lunch that balanced him both mentally and physically. John's journey had various goals that would make him comfortable if they satisfied him. If he couldn't reach one of the goals, he might not pass to the next micro-stage. While considering his lunch options, John's goal was to research and find the best type of food to eat that fit his values. During his research, he made his to what to eat. By ordering early, his goal was to spend his break efficiently. While waiting, he checked the website of the pizzeria to reduce his anxiety while waiting and to feel positive by tracing the delivery. (Remember how Amazon provides a way to track its Prime Air deliveries). During the delivery and payment micro-stage, his desire was to pay fast and securely. During consumption, his goal was to eat organic and enjoy a hot, tasty pizza. When disposing of the box, his goal was to go green. Finally, by sharing the memorabilia from his first office lunch, his goal was to be noticed by others and to gain their approval. While John was reaching his ultimate goal of having a lunch that gave him mental and physical homeostasis, he evaluated whether he could achieve each of the micro-goals along his journey. Achievement of these goals will surely affect the future buying behavior of John.

Thoughts, Emotions and Behaviors of Customers

At each micro-stage, customers develop ideas, have feelings and perform actions in response to the touchpoints. By capturing the essence of what customers think, feel and do at each stage (or microstage), the company can understand what motivates them to move on to the next stage, as well as what possibly could be responsible for interrupting their journey. Since the ultimate goal is to get customers to complete the "call-to-action" end stage, anything that might interrupt that journey should be noted and fixed as soon as possible.

The Customer Journey Map is a visual representation that offers key insights into the movement of the customer across the whole consumption journey. When companies take time to evaluate those insights, they can more efficiently develop and launch their brand. In our example, John, during his "considering" stage, asked his colleagues for suggestions, and when he heard that some restaurants delivered to the office, he got excited. In the search stage, he used his phone to check the Internet, but was too impatient to keep scrolling on his phone, so he switched to his desktop computer to continue the search. Once he found a pizzeria that served pizzas with organic toppings, he was thrilled and ready to order. At the ordering stage, he called the order line immediately, hoping to get the pizza delivered early into his lunch hour. The friendly and upbeat employee on the order line put him in a positive mood. While waiting, however, he started to worry about whether his food would arrive on time or not, so he visited pizzeria website to check and track his pizza's delivery. This eased his mind, balancing his mood a bit, and when the pizza actually arrived, he felt positive again. While paying, he worried about whether this delivery boy might copy his card. He reluctantly paid the bill with the card, but his doubts weighed heavily on his mind. While eating, he was amazed at the quality and taste of the ingredients on his pizza and regained his earlier positive mood. During the disposal stage, he automatically thought about the sustainability of the environment and planned to put the box into the recycle bin, but when he realized that he couldn't because it was made of Styrofoam, he felt guilty for hurting the environment. This made him feel negative again. In the sharing stage, he thought of letting his friends know how great his lunch was, so he shared the selfie that he took of his meal and the pizza magnet. Unfortunately, he didn't quite get the enthusiastic reaction he had hoped for from the selfie and that made him feel negative at the end of his pizza experience. Isn't it amazing that John thought, felt and did all of this during a simple pizza consumption experience? It is important to keep in mind that even the simplest statement, like, "I ate pizza at lunch," can be hiding either positive or negative emotions—or a roller coaster, like John's.

Points of Pleasure, Pain and Equity

Man shapes his behavior by relying on two concepts: pleasure and pain. Since the ancient ages, scholars like Aristoteles, Epicurus, Locke, Condillac and many others referred to these two basic concepts as determinants of man's behavior. Man tends to act in ways that give him pleasure and avoids the ways that cause him pain. If a person likes a particular food, he will want it again; if he doesn't like it, he won't eat it anymore. If a company removes pain points and induces pleasure points, they increase the probability of gaining and retaining customers.

Moreover, they could steal customers from poorer-performing competitors, thanks to word-of-mouth about the great experience they had delivered. "Pain points" are the touchpoints that possess a negative gap between what customers expect and what they actually receive; on the contrary, "pleasure points" are when what customers receive exceeds what they expect. An "equity point" refers to an equal balance between what is expected and what is received. The relationship can be expressed as follows:

· If *Delivered Value* varies from *Expected Value* in a positive direction, then it's a *Pleasure Point*
· If *Delivered Value* varies from *Expected Value* in a negative direction, then it's a *Pain Point*

· If <u>*Delivered Value*</u> *has no significant variation from* <u>*Expected Value*</u>*, then it's an* <u>*Equity Point*</u>

takeaway!

Customers experience both pain and pleasure throughout their journey experience. In the very beginning of a Customer Experience Program, it might be difficult to predict these points. In later chapters you will learn how to quantitatively determine them; however, as you begin your research, qualitative experiential research methods should enable you to locate your customers' points of pain and pleasure along your value chain.

Moments of Truth

Defining the "moment of truth" is as important as defining points of pleasure and pain along the customer's journey. A moment of truth is the moment of decision when the customer decides whether to go on to the next stage with the brand or not.

In fact, the customer experience journey should be thought of as a timeline rather than separate actions at each touchpoint. This is because the customer is in a continual process of valuation that triggers changes in his attitudes, emotions and behavior as he interacts with brand-related stimuli.

Therefore, in order for a company to understand the sum of these experiences in the major stages, applying the "moment of truth" concept is helpful. At the end of each major consumption stage, the customer assigns meaning and relevancy to the brand—his "moment of truth"—which determines whether or not he continues the journey. If he believes what he is being told about the brand AND feels it relates to his needs, he goes on to the next stage.

The Four Moments of Truth

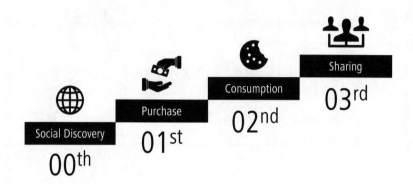

If something in the touchpoint causes him to disbelieve what he is being told OR it does not meet his needs, he discontinues his journey because he can't justify going any further in the process. At that point, he may even start exploring a competing brand.

There are four phases, or "moments," of truth that customers go through when exposed to a brand. In each phase, they summarize their experiences, evaluate them, and then decide whether or not to continue their journey with the brand:

1. The Zero Moment of Truth

This is the moment of truth that a customer gains through secondary research. This would include online reviews, the company website, vendors' websites, social media, advertisements, word-of-mouth and so on. In the "Zero Moment of Truth," according to Google who coined the phrase, the customer does not directly interact with the product or service.[1] The experiences that the customer has in this phase are indirect. The zero moment of truth is not the beginning stage of consumption. Just as the number zero is prior to the numbers 1, 2, and 3 on the number line, the zero moment of truth is a preliminary phase. If, at this point, the customer decides to go on to the next consumption stage, i.e., getting online or going to the store to purchase the product or service, then it means that the brand has planted the "purchase intention" into the mind of that customer.

takeaway!

For example, your friend is texting on her brand new mobile phone. Peeking over her shoulder, you notice its innovative features and the way it operates and start thinking about trading in your old phone for one like hers. Later, on your laptop, you start exploring that model online, read reviews about the phone, visit forums online, watch ads on YouTube and ask other friends what they think about the phone. With all this new knowledge, you consider buying it. That is your "zero moment of truth."

2. The First Moment of Truth

When a customer becomes aware of a brand's product or service directly or indirectly and then decides to actually interact with it, this is the beginning of his "First Moment of Truth," During this Moment of Truth, the customer makes one of two decisions: **"Purchase Conation"** (he intends to buy) or 2. **"Purchase Behavior"**(he actually makes the purchase). In the purchase conation phase, the customer has the intent to buy, but hasn't literally made the purchase yet. (This is different from intention in the purchase behavior stage.) Depending on what happens next, the customer will either make the decision to buy the product/service, or, because he is dissatisfied or uncertain, he will hold off deciding or abandon the effort altogether.

Suppose a customer sees an ad for a laptop that he wants to buy. This triggers an urge to find a way to purchase it. This is purchase conation. The customer then makes his way to the electronics store. As he arrives, he either turns his decision into action by purchasing, or something interferes to make him change his mind. For example, in the showroom, a salesperson may suggest a competing brand that either has a lower price or added features that his original choice does not have. Or, on the way to the store, he may have noticed an ad on his mobile phone for another brand laptop. Competing stimuli like this might persuade him to disregard the purchase connation that he originally formed and buy another brand. Moreover, the stimuli bombardment could cause so much confusion that he starts to re-think the entire purchase. He might be vacillating about which option is the best one and may ultimately decide not to buy any laptop at that moment. To clear up his confusion, he may rebound to the Zero Moment of Truth to get more information online, or he may ask a friend or family member who is a market maven of electronics for suggestions. If, on the other hand, the customer goes ahead and purchases the laptop, then he has exhibited purchase behavior.

takeaway!

Smart companies know that "purchase connation" and "purchase behavior" are vital customer responses for companies to keep in mind when designing a customer journey. If the CE Team is aware of the competition's marketing when creating experiences, the First Moment of Truth will result in more customers purchasing their brand.

3. The Second Moment of Truth

Throughout the Zero and First Moments of Truth, customers formulate what is called "Expected Value." This is the value that they expect the service or product they purchase to provide. After purchasing, customers enjoy using the product or service—in other words, they receive something else—actual value. This is called "Received Value." As they experience the received value, they compare it to the expected value. If the received value is little lower than the expected value, the customer feels dissatisfaction; but if the received value is far below the expected value, then customer feels frustration. On the other hand, if the received value is equal or little higher than expected value, then customers feels satisfaction, and if the received value is much higher than the expected value then customer feels delight.

Customer Emotional State Mechanism

Experiencing the product or service and comparing the expected and re-ceived values is a strong determinant of behavioral loyalty in customers. If the product or the service performs equally or above the expectations of the customer, then the customer has great potential to repurchase the product. The customer then forms an opinion that determines whether he will repur-chase the product or service. If the product or service performs lower than the expected value, the customer's opinion will prompt him to refuse to purchase it again. This repurchasing decision moment is the "Second Mo-ment of Truth." Companies that provide customer satisfaction and custom-er delight foster "**attitudinal loyalty**" and/or "**behavioral loyalty**" in their customers.

4. The Third Moment of Truth

Not all, but some customers, after their Second Moment of Truth, pass on to the Third Moment of Truth. This usually involves considerable emotion;

they are either frustrated or delighted with what they had experienced with the brand and choose to share their feelings.

Delighted customers most often generate positive word-of-mouth and/or write positive feedback on forums and product-review sites. Some of these delighted customers go beyond mere advocacy and enthusiastically defend the product or service in the name of company on various platforms, in social media, to friends and relatives and so on. On the other hand, frustrated customers disseminate more negative comments on social media and to their family, friends and neighbors.

It is critical to note that sharing—by nature—has both plurality and reciprocity. Plurality means that at least one other individual is needed for sharing to occur. Companies need to be ready to respond, whether the customer shares with one close friend or with several thousands of people online.

The second important quality of sharing is that it is reciprocal. In other words, it is a two-way street. When a customer comments on his or her consumption experience either to friends who are physically nearby or to tens of thousands of people who surf online, the recipients have the opportunity to support or refute the customer's opinion based on their own experiences with the brand. The sharing is reciprocal because the original customer may then respond to the reactions of others by adjusting his own attitudinal and behavioral position about the product or service based on their reactions. Hence, the Third Moment of Truth has far-reaching consequences. The feedback from the original customer affects other potential customers, either positively or negatively. The reciprocal feedback from those responding to the original customer may reinforce his original evaluation or may cause the customer to rethink his position. Reinforced positive feedback will lead to repeat purchase behavior. Products and services that perform well in this feedback stage give birth to "**attitudinal loyalty**" and/or "**behavioral loyalty**" in the mind of the customer.

Barriers

When putting together a Customer Journey Map, it is critical to clearly identify and define the barriers that may prevent customers from continuing the journey. One bad experience, such as a website malfunction or a major shipping delay—even a salesperson who accidentally misleads a customer about a product—can make customers abruptly leave the brand.

Defining barriers enables businesses to more easily develop touchpoints that the company can support with its current resources. Certain barriers might be due to unavoidable issues on the operational side. For instance, the company may lack experienced workers to support a particular consumption stage of the offering; regulations may prevent the company from providing that support; channel partners may not allow certain provisions that the experience requires; or suppliers may not be able to provide the needed materials fast enough. This puts the brand at a disadvantage because their competition may not be up against these same barriers. The best way to isolate and overcome these barriers is to use inductive methodology. This will enable the company to gain an explorative picture of the kinds of issues that have the potential to prevent customers from becoming or remaining loyal to the company.

takeaway!

Never simply assume that each touchpoint for your offering is operating flawlessly. Always verify that the operations that support each consumption stage are operating properly. By staying on top of all the background operations behind your customer journey stages, you may prevent your customers from having an unsatisfying experience with your brand and switching to your competition. This is why Customer Journey Mapping is so essential.

Opportunities

A detailed Customer Journey Map enables the CE Team to see what is happening at each consumption stage. If it is regularly updated, it can be amazingly dynamic. It provides an interactive record of what customers think, feel and do at each stage of an offering, and provides insight as to what their goals are at each touchpoint along the journey. Consequently, the CJM can hint at new opportunities for enhancing the relationship between the customer and the brand. Conversely, this diagnosis can also reveal what is stopping customers from moving forward toward purchase or why they suddenly prefer another brand.

Remember John and his only partially satisfying pizza experience? There were missed opportunities by the restaurant during the considering stage: the restaurant could have grabbed John's attention early on by having a Google ad for him to see during his online searches. They could have immediately texted a discount coupon to his phone or offered it during his call to the order line. Moreover, they could have proactively suggested that next time, if he orders his pizza early, say at 10 am, they could guarantee that he would get his pizza on time. This would get John thinking about getting a future pizza from this restaurant even before he had gotten the first one. His anxiety level would be reduced because he now knows that the company is committed to getting him his pizza on time despite the lunch rush. During the delivery/payment stage, the employee could have let John scan his credit card into the device himself or the restaurant could have provided a mobile phone payment option, so that John would feel secure about using his credit card. In the consumption stage, the restaurant could have attached a colorful flyer to the pizza box explaining all the health benefits of eating an organic pizza like the one he had ordered. For the disposal stage, the pizzeria could have been more aware of how many customers are green-conscious and put the pizza in a recyclable box. For the sharing stage, the pizzeria might have offered a hashtag that says "#Ilove(the pizzeria's name) to encourage enthusiastic sharing. Apparently the magnet was less than inspiring. They may need to redesign it to "wow" their customers and include their website URL and phone # to prompt them to keep it on their refrigerator for the next time customers like John want to order pizza. Defining missed opportunities like these and implementing changes can make a phenomenal difference in how customers respond to the various touchpoints. Each company should periodically evaluate and explore creative ways to enhance their customers' experiences. They should adjust their CJM accordingly so that the new ideas are included in the next round of offerings.

Responsibilities

It is common practice for the departments in most companies to work like disconnected silos. Each department pursues its own targets and sometimes those targets conflict with other departments. In the midst of tangled priorities, the customer is often hurt. In order to create and manage an effective customer experience program, any conflicts that exist between departments should be resolved. Otherwise, marketing, sales, fulfillment, shipping, and customer service might be miscommunicating and causing the customer to have frustrating experiences. It is critical that certain employees be assigned to oversee each part of the customer's experiential journey. Ideally, the sole responsibility of each individual should be to secure the experiential value of that particular micro-stage from a holistic, integrated company perspective. To ensure that the company is able to continuously develop excellent customer experiences, it is wise to establish a Customer Experience (CE) Team. Moreover, when targeting several divergent segments, be sure to adapt the touchpoints wherever possible to each particular segment's persona.

Personas

A generic map may show how an average customer would pass through the consumption stages of an offering, but—unfortunately—no customer is exactly "average." This means that a "one-size-fits-all" approach simply will not work. Companies need several journey maps to cover the spectrum of ages, ethnicities, income levels and interests of potential customers for that particular offering. If this seems somewhat overwhelming, it is.

Each segment of a customer base has a few key characteristics or traits that distinguish them from other segments. This allows brands to group their customers by similarities so that they can target them with various touchpoints. Not every customer will respond to the same brand stimuli. On the other hand, one cannot design a customer journey to meet the individual needs of millions of people. The way to narrow it down is to split potential customers into groups, or "segments," and then assign a "persona" to each one.

Each segment can be represented by a persona, as with the example of

John. John may have seemed like a real person, but he was actually a construct that was based on the responses that a customer in his segment would have had. Each customer segment has specific characteristics based on experiences shared within that segment. As a result, each segment has different experiential needs as they relate to a product or service. By creating a persona with those characteristics, it will be easier to anticipate how that customer segment will respond to a brand's offering." [2] Touchpoints designed with specific personas in mind will be far more effective. [3]

While designing personas, also create scenarios to go with them. This is like role playing. Each scenario provides a set of circumstances that the persona must react to. By adjusting the scenario, companies can experiment to see how that persona would respond to various touchpoints along their customer journey.

takeaway!

Creating personas helps you design a real-world experience for a seemingly real person. This will make each touchpoint more pleasant for the customers who are actually interacting with your brand. Designing realistic personas, as well as scenarios for them to interact with, also enables your CE Team to provide relevant content that your customers will perceive as a solution for their problem.

The next step is designing scenarios, which describe how each persona responds to each of the product or service touchpoints. Their reactions will differ, but these touchpoints still need to be able to move them on to the next stage in the purchase process. Remember how John had emotional reactions at each micro-stage in his pizza-buying experience. Companies must be aware of the range of responses that customers might have to each step in the offering. Creating personas and their scenarios is a commitment to creating the absolutely best customer experience journey possible for the brand. It cannot be rushed. Trying to speed through this process will produce unreliable results and just be a waste of time. However, if a company's customer experience team creates realistic personas and scenarios, their hard work will pay off in more customers purchasing the offering.

Relevant Values

Until businesses know what values a particular customer segment has in relation to their company's industry, it will be nearly impossible to design touchpoints to connect with that persona. Finding out these values, as previously mentioned in this book, gives hints about what drives customers along their purchasing path.

Customer Involvement

Customers do not become involved equally in every offering that they consume. Their level of involvement changes depending on what they perceive the cost and value of the brand offering to be. Involvement refers to the degree of cognitive effort that a customer expends when making a purchase decision. As the cost of an offering increases, the involvement level of the customer increases accordingly. For example, making a decision on specialty goods (cars, houses, etc.) requires more cognitive effort compared with convenience goods (chewing gum, toilet paper, etc.) or shopping goods (clothing, cosmetics, etc.). Consequently, companies should take into account where their particular product is on the involvement-level spectrum when planning out their customer consumption journey. Products and services, as we mentioned earlier, cannot rely simply on previous popularity or name recognition. In order to assure involvement, the customer needs to be made aware of the ways that this particular product will make their lives easier, thus intensifying their involvement. Big Data Analytics is not going to tell a company how to make customers value their product, especially if it is low-involvement to begin with. The only way to unlock the factors that customers truly care about is through Experiential Research.

Borders

Customers pursue certain experiential cues in their consumption journeys. These cues either reinforce the quality of the product in the eyes of the customers or harm it. Experiential cues move in one of two directions: either desire or aversion; consequently, customers are either attracted to the cue or reject the cue. Suppose a customer who is an avid animal lover needs to buy a coat. If a retailer's offering includes coats made of genuine fur, the animal lover would immediately reject that experiential cue, since the customer most likely would never buy fur or any product made from fur. On the other hand, a customer whose dominant value is being fashionable and standing out from the crowd would probably perceive the same fur coat as a positive cue and would define the fur as "a must" in coat design. Where desire and aversion meet is considered a "border" between two opposing segments of customers. Companies creating journey maps need to be sensitive to the desires and aversions of certain segments of their customers as they relate to specific attributes of their products. Borders need to be clearly marked on those journey maps so that the touchpoints allow for divergent responses to experiential cues.

Demographics

Obviously, a particular product or service will not appeal to every demographic. Each segment of customers is unique. In order to create personas, companies have to first start with analyzing the demographic groups that might be interested enough to buy their product or service. Age, gender, ethnic origin, income level, education level, marriage status, area of residence, etc., all go into defining the demographics of a group of people.

Current Interests

Customers have a certain degree of interest in whatever is being offered by companies. Additionally, they only have a certain wallet volume, so to speak. When a group of customers is targeted by a brand, they are automatically nominated to share from their wallet. How much money customers are willing to part with is positively correlated with how interested they are in the offering. So, understanding the relationship between the customers and the current offering is vital when adapting the customer experience journey to specific segments. The key to getting segments to purchase is to find creative ways to demonstrate how the brand's offering meshes with their interests.

Goals

Customers consume goods or services for various reasons; they actually have a goal in mind that they want to achieve while they are going through each stage of their experiential journey. Hence, companies need to identify the common goal that they anticipate customers in each segment will most likely want to achieve at each touchpoint. This will enable them to better design experiential offerings.

Behaviors

The behavioral patterns of customers reveal a lot about them, so that by tracking these patterns, companies can shape the customer journey as well as improve the impact of their offerings. The classic legend about diapers and beer illustrates how the technique of data mining customer behavior has the potential of enabling businesses to grow if applied correctly. Unfortunately, a number of businesses heard about this legend and tried to copy it, but were less than successful. The legend claims that a number of years ago, Walmart had combined data gathered from its loyalty card with its point of sales. When they data-mined it, they found explicit correlations, such as people who bought gin most often also bought tonic. They were surprised to discover, though, that young American males who bought diapers also bought beer. This was so far outside their expectations that someone suggested that they move the diapers next to the beer and see if it increased sales. Well, according to the legend, sales of those items rose substantially.[4] Companies heard about this and immediately put the diapers next to the beer, hoping for a similar result. Some carried it further and started pairing other products based on the data mining technique. Much to their chagrin, the pairings, other than for items that normally go together like peanut butter and jelly, did not sell faster as a set.

The actual truth behind this legend was that Thomas Blischok, who was vice-president of NCR Corp at the time, did a study for Osco Drugs, an American retail chain. He found that there was a correlation between purchases of fruit juice and cough medicine. (No, beer and diapers did not show a correlation.) NCR's data mining examined the contents of 1.2 million shopping carts in 25 stores and identified 30 different shopping correlations. Because of these findings, Osco removed 5,000 slow-selling items from their shelves and rearranged the remaining products. This created a better shopping experience for customers, who were convinced that Osco was actually giving them a larger selection to choose from.[5] This suggests that understanding the behavioral patterns of customers is a key component of a successful customer journey mapping effort.

Experiential Commonalities

As we have seen, separating potential customers into segments is a necessary tool for creating meaningful and effective customer journey mapping. The official term for this action is "Experiential Segmentation."

Experiential segmentation relies on the accumulated common experiences and value system of customers. This suggests that, when defining a customer segment, the roots of and consequences of those accumulated experiences and their resulting value system should be thought of as cause and effect.

When companies identify the "Experiential Commonalities" of their customer segments, these commonalities help them create legitimate segments to aim their offerings at because each segment is already predisposed to respond within those parameters. Brands that integrate Experiential Commonalities and Value System into their CJMs are grabbing the baton that is being extended by customers themselves in the relay race of experiential marketing.

REMEMBER: CJM is NOT a Service Blueprint

One day, one of the authors was at a meeting with a company that is leading in its industry. Customer Journey Mapping (CJM) came up in the discussion. The company told the group that it has been doing CJM and pulled up a service blueprint as their CJM. Customer Journey Mapping is not a service blueprint or process flow chart. It doesn't show how internal departments operate and relate with each other to provide offerings to customers. Rather, CJM looks at consumption through the eyes of customers. It is a representation of the touchpoints that allow customers to connect with the offering. Whereas a service blueprint is, by design, company ego-centric, Customer Journey Mapping is customer-centric. If this company wants to turn its service blueprint into a real CJM, it needs to take the insights that CJM analysis provides and totally redesign its service blueprint to view its offerings from the perspective of the customer. Moreover, it needs to adjust its interdepartmental relationships so that they work together to positively affect the journey of the customer.

"Persona"-fication Framework Chart

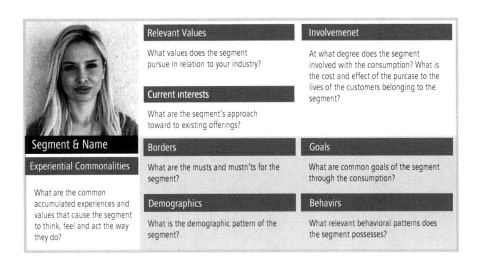

	Relevant Values	Involvemenet
	What values does the segment pursue in relation to your industry?	At what degree does the segment involved with the consumption? What is the cost and effect of the purcase to the lives of the customers belonging to the segment?
	Current interests	
	What are the seqment's approach toward to existing offerings?	
Segment & Name	**Borders**	**Goals**
Experiential Commonalities	What are the musts and mustn'ts for the segment?	What are common goals of the segment through the consumption?
What are the common accumulated experiences and values that cause the segment to think, feel and act the way they do?	**Demographics**	**Behavirs**
	What is the demographic pattern of the segment?	What relevant behavioral patterns does the segment possesses?

Customer Journey Map Example

John is a 28-year old sales representative who works for an insurance company. He is a tech-savvy, green-conscious customer who likes to eat healthy foods.

	CONSUME	SEARCH	ORDER	WAIT	RECEIVE/PAY	CONSUME	DISPOSE	SHARE
Think	What shall I eat at lunch?	Lets check the internet for options	I must order early to get it at the beginning of my break	Will my food arrive on time?	Do they copy my card?	Are these ingredients organic? I hope mu pizza tastes great	I must help care for the environment	I've got to let everyone know abaout my first office lunch!
Feel								
Act	Asks suggestions from friends	Browses on Google Chrome	Calls order line to order	Surfs on smart phone	Pays with credit card	Enjoys the meal	Dropping package into recyclable garbage	Takes pic of meal and shares on social media
Touchpoints	Buzz	Internet, Smart Phone	Order Line	Mobile	Employee	Product	Package	Memoribilia
Customer´s Goal	Finding out options regarding what to eat	Make a proper decision on what to eat	Spending the break efficiently	Enjoying waiting for his pizza	Paying fast, safe and start enjoying meal	Eating healthy because it fits his values	Going green	Being approved of or recognized by others
Opportunities	Sending an discount coupon code at 11.00 AM	Google ads help brand to get into consideration set	Giving customer chance to prefer delivery time interval	Send push notification reading the delivery time	Let the customer scan in the credit card	Attach a flyer to the box promoting the healthy ingredients	Use recyclable package	Provide reason to share

Chapter 7

EXPERIENTIAL SEGMENTATION AND TARGETING

Market segmentation is the process of dividing a broad market into economically meaningful clusters based on types of shared characteristics. When segmenting markets, researchers analyze the markets through: demographic (male vs. female, etc.), geographic (urban vs. suburban, etc.), behavioral (loyal vs. non-loyal, etc.) and psychographic (believer, achiever, etc.) traits.

In marketing history, the term "segmentation" was first introduced to the masses by Wendell R. Smith through his article, "Product Differentiation and Market Segmentation as Alternative Marketing Strategies," which was published in the Journal of Marketing, 1956. Smith compared the market to a cake and proposed that companies apply segmentation practices by targeting one or more slices of the "cake" through their offerings in order to succeed in relevant markets:

> "The differentiator seeks to secure a layer of the market cake, whereas one who employs market segmentation strives to secure one or more wedge-shaped pieces." [1]

Smith was quite right. In fact, several companies were already practicing segmentation, even before there was a term for it; for instance, General Motors produced different car models that targeted different audiences: Cadillac targeted high-income customers, Pontiac targeted performance-seekers, Chevrolet targeted mid-income level customers and Oldsmobile targeted low-budget customers. Segmentation was the prominent strategy that helped General Motors to capture market leadership from Ford by 1931. It didn't take long for Ford to retaliate by copying what General Motors had done, abandoning their "one car model fits all" strategy and recognizing the existence of diverse car-buying segments.

Smith's segmentation article triggered a major shift in the business world to segmentation awareness. He was given the Alpha Kappa Psi Foundation Award for his contributions to marketing science. His article reinforced the then-current "Mad Men Era" of Madison Avenue. This was a group of advertisers in New York City who were "able to tap into what audiences wanted most, as opposed to what they needed," according to Sandy Rubinstein, CEO of DXagency. In critiquing the "Mad Men" TV series re-enactment of that period, she described the main character, Don, saying, "His ability to craft messaging around emotions versus necessities is what ultimately sold a product."[2]

This is exactly what advertisers of that time did—they crafted messaging that touched the emotions of a specific segment of the target audience. Businesses not only identified which segments of customers would buy their products, but they also aimed their advertising at those specific segments: A vacuum cleaner company targeting housewives would place ads in fashion magazines, whereas an aftershave brand targeted bachelors with the slogan, "Lucky Tiger Gets the Gals."[3]

From the late 1950s until the late 1960s, advertisers, business executives, consultants and marketing research companies went after demographic segmentation and divided the markets according to the ages, genders, income levels, occupations, etc., of customers. In 1964, a Harvard Business Review article, "New Criteria for Market Segmentation" by Daniel Yankelovich, shook the business world's obsession with demographic segmentation. According to the study, he had determined that demographic traits were simply not enough to properly segment markets:

> "Demography is not the only or the best way to segment markets. Even more crucial to marketing objectives are differences in buyer attitudes, motivations, values, patterns of usage, aesthetic preferences, and degree of susceptibility."[4]

The opposition of Yankelovich to the status quo of depending solely on demographic traits paved the way for behavioral and psychographic segmentation to be born. In 1971 Ruth Ziff empirically proved that customers could be segmented according to psychographic traits[5]; in 1974 Emanuel Demby, the father of psychographic segmentation, released the article, "Psychographics and from Where it Came," in an American Marketing Association publication, bringing a methodological view to psychographic segmentation.[6] The progression and evolution of psychographic segmentation went on through the contributions of academicians and practitioners. In 1978, under the leadership of Arnold Mitchell, a group of scientists from Stanford University developed the VALS model. This model measured and segmented customers in a psychographic way through three criteria: "Values," "Attitudes" and "Lifestyles."[7] VALS immediately became the latest fashion in the psychographic segmentation measurement. Later, VALS2 was released as an upgrade, but the name reverted back to the original acronym, VALS, while carrying the modus operandi of the second version. Today VALS is mostly used by the advertising industry to intensify demand for offerings.

When psychographic segmentation first arose, it cast a spell on academicians and practitioners alike; however, as time passed, its real-life outcomes failed to reach its expected potential. Ironically enough, one of the people who roared against its impotency was Daniel Yankelovich—the man who carried the rebellion banner against the demographic and geographic segmentation. In 2006 he wrote an article with David Meer in the Harvard Business Review, under the title of "Rediscovering Market Segmentation." In this milestone article, he thoroughly criticized this latest fad of psychographic segmentation practices and their results:

> "Psychographics may capture some truths about real people's life styles, attitudes, self-image, and aspirations, but it is very weak at pre dicting what any of these people is likely to purchase in any given product category. It thus happens to be very poor at giving corporate decision makers any idea of how to keep the customers they have or gain new ones." [8]

As a result of these failures, some businesses that couldn't enjoy the boons of psychographic segmentation went back to geographic, demographic, behavioral, or some combination of these segmentation methods. In fact, they remained clueless in a segmentation desert. Some short-lived fads like Blue Ocean strategy took advantage of the segmentation confusion and suggested that businesses pursue "DE-segmentation" to succeed in their markets. According to views like this, there shouldn't be any segmentation effort at all, and company offerings should not be tailored. Blue Ocean advised them to take a "one size fits all" approach, using the "average man" of the masses as a reference. (Readers may be sensing a little déjà vu back to Ford and his "customers can have...any color as long as it's black" comment). Despite all these efforts, the need for a proper, reliable, valid and actionable segmentation methodology couldn't be satisfied. Yankelovich and Meer expressed the problem and their perspective on it:

> "The failings of psychographics, however, and the disappointments it has produced in its users, should not cast doubt on the validity of careful segmentation overall. Indeed, marketers continue to rely on it, and line executives increasingly demand segmentations that the

whole enterprise can put into action. Because of the technique's un
derlying validity, and managers' continuing need for what it can do,
there's good reason to think that segmentation's drift from its origi
nal purpose and potency can be halted. Good segmentations identi
fy the groups most worth pursuing—the underserved, the dissatisfied,
and those likely to make a first-time purchase, for example." [9]

Because most marketers largely ignored this thinking, confusion about
the segmentation issue toppled over into the Customer Experience Age
without a proper solution. From the late 1980's to today, some companies
pursued micro-segmentation efforts, thanks to technological advancements
and accumulated data regarding customers. Most of these companies relied heavily on CRM systems, Data Mining efforts and Big Data processing
software to segment the customers. The segmentation fell into the claws
of pure positivism, which claimed that "...only "factual" knowledge gained
through observation, including measurement, is trustworthy." Hence, only
"...quantifiable observations that lead themselves to statistical analysis" were
allowed. [10]

Unfortunately, pure positivism cannot give birth to reliable and satis-
factory outcomes because it disregards the integration of qualities, which is
the only way to give context to pure data. As a result of inefficient real-life
simulations based purely on quantities, many companies ignored or limited
segmentation after a few trials and errors. Others continued to pursue the illusion that positivism would give them the answers they needed, since there
seemed to be no alternative way to segment customers.

A company may have incredible Big Data and may mine it using the
latest trendy software; however, a segmentation effort that depends solely on
quantities—which Big Data does—is nothing beyond a mirage without the
integration of qualities. One of the prominent challenges that the Customer Experience Era intensifies is the segmentation issue.

Traditional segmentation evaluates customers through a single-stage
mindset. This is natural because almost all businesses see their offerings as
single-staged offerings and not as part of a process. According to experiential
segmentation, all offerings are actually multi-staged and should be considered as such when segmentation research is conducted. Traditional segmentation may analyze behavioral patterns of customers and come up with an

outcome of segments, such as entire-year consumers, seasonal consumers, weekend consumers, weekday consumers, day-time consumers, night-time consumers, etc. In contrast, experiential segmentation breaks the whole consumption experience into stages, such as buying/using/disposing, and breaks these three stages into sub-processes revealing the expectancies of customer segments at each sub-stage. Consequently, experiential segmentation provides a clearer and more actionable understanding of each of the segments. In experiential segmentation, a customer that is member of a specific experiential segment in the early stages of the journey may shift to another experiential segment along the consumption process. Traditional segmentation, on the other hand, adopts a static perspective: If a customer belongs to a segment, he or she stays in that segment regardless of the consumption experience.

Traditional segmentation mostly relies on quantities, such as analyzing Big Data through cluster analysis, logistic regression, discriminant analysis or other parametric tests. These are considered reliable enough for segmenting customers. Most studies disregard external validity and proceed by utilizing internal data. However, experiential segmentation adopts an "outside-in" perspective, as we have mentioned before, and studies the relevant qualities that significantly affect the formation of segments. To accomplish this, it functions beyond the scope of in-house Big Data. Besides this, it studies the reciprocity of quantitatively-formed segments in real life environments. Thus, experiential segmentation is both externally and internally validated. Experiential segmentation does not disregard parametric methods which are the requisite for a proper deduction, but reinforces their validity both from external examination and in-time context philosophy, applying inductive methods. Unlike traditional segmentation, experiential segmentation divides the market into sub-groups based on customers' experiential expectancies, experiential commonalities and value systems. across the customer journey. This provides executives and decision-makers with the equivalent of a video rather than a mere photograph of the customer's journey. Customer experience is in constant flux along the consumption stages, and experiential segmentation provides the answers for how customers expect, experience, think, feel and behave along the customer journey. It also provides comprehensive knowledge about the customers and the segments they form, which enables companies to create more effective touchpoints.

The market is full of customers with diverse expectations. This simple and obvious truth is recognized by most practitioners—especially by those who conduct market research, product development, pricing, strategy formulation, communication and sales functions in companies. A proper segmentation provides brand competency by tailoring offerings based on the expectancies of these customer groups. Consequently, segmentation is a requisite for all organizations to survive and grow. However, in the customer experience era, it should be steered based on customer experiences rather than explicit demographic, geographic, behavioral or ambiguous psychographic parameters.

Experiential segmentation refers to dividing the market into sub-groups by noting the accumulated experiences of the customers and their value systems that make them behave cohesively in a similar way. The aim of experiential segmentation is to reveal a picture of groups of customers in a specific market based on their experiential similarities. As we previously mentioned, people in a particular segment choose to consume specific products or services due to common experiences. The purpose of experiential segmentation is to view the market through the customers' evaluation struggle to reveal groups with commonalities. Thus, multiple experiential segments are formed, each with diverse traits which are shared by everyone in that segment. Experiential segmentation, compared to traditional segmentation methods like Demographic, Geographic, Psychographic and Behavioral, is both more reliable and more effective, since understanding the cause of a specific consumption behavior or attitude enables businesses to proactively respond to shifts in the behavioral or attitudinal patterns of their customers.

By the way, it is imperative to underline the fact that marketers should not evaluate experiential segmentation on the platform of sensory experience (sight, smell, tactile, taste and hearing). Nor should they confuse it with early proposed, raw, non-actionable experience-related customer profiling studies that limit the concept to relating, sensing, feeling, thinking and acting. Experiential segmentation is not as simple as early abstract experience-related customer profiling. On the contrary, it possesses a massive body of knowledge compared to these early sketchy customer-profiling attempts. In fact, experiences are much deeper than surface responses of the senses. Senses are receptors that receive data from the outside world and transmit them to the brain through the nervous system. That is how individuals—and, more specifically, customers—sense their environment. The senses gain meaning through cognition, and during cognition, customers compare, combine and relate what they have just sensed to what they already know. Senses are just electrical signals that carry data about the outer world, so that performing sensory-focused segmentation does not provide actionable data regarding customers, since they can't reveal the customers' experiential mindset.

Experiential segmentation requires a holistic view toward the interaction between the shared traits of customers and the specific market that is about to be segmented. Every market and industry possesses a certain distinctive experiential nature. Hence, customers interacting with that industry carry similarities based on their specific experiential accumulation. Therefore, the dynamics of experiential segmentation should be adapted according to the experiential nature and background of the customers in the market. Framing the values, personality traits, attitudes and beliefs of customers from the perspective and filter of the nature of the market is the only way to conduct an actionable experiential segmentation.

Customers in the market possess diversified experiential traits. However, some of the traits for some groups of customers carry commonality. This commonality causes specific customer groups to be like-minded; they may have similar interests, similar backgrounds, similar birth places, similar education levels, etc. Internal and external traits cause the group to display similar behavioral patterns, i.e., their life views are shaped by similar experiences. Similar experiences cause them to develop similar associations between concepts. For example, when reading the words "purple" and "gold," Los Angeles Lakers fans will have a different reaction than most other people. This is because that color combination has significance in the value systems of Lakers fans based on their common accumulated experiences. Accumulated experiences can trigger similar impulses, cognitions and behavior within the segment. The intensity of the response is due to the strength of the experiences. Every experience causes an association or strengthens an association. Associations are like muscles; if they are exercised regularly, they become stronger just like biceps or triceps. If a sports fan is frequently exposed to the team colors, then the association between purple/gold and the LA Lakers team cements. Similarly, when segmenting a market, understanding the industry, potential customers, and the specific cultural associations that the population has are the keys for a healthy, well-performing, actionable experiential segmentation.

By the same token, this is one of the reasons why the strategies used in designing customer experiences in different cultural environments also need to be carefully thought through. For example, if a company is targeting customers in several countries that have widely different cultures and values, they need to decide how to incorporate and respect those cultural differences throughout their value chain. Again, there is no "one size fits all" when a company is serious about experiential segmentation. This is especially true in areas that have multiple subcultures. Subcultures are groups of people in a country or region who have either developed independently from the dominant culture or have become disenfranchised and have separated themselves from the main population. In the inner cities of the US, for example, there are numerous subcultures of poor minority citizens who not only believe that they are not a part of the main population, but they feel pride in their separateness. They have developed their own subculture, set of values, even music and jargon. To reach customers in this experiential segment, a company would need to intently study this subculture to discover its value system and experiential commonalities before attempting to create a consumption journey for them.

What this all boils down to is that businesses need to be proactive when designing customer experience for each specific segment. Without careful planning and the willingness to make changes based on new information as it comes in, the brand could be unpleasantly surprised by an adverse reaction by the segment to part of their value chain.

Experiential Qualities

In the very beginning of the segmentation process, it is vital to find out which common behavioral and attitudinal patterns the customers in a particular relevant market possess. Identifying behavioral and attitudinal patterns is crucial for a proper experiential segmentation. To reveal these patterns, experiential research should be conducted. A comprehensive framework on how to conduct experiential research was covered in Chapter 5.

After isolating the patterns, determine the experiential accumulation that caused the patterns in the first place. Use qualitative analysis to go deeper and understand the experiential commonalities between the customers with similar traits that form each group. In further stages of the segmentation, the values of the groups will become obvious. The next step is to carefully describe the direction, depth and concentration of those values. This deeper step is somewhat like data mining, but it is "value mining." Value mining goes far beyond data mining because it digs up the motivations behind the experiential commonalities.

Taking the extra effort and time to uncover this type of implicit relevant experiential accumulation will enable the brand to deliver "spot-on" customer experiences that are distinct from the competition because they are true to the customers themselves.

Experiential segmentation, compared to traditional methods, provides a clearer picture of where individuals in a particular segment are in their thinking and in their beliefs. The thing that makes an individual an individual is the accumulated experiences of that individual, so people with similar experiential accumulation are more likely to behave in similar ways.

Adler's Birth Order Theory is a great example to illustrate how experiential segments are formed. The relation between birth order and personal traits was proposed by Alfred Adler in 1930. Adler proposed that the oldest child has a dominant personality and tends to be smart by nature, but the oldest child also has a strong need for the approval of others. The reason is due to the experience that almost all oldest children must pass through— the birth of the second child. At this point, the oldest loses his position as the center of attention. Now the younger child sits at the center of the family. Suddenly all the behaviors of the oldest are not tolerated as in the past, so gaining parental love and favor becomes a driving force that shapes the behaviors of the oldest. On the other hand, the second child doesn't possess this drive for approval, since as the "newcomer," the parents are far more tolerant of his behavior. Soon the parents load the responsibility of making sure that the younger sibling doesn't get hurt or into trouble onto the older sibling. Since this meshes well with the dominant personality trait of the oldest, he usually takes this new role in stride. When the third child joins the family, it drastically changes the dynamics. The youngest child is now the middle child, stuck between the new youngest and the oldest. The middle child is neither old enough to lead the siblings like the oldest, nor young enough to be easily tolerated like the youngest. So the middle child competes on both fronts. As time passes, experiential accumulation causes the middle child to become diplomatic as well as competitive —depending on the circumstances—since being stuck in the middle sometimes requires diplomacy and other times requires vying for position. The youngest child sits in the center of attention and receives protection from the whole family. Hence, the youngest gets his way most often, which makes the youngest feel important. This results in a more demanding child who is often selfish, since the child is not as experienced at sharing as the other two. It is true that several other factors affect the relationship between children from the perspective of birth order, such as gender or the age difference between the siblings, or the socioeconomic status of the family and so on; however, this example helps us to gain a clearer idea about how shared experiential accumulation can bind together customers within segments, causing them to respond in similar ways to brand-related stimuli.

Companies that segment customers by experiential accumulation - and value systems consequently - are able to provide a more optimal solution to the customer based on what the customer should feel, think and do towards their product or service. Therefore, the essence of experiential segmentation reveals implicit and relevant experiential accumulation. What is more, it demonstrates the reciprocal needs of customers to form customer groups (segments) accordingly. This approach is different than one-to-one marketing, since one-to-one marketing pursues a micro-segment of the potential customer base. In comparison, experiential segmentation goes after groups of customers based on their implicit, multidimensional experiential needs. Experiential segmentation is also far more cost-effective than one-to-one marketing.

Unusual behavior by specific segments of the population who share experiential accumulations has been recorded throughout history. In 1966, it was noted that Japan's birth rate had dropped drastically only to recover completely the next year. It was assumed at first that some external event had caused this unpredicted occurrence. Maybe an earthquake or tsunami had interrupted the normal birth rate, but the phenomenon was too widespread. Crop failures or financial disasters also would not have affected such a large portion of the population. The answer lay in Japanese tradition: 1966 was the "Year of the Fire Horse." Every 60 years, the twelve zodiac animals intersect with the five traditional elements (fire, water, earth, wood, metal), to create the Year of the Fire Horse. The Japanese people believe that any female baby born during the Year of the Fire Horse would have poor prospects for marriage. Hence, women actively avoided having any children during that year.

As a result, there was a decrease of about 463,000 live births in Japan in 1966, constituting a sharp departure from the linear trend before and after. Both contraception and induced abortion were used by parents to ensure that a child would not be born during this taboo time period. The induced abortion rate, 43.1 per 1000 births (a total of 65,000), was significantly higher than the expected 30.6 (46,200 total) based on the trend from the years 1963 to 1969. No epidemics were reported in 1966 which might have caused the increase in infant mortality. Researchers could find no other explanation than voluntary compliance with the observance of Hinoe Uma (Elder Fire-Horse) by a massive group of women.[11]

These Japanese women formed a segment of the population that had a common experiential accumulation. It was one that they had been raised to believe—that having a child in the Year of the Fire-Horse was a bad omen that would keep their daughter from getting married. The shared belief in this tradition was powerful enough to convince an unprecedented number of women to use contraceptives or to have an abortion rather than give birth to a child in 1966.

Experiential accumulations are extremely strong motivators. They can either inspire a group of people to seek after something they want, such as customers, or force them to reluctantly take an action that they wish they didn't have to, like the Japanese women. Shared incentives can help companies market their products if they segment their customers by commonalities in their experiences, because, as we have seen with a real-life example, people in the same segment will likely respond similarly to the same stimulus, since they possess similar value systems.

In another supporting example, it was noticed that most of the players in a Canadian ice hockey league had birthdays in January, February or March.

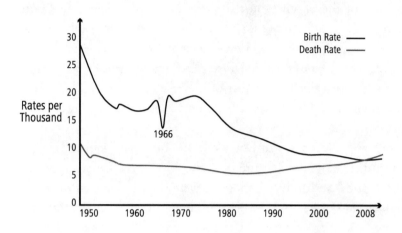

Birth Rate Trends in Japan 1950-2008

This seemed a bit odd at first glance. If one believed in astrology, it would appear that these players had some extra abilities because they were born under the Capricorn, Aquarius or Pisces sign. Obviously, there had to be another answer. Sure enough, the eligibility cutoff date was January 1st, which meant that the boys whose birthdays were in the early months of the year had several months' growth and maturity advantage over those whose birthdays were later in the year. That advantage allowed them to perform better than many of their teammates in that class, and, later, scouts would notice their strong performance and move them ahead into rep squads, where they would get more professional coaching. This segment of boys whose birthdays fell in January, February and March all benefited from a major advantage in their hockey experience.

This demonstrates that it was a shared experiential accumulation that boosted these players forward in their careers. Had it not been discovered that their advantage was linked to the eligibility cut-off date, there would have been no way to prove one way or the other that these boys were not simply a random cluster of better players. [12]

Quantitative Validation

Once the experiential needs, expectations, commonalities and value systems of customers in a particular segment are revealed, the qualities should be quantitatively investigated and validated so that they are representative as well as generalizable. The way to quantify relevant experiential qualities is to use a representative sample that is obtained from the total customer audience in the market.

takeaway!

When examining your customer segments, it is critical that you find a way to measure your qualitative results quantitatively. Otherwise, you risk making assumptions about your segment that do not have a valid basis. The assumption that every female customer ages 6-11 would want to buy your brand's hot pink bookbag—simply because most girls that age love the color pink—needs to be quantitatively tested. Testing may prove that you are right, but other factors could cause most of those young customers to select a blue or purple bookbag—especially if it has the picture of a character from a cartoon movie like Frozen on it. Quantitative testing enables you to validate any qualitative assumptions you have made about your customer segment. (And it may prevent a costly marketing mistake!)

Multi-criteria Experiential Positions of Segments

In marketing books and resources, most customer segmentation maps provide a two-dimensional visual representation of a specific group of customers as they respond to a company's product or service. However, an experiential segmentation map shouldn't be confined to two dimensions. When constructing an experiential segmentation map, a multi-dimensional approach offers much more flexibility. There are a number of methods for building maps that include far more variables than two-dimensional maps can contain. With multi-criteria maps, companies can define and sort out what types of experiential qualities the customers share and statistically show which customers belongs in which segment.

Multidimensional scaling (MDS) can help CE Teams devise a multi-criteria segmentation map. Similar to a map used for traveling, this segmentation map shows the distance or relative positioning of certain customer segments from the brand's offering. As mentioned earlier, this kind of map is not limited to two dimensions. Multidimensional scaling allows customer responses and preferences to be transformed into distances and pictured in three dimensions. Hence, MDS is far more flexible and enlightening. With MDS maps, it is possible to measure and determine which aspects of a brand are more effective with which customer segments due to their value systems. The ultimate benefit of using multi-criteria maps is that they enable brands have a "bird's eye view" of the entire consumption journey. This makes it much easier to tweak touchpoints to solidly connect with the experiential accumulation and value system of each customer segment and to be more proactive in redesigning any micro-stages that might be underperforming.

Potential Value and Accessibility of Segments

Once segmentation analysis and mapping are complete, there should be a detailed description for each customer segment, including their experiential traits, values distinct from the other customer segments. By now, the entire Customer Experience team should have a clear and quantitatively reliable image of the market in hand; hence, they are almost ready to choose which target segments the strategy will be built upon. Before selecting which segments to target, be sure to evaluate the size of each segment. This will make it possible to project the "potential value" of each segment. Potential value is an estimate of what a customer is worth to the company or brand. It is based on a series of scores, including past activity, income level, expenditures etc.

More broadly, in terms of customer segmentation, "potential value" is the value that the company places on a segment of potential customers who share specific commonalities and who will interact with the brand.

While determining the potential value, two aspects of accessibility must also be nailed down. The company must: 1. decide how they will communicate their experiential offering to their target customers, and 2. decide how they will deliver their experiential offering to their target customers. These are not the same thing.

Four Pillars of Experiential Segmentation

Experiential segmentation efforts in order to produce results, should rely on at least four pillars as: Value Centricity, Stage Focus, Reciprocity and Approach & Avoid Perspective. Through satisfying these core qualities a proper level of segmentation can be executed.

Four Pillars of Experiential Segmentation

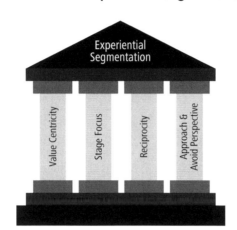

Value Centricity

Experiential segmentation identifies the values that the segment's customers pursue to express through their purchase rather than specific features and benefits that they might be looking for.

Stage Focus

Experiential segmentation is a kinetic effort, since it focuses on the evolution of the costumer rather than static traits.

Reciprocity

Experiential segmentation emphasizes the importance of using both qualitative and quantitative research and relies on both external and internal data sources to validate the segmentation effort.

Approach and Avoid Perspective

Experiential segmentation looks at the customer's accumulated experience from a pleasure/pain perspective, which allows the brand to fine tune stages to appeal to that segment.

Comparison Table of Traditional and Experiential Segmentation

	Traditional Segmentation	Experiential Segmentation
Context	Fixed	Relative
Source	External or Internal	Both Internal & External
Customer View	Standing	Flowing
Inputs	Quantitative	Quantitative & Qualitative
Nature	Direction	Proaction
Screening	Cross-Sectional	Longitudinal Journey

Experiential Audit

In order to ensure that a company is properly targeting its customer segments, it is necessary to periodically perform an Experiential Audit. This type of study will reveal if the company's offerings are effectively engaging the intended customer segment(s). In the process of performing an experiential audit, the chances are good that the audit will also reveal untouched niches that the company can target in the future.

The Experiential Audit asks the questions: Which experiences do the customers in this segment desire? Which of these experiences is the brand actually delivering? Which of these experiences is the competition delivering?

Through answering these questions, the CE Team will be able to determine which segments are being served through the touchpoints along the consumer journey and which are not. This study will provide a wealth of knowledge and data to build a strategy to fix the problems and capitalize on the successes.

In the process, it will also be possible to spot untouched experiential niches that the brand can fill. Take an honest look at the capabilities of the company and explore the possibilities these niches might offer. Targeting new customer segments that are interested in those niches will require new strategies such as HR strategy, Operations Strategy, Innovation Strategy, Communication Strategy and so forth. Claiming new niches in the market will demand broad and dedicated participation from various departments, so each department will need to do its homework and disclose its reciprocal positioning decision.

Chapter 8

EXPERIENTIAL POSITIONING

ositioning is the sum of the efforts that are made by brands in order to occupy a distinctive place in the mind of the customer. Holding a distinctive position is critical, because by doing so, brands avoid falling into the "inert set" when customers are making a purchasing decision. "Inert set," as mentioned before, refers to brands in a specific product category that are perceived by customers as not noticeably different than others in that same category. For example, television brands struggle to hold a distinctive position in the minds of middle class American families. Sony, RCA, Samsung, Panasonic, Toshiba, Philips and Vizio—to name a few—all appeal nearly equally to this customer segment. Unless customers have had excellent or poor experiences with one of these brands, or a particular model has a "wow" feature, these televisions form an inert set and are lumped together in the customer's mind. Rather than one brand being evaluated as a distinctive alternative to the other TV brands, each is considered "more of the same thing" among many "me-too" options. Because there is not enough differentiation, the likelihood of one brand being the purchase choice of a customer decreases.

Like most pillar concepts in marketing, positioning originated in the mid-20th century. An early forerunner of positioning was the "Unique Selling Proposition" (USP) concept, which was coined by Rosser Reeves in the 1950s:

> " For we all have a third ear, and it does listen, whether we will it or not, to the music of drums that we ourselves can rarely hear. So it is better to drape a product, on the nonverbal level, with as many ac tivating and pleasant associations as possible. We simply say: "The totality of the advertisement must project a Unique Selling Proposi tion, as well as a feeling." Embellish it then, if you will, with gold or sprinkle it with stardust. Drape behind it the richest tapestries of the nonverbal school. We believe that a raw and naked USP is one ex treme; and the richest brand image, which does not project a claim, is the other."[1]

In later years, Ogilvy, in his work "Confessions of an Advertising Man," wrote about the position of a product in the marketplace. He defined positioning as a kind of consistency of brand in the long run, but Ogilvy didn't call his concept "positioning" even though his view covered the essence of positioning:

> "Plan your campaign for years ahead, on the assumption that your clients intend to stay in business forever. Build sharply defined per sonalities for their brands, and stick to those personalities, year after year. It is the total personality of a brand rather than any trivial prod uct difference which decides its ultimate position in the market."[2]

The term "positioning" was actually coined by Trout in his article, "Po sitioning is a Game People Play in Today's Me-Too Marketplace," which was published in the Industrial Marketing Journal, 1969. The article was followed by another in 1972, co-authored by Ries and Trout, which was published in Advertising Age under the title, "The Positioning Era Cometh." Trout's choice of the word "positioning" was inspired by a definition that he saw in a dictionary. The word "strategy" was defined as "finding the most advantageous position against the enemy."[3] Thus, he decided to expound on this concept in his article:

> "To succeed in our over-communicated society, a company must cre ate a 'position' in the prospect's mind. A position that takes into con sideration not only its own strength and weaknesses, but those of its competitors as well."[4]

In 1981, Ries and Trout published their masterpiece book, "Positioning: The Battle for Your Mind," which comprehensively elaborated on the posi tioning concept with examples from real life. They repeatedly underlined the cognitive aspect of positioning and the perceptive side of offerings:

> "Positioning starts with a product. A piece of merchandise, a service, a company, an institution or even a person. Perhaps yourself. But positioning is not what you do to a product. Positioning is what you do to the mind of the prospect. That is, you position the product in the mind of the prospect."[5]

Positioning is about creating associations between the brand and the oth er concepts that are already in customers' minds. When this binding process is conducted, relevancy should be taken into consideration. A toothpaste brand can be relevant because of the values it offers, such as whitening, an ti-tartar, fights germs, and so forth; or in case of cars, air bag systems (ABS) which are tied to safety concerns of customers are relevant for car brands. However, possessing relevancy is not the sole criterion of distinction; one brand's positioning should be distinctive from the competition as well. In the toothpaste example, it doesn't seem like any one brand is distinct from another simply due to its whitening or anti-tartar formula. Similarly, in the automotive industry, providing an ABS is not something that helps a company occupy a distinctive place in the mind of customers.

With technological advancements, most attributes are being matched by the competition in a relatively short space of time, so differentiating is getting harder and harder day by day. The traditional positioning formula invented on Madison Avenue is not working in saturated markets anymore, so developed companies relying on positioning are losing ground. Jack Trout, as the father of positioning, addresses his complaints about the ground that positioning has lost over time and expresses his ideas in an American Marketing Association publication:

> "While America has to re-learn positioning, China has decided to learn it. Recently, Peking University in China has put my positioning strategy material into its business school curriculum. China is moving from manufacturing to marketing with a vengeance. Look out, world." [6]

Trout was complaining about American professionals neglecting his positioning concept; however, his complaints were not on solid ground, because America is not the old America any more. The market has progressed over the years and evolved into a highly saturated market. Thus the concept of traditional positioning, which was proposed by Trout and Ries in the previous millennium is not working anymore. It has, however, taken foothold in underdeveloped and developing countries. China is a developing country and it is quite normal for them to embrace the traditional positioning framework just as America did at the beginning of the mid-20th century.

Despite the fact that traditional positioning is written about in almost all marketing textbooks and taught in the leading business schools, it is not easily converted into solid action. It cannot simply be snatched from the page and applied to today's marketplace because of its traditional approach to brand distinction. Thus, traditional positioning is being scrapped today because it couldn't adapt to the zeitgeist of 21st century marketing. With the welcomed Customer Experience Era, experiential positioning, rather than traditional positioning, seems to be the proper solution that enables brands to hold a distinctive position in the minds of customers.

According to studies about human memory capacity, there are limitations to our ability to consciously distinguish between offerings within the same category. George Miller in 1956 conducted a research study in Princeton University on the memory limitations of the human brain. The results showed that working memory can only hold an average of seven objects from a specific category, with a ±2 deviation. Working memory is the type of memory that is responsible for processing data in a flowing base. It has an average of 1-2 seconds of storage capacity. [7] As such, it resembles the RAM (Random Access Memory) that computers possess. Without working memory, man cannot process data and make a decision.

takeaway!

Test your own working memory by listing as many brands that you can think of in any one specific product category—for example, potato chip brands. Can you think of more than seven brands off the top of your head?

In order to be one of those seven companies that most everyone remembers, offering category standards such as whitening, anti-tartar, or an ABS in cars, is a "must" to stay competitive, but still not enough to be distinctive. Besides these standard features, given this new customer experience era, businesses should provide additional features that customers can connect with experientially. Coca-Cola's unique-tasting formula is a quality that creates a memorable experience for customers and distinguishes it from all other cola drinks. In the process, it gives Coca-Cola an experiential positioning that the competition cannot match.

Experiential positioning is different from traditional positioning in several key ways: Traditional positioning focuses on the strength and explicit nature of the positioning, thus the process is seen as a managerial practice rather than a customer implementation. In contrast, in experiential positioning, the positioning is implicit and designed to make the brand relevant to the customer. Consequently, the customer prefers the brand every single time with or without necesseraily being aware of the reason why. Traditional positioning is based on the current needs of customers, but experiential positioning can address both the current and future needs of customers—thanks to experiential research infrastructure. Traditional positioning relies on the traits of the offering lingering in customers' minds, while in experiential positioning, the values of the customer segment outweigh the product traits. In saturated markets, traditional positioning, for the most part, survives only in theory. This is because it transmits a single message that remains static across all the consumption stages. But consumption doesn't consist of a single message or a single point of interaction; rather, it is an interactive process. Experiential positioning takes the entire consumption journey into account. It is also process-oriented because it aims to deliver an interactive positioning statement that responds to customers as they pass through each stage. Hence, customers see how it dovetails with their values and thoroughly enjoy their journey.

The crucial thing in experiential positioning, then, is finding the value or values that are relevant to that customer segment. Consider the automobile industry. BMW, Mercedes and Lexus hold similar positions in customer thinking because all three provide luxury and prestige to their owners. As noted before, they are an inert set. A customer may evaluate the brands as pretty much the same. Volvo, however, even though it is not designed to be luxurious or prestigious, has a significantly distinctive positioning in the market because of the unique values of safety it offers compared with other cars in its class. As you remember, the company has announced that by 2020 the brand will launch a new generation of vehicles—death-proof cars. Parents whose priority is keeping their families safe will see tremendous value in this new type of car. Consequently, in experiential positioning as well as in experiential.

takeaway!

*Once you have determined which values are important to your
target customer segment, the next step is to go deeper and
explore the associations that your target segment shares.
Remember that in Chapter 5, you were given a comprehensive
walkthrough of how to map these associations. It is time for you
to map your target segment's
"value associations."*

*Your aim is to identify the relationships between various
concepts and values in the minds of your target customers. You
will notice that they share a lot of them due to their experiential accumulations. By writing and/or sketching these connections on an associational map, you will be able to determine
how your offer can be relevant to them. With this knowledge,
you can position your experiential offering so that it will engage
and even "wow" your customers.*

segmentation, detecting value streams and value-based customer accumulations is much more important than solely understanding behavioral, demographic, geographic or psychographic relationships.

Associational Quantification

Once the associational connections of the segment have been mapped, it
is necessary to measure the strength of the bonds between each concept.
Think of these concepts as being connected with rubber bands. Some of
the rubber bands are thin and narrow and can easily break. Others are thick
and strong. Marketers hope that most of the associations that customers

have between their values and the marketer's offering are strong, but there is no way to know for sure without actually measuring them quantitatively. This kind of study enables companies to verify the strength levels between relevant concepts. This testing can be conducted either at the conscious level or subconscious level. However, ideally, the study should be run at both the conscious and subconscious levels simultaneously. These results will validate both the explicit and implicit associations that these customers are making. Moreover, these associations can be incorporated to varying degrees into the touchpoints.

An Illustration of Positioning of a Brand in the Mind of Customers

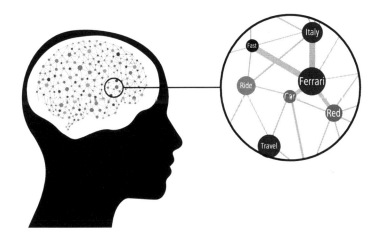

Experiential Positioning Statement

After the associational map is quantitatively validated, it is time to position the brand/product/service in the real world. In other words, it's time to create a positioning statement.

To be effective, an Experiential Positioning Statement should be:

1. Relevant to the target segments and integrated with their value systems
2. Differentiated from the competition
3. Experientially grounded
4. Consistent over time
5. Actionable through existing capabilities.

takeaway!

*When developing your positioning statement, consider the
strength and valence of associations among your company,
your competitors and relevant concepts in the minds of customers
that are in the category you are competing in.
Then evaluate your organization's capabilities,
based on the 5 criteria listed above, whether you can
hold that position in the market or not.*

*What is more critical than forming an experiential positioning
statement is; adopting it as an organizational attitude and
transforming the company in alignment with the statement.*

How to Get Started: When positioning a brand, trace the concept associations that the customer feels are important and then measure the strength of the bonds that have formed between them. For example, one customer may see the name Volvo and think of the Euro NCAP, which assesses car safety levels. A customer who is concerned about safety might connect these concepts. Knowing that Volvos have passed numerous crash tests puts his mind at ease and strengthens the association between the Volvo name and safety.

Comparison Table of Traditional and Experiential Positioning

	Traditional Positioning	Experiential Positioning
Context	Strong & Explicit	Relevant & Implicit
Source	Current Needs	Current & Prospect Needs
Base	Characteristics	Values
Customer View	Theoretical	Actionable
Inputs	Static Across Stages	Kinetic Across Stages
Nature	Goal Oriented	Process Oriented

Chapter 9

DESIGNING EXPERIENCES

Today many companies are desperate for new ideas to make their brands stand out. One way is to design innovative additions to their existing products. This sounds like the perfect solution. It is more economical than coming up with a whole new product. Plus, these innovations will make their existing products more appealing and increase sales. Unfortunately, some companies confuse <u>efficient innovation</u> with <u>pointless novelty</u>. An efficient innovation will render their current offering more valuable through delivering differentiating relevant experiences. A pointless novelty may appear to be an innovation, but it doesn't accomplish its goal of benefiting the customer. The automobile industry has been guilty of making this mistake on more than one occasion. They often add new features to their cars to "enhance the experience" that their car provides. Unfortunately, most of these are mere novelties—not true innovations. What's the difference? Pointless novelties don't find reciprocity in the experiential expectancy and value system of customers. Rather than delivering experiential value, pointless novelties merely deliver extra costs for customers. For example, a leading global car brand, in some of its models, offered air vents that were wrapped in genuine leather. Other than providing an excuse to increase the price of the vehicle, this enhancement didn't seem to provide a better customer experience. In fact, customers still have not figured out how leather on air vents improves the overall experience of the car. What is telling is that research has shown that the customers who own this car are not even aware of this attribute. Another leading global car brand fell in to the same pitfall and created a so-called innovation that made customers scratch their heads in disbelief. It is a motorized lid that slides back to reveal a dual cup holder in the console between the two front seats. Made of leather with classy stitching, it has a small chrome handle, but the customer is not supposed to grab the handle and slide the lid back himself. No, no. Instead, he only needs to lightly touch the handle with his finger and the lid automatically slides horizontally back and out of the way. Will wonders never cease?! What an amazing, useless device—at least that was what most customers thought about it. The brand presented this "innovation" as "an experience enhancer," but the attribute did not make any sense to customers. Since most handles are supposed to be grasped, and not just lightly tapped, it sent mixed signals as to how to use it. Moreover, the lid moved very slowly; it took longer for the lid to slide back automatically than for customers to slide it back themselves. It was seen as a time-waster for impatient, busy customers, as well as just one more unnecessary thing that might break. Hence, they considered it "an experience killer." In fact, one customer was so annoyed that he actually made a YouTube video about it.

So the key question to ask is: Which customer segment did these brands target with their "innovations"? Which experiential customer needs did they satisfy or which customer values they serve? We guess none, since most probably they never looked at their exciting new feature from an experiential viewpoint. The vents and the cup-holder lid were exciting only to the company—not to the customers. Like many companies who impose innovations on customers without ever defining what the customers need, they invested an immense amount of time, money and human capital to make their pointless novelty a reality. It would not be surprising if these pointless novelties were then paraded as true innovations by these two companies to their shareholders.

Companies need to comprehend the deep experiential expectations and value systems of their potential customers. They must then evaluate those expectations and value systems in the light of the company's overall experiential goal. This is the essence of effective experiential design.

Consider a group of customers in a restaurant. A few of them are probably hoping that they will be served quickly; some are looking forward to their meal being a memorable "taste sensation"; others are there just to relax and soak in the ambiance of the restaurant while they eat. Even though all of these customers are in the restaurant at the same time, each segment of diners has different experiential expectations. Based on this reality, businesses should design their offerings to accommodate the varied experiential needs of their target customers. Whether intentional or not, every experiential stimulus that companies put into their offerings has certain outcomes, and the resulting experiences cause customers to behave in a certain way. Surprisingly, as a result of these behaviors, customers' experiential expectations and value systems evolve over time. This is another factor that needs to be kept in mind when designing a customer experience. Don't assume that a segment's expectations will remain static forever. They are interactive and, therefore, dynamic.

Managing "Customer Experience" is not solely about planning how customers can effortlessly flow through the company's value-delivery stages; rather, customer experience management enables the company to be aware of what the customer is experiencing at each stage of contact with their brand. Obviously, the goal is to create loyal customers, but a customer might become disloyal and leave a brand for a number of reasons: satisfaction level, perceived value, aftersales support problems and so forth. These are explainable dimensions of disloyalty, but, disloyalty can also occur for implicit reasons which may not be revealed through conventional marketing research. Consider a couple who have been married for 25 years. They seem to have a great relationship—as perfect as one could get. The man earns enough to keep the family comfortable; he is handsome, gentle and understanding and is appreciated by everyone who knows him, including his wife. Similarly the wife takes loving care of her family and home. She is beautiful, patient and giving. The husband and wife seem as if they were made for each other. What is surprising is that the man is cheating on his wife; in other words, he is not loyal to her. Does that sound impossible? Do all disloyal spouses cheat for an overt reason or can there be underlying motivations? Suppose the man wants a divorce; are all divorces due to obvious factors? Of course not. So, why do couples become disloyal?

The "Experiential Value Curve" might offer an explanation for this. This concept says that when an individual experiences an event, the initial experiences provide a higher experiential value than later experiences related to that same event.

Notice that the experiential value ratio decreases not in a linear way but exponentially as it continues asymptotically. In other words, the perceived value drops off faster as time goes on, which means that eventually these experiences are doomed to end up with no value at all.

This is exactly what businesses do not want, since this phenomenon occurs when brands are undifferentiated from other brands. The aim of companies shouldn't be just to differentiate their brand from the competition. These brands should also be continually differentiating from themselves—in other words, refreshing their products/services so that customers don't lose interest. Getting back to our couple, the fact that there was no specific reason for the husband to cheat on his wife suggests that the "experiential value

Experiential Value Curve

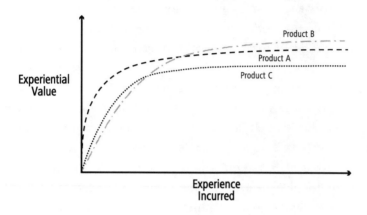

curve" was at work in the relationship. Their recent experiences with each other had become undifferentiated compared to their earlier experiences. In the eyes of her husband, the wife had not differentiated herself enough from the competition nor made changes that countered the ever-diminishing value of the experiences she offered. Implicitly, he felt that this gave him the right to cheat on her and to eventually ask for a divorce. (On the flip side, the wife may have felt that she had the right to cheat on him because her husband was not putting any excitement into their marriage.) In the same way, there doesn't have to be an explicit reason as to why a customer drops a brand. The reason is often experiential and implicit. Businesses that ignore the experiential value curve risk having disloyal customers.

The secret for avoiding the experiential value curve can be found by viewing this couple's relationship as a progression. Back when they first met, they knew very little about each other and the exciting stage of exploring each other triggered passion. As they learned more about each other, their relationship grew. They were happy until one day they realized that they did not have much to explore about each other anymore. In order to prevent relationships from wearing out like this, marriage counselors often recommend that couples add mystery and change up their routine to revitalize their relationship to make it more exciting. If they don't continually discover new shared passions, the relationship may suffer from boredom, which can lead to disloyalty.

If we translate the phrase "change up their routine to revitalize their relationship" into business terms, in essence this is "innovation." Customers need to explore new things. They want to learn and add to their body of knowledge. They seek adventure. Why else would so many people go to different vacation spots each year, wander around the world and soak in new sites and exotic cultures? Why is a customer who visited the Great Canyon last year not loyal enough to the Great Canyon to visit it again this year? Was viewing the canyon depths through a glass floor not worth experiencing a second time? Or does the customer think, "Been there, done that" and want to move on to something else?

Here is an odd phenomenon: Products that have the word "New" on their label jump off the shelves faster than those without it. The word "New" has the connotation of being innovative, untried, fresh, different, exciting and having a value that the existing products don't. Customers respond eagerly to the chance for adventure, for a memorable experience with a product. Companies that offer a new flavor or new size or any kind of innovation to an existing product reverse the downward momentum of the "experiential value curve" and can rescue the brand from disloyalty.

Businesses that focus solely on customer recommendation ratios or designing an effortless experience may still risk generating product disloyalty. This may sound strange, but unless they interject innovation when the downward experiential value curve kicks in, they are not offering their customers the kind of experience that keeps them loyal to the brand.

As can be seen in the diagram below, adding an innovation to a product causes it to jump in value, creating a higher experiential saturation line, which can translate into higher profits for the brand. Innovations disrupt the diminishing loyalty that comes from customer boredom and pump new energy into the entire customer experience.

Random, Accidental and Designed Customer Experiences

Customer experiences fall into three categories: random, accidental and designed. Random experience refers to when a customer gets product or service from a random provider. Consider a customer who feels hungry and goes to the first fast food eatery he sees to satisfy his hunger. The customer will experience an undifferentiated experience since many fast food places

Experiential Value Curve

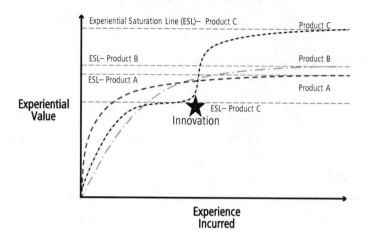

are similar. Besides this, his experience is likely to be inconsistent from one day to another because there might be different cooks on the line or different counter workers due to shift changes. The customer may be the first one served and get a hot delicious hamburger one day, but have to wait in a long line for a burnt hamburger on a dry roll the next. Random experiences are unintentional, which means that they are not products of active planning, thus they are not sustainable and are open to being influenced by numerous factors in the provision process. Random also means that the company has no real control over these experiences. Most try to limit the number of random experiences that their customers encounter in connection with their brand because a random bad experience could prompt the customer to immediately switch brands.

Accidental experiences are a step up from random experiences. Think of the hungry customer again. This time he goes to a popular local restaurant. This restaurant is famous for its hearty family-style dinners and, for the most part, delivers satisfying meals in a noisy, kid-friendly atmosphere. Accidental experiences are more consistent because during each visit, the customer gets more or less a similar experience. Accidental experiences are also unintentional but differentiated. The locally famous restaurant is differentiated because it stands out among hundreds of other restaurants for specific services or foods it provides. However, the experience that the restaurant provides is not the product of an elaborate design. More often than that it is guided by the owner's or manager's intuitions and not by an overarching plan; thus, it is considered "accidental" at the experiential level. The unplanned structure of the experience makes it unsustainable because the next generation of owners may not be able to operate it exactly as their predecessors did. The result of accidental experiences has enough consistency to keep some loyal customers but enough inconsistency to turn away new customers after a bad experience, such as food that is tasteless or cooked incorrectly.

Designed Experiences are consistent, differentiated, intentional and sustainable. The experiences they provide are products of careful design and are intentionally constructed. They are differentiated from the competition and are consistent. Each time a customer goes to a Starbucks, he knows what to expect: The coffee and other menu options are listed on the wall high above the glass counter, which is brimming with tantalizing rolls, bagels, cakes and snacks. Bottled water, juices and teas are displayed nearby. He has the option of ordering "to go" or sitting at one of the many small tables scattered around the room. There are usually a few comfortable chairs available for those who want to linger over their morning brew. Free Wi-Fi hook-ups allow customers to use their laptops and mobile devices while enjoying their meal. Each of these features exists at every Starbucks and separates it from other types of restaurants. The intent of each attribute is to offer a pleasant start to the customer's morning, or a "pick-me-up" during the day. The calm, low-key atmosphere is another intentional feature that defines Starbucks and differentiates it from other restaurants. Starbucks is sustainable because it fosters a loyal segment of customers who appreciate the way they are treated and the unique services they get. As a company-operated chain, Starbucks has set requirements of each store manager and each establishment, which also keeps it sustainable no matter who the managers are.

Experiential Value Proposition

Designing competitive, distinctive and sustainable offerings is more difficult in saturated markets. This is because, within these markets, one can't help but find a wide variety of products that cover almost every need or want that customers could have. In the dairy section of any grocery store, one

Comparison of the Three Types of Customer Experiences

Random Experience	Accidental Experience	Designed Experience
Inconsistent	Consistent	Consistent
Undifferentiated	Differentiated	Differentiated
Unintentional	Unintentional	Intentional
Unsustainable	Unsustainable	Sustainable

sees whole milk, reduced-fat milk, low-fat milk, fat-free milk, organic milk, lactose-free milk, raw milk and so forth. Confusing, isn't it? Now add the number of brands as a multiplier and imagine what the shelf looks like. Being a brand that is competitive, distinctive and sustainable is even more complex than that. Think about the customer's experience when he faces that shelf. He may have a brand and type of milk that he buys consistently, but glancing over all the other options, he may decide to try another brand the next time he buys milk. So, how does the company retain its customer? What can it do?

In order to answer this tough question, it is crucial to understand the nature of offerings themselves. An offering, whether a tangible or intangible product or service, gets into the customer's cart as a result of four sequential qualities: Basic, Expected, Augmented and Experiential. By carefully designing these levels the right way, the brand has the potential to be placed in the customer's basket in each purchase.

Basic Offering

Basic Offering is the lowest level and value that an offering can have. It provides a utility to the customer without satisfying any other need. "Fundamental need" is the keyword for defining basic offerings. Tata Nano is a perfect example of a basic offering. This India-based car brand offers nothing more than a body, an engine, a transmission and four wheels in exchange for the equivalent of $3,056. The car enables the driver to travel from Point A to Point B safely, but that's all. Back in the 1970s, Volkswagen provided a similar service in America. College students jumped at the opportunity to buy the Volkswagen "Bug," a small car that could carry only 4 passengers (although they tried to fit in more), was economical on gas and was priced very reasonably. It got them where they wanted to go.

Expected Offering

Expected Offering defines the lowest standards of a particular industry or category. The existence of expected qualities does not trigger an increase in satisfaction but prevents customers from feeling dissatisfied. Features like ABS, intermittent windshield wipers and a remote control key are expected by most automobile customers in their purchases. If a car that they are contemplating buying is missing one of these expected offerings, the potential customer would be dissatisfied and might not purchase the car. On the other hand, if a customer is looking at used cars and the remote control key doesn't function, that might not keep the customer from purchasing.

Augmented Offering

Augmented Offering passes beyond the expectation level while still containing the features of the previous two offering levels. An augmented offering will get customers excited about the brand. Cars that have heated seats, a sunroof, leather interior, five-spoked chrome rims, and so on might be counted as augmented offerings. Citroens has hydraulic models like Xantia or GS which hoped to "augment" the customer's experience. If the car had a flat tire, this vehicle could travel on three wheels for a while, instead of four, and get the customers to the nearest repair shop. Surprisingly this feature did not turn out to be as popular with customers as the company had hoped. When designing augmented offerings, too often companies fail to capture what is really relevant to customers. Being able to create something distinctive shouldn't tempt brands to ignore relevancy. Augmented offerings are more likely to foster customer loyalty if they satisfy relevant features or benefits as well. One augmented offering that customers do consider relevant is a backup safety camera that is linked to the built-in GPS screen in certain car models. The second that the driver shifts into reverse, the camera activates and shows the driver what is behind the vehicle. Customers are eager to have this feature because they perceive it as a way to prevent accidents when backing their car out of parking spaces or out of their driveway.

Experiential Offering

Experiential Offerings are designed to be relevant to value systems of customers. These offerings trigger specific emotions, thoughts and behaviors in customers, and their effectiveness can be evaluated by breaking these offerings down into buying, using and disposing stages. The ultimate aim of experiential offerings is to make the customer comfortable and satisfied throughout the entire customer journey.

For example, a customer who is concerned about safety will be fascinated with all the newest auto safety features and will most likely select a model that has as many of them as he can afford. Once he is driving this new car, he will experience these safety features at one time or another; hence the car's experiential offering can continue to satisfy him. Suppose his car is about to get into an accident. His Forward-Collision Warning (FCW) system will detect it, using a camera, radar and/or laser to alert the driver that he is approaching another car in his lane too fast. When he slams on the brakes, the Brake Assist feature takes over and applies the brakes so that they don't lock up, but hard enough to stop the car as quickly as possible. If the car detects that the driver is not applying the brakes fast enough, the Automatic Emergency Braking (AEB) takes over and stops the car automatically. Systems like GM OnStar, BMW Assist, Hyundai Bluelink, Kia UVO, Lexus Safety Connect, Mercedes-Benz's mBrace, and Toyota Safety Connect all "allow the driver to communicate with a central dispatch center at the touch of a button. This center knows the location of the vehicle and can provide route directions or emergency aid on request. If an air bag deploys, the system automatically notifies the dispatch center, locates the vehicle, and summons emergency service, if the driver does not respond to a phone-based inquiry."[1]

Another safety feature is Active Head Restraints: If the vehicle behind the customer doesn't stop in time and rear ends his car, the effect of the impact will be minimized by the Active Head Restraint mechanism, which proactively moves the headrest up and forward "...to cradle the head and absorb energy in an effort to mitigate whiplash injury."[2]

Despite the fact that most auto manufacturers provide some kind of advanced safety systems, not all cars have the exact same safety features, so there is distinction among the models, giving customers differing experiences. Having an Experiential Offering provides companies with a sustainable and yet distinctive advantage over their competitors. Experiential offerings are quite hard to imitate because a slight variation can create a significant difference in what the customer experiences. What's more, unreliable imitations tend to prove that the original was the better choice after all. On the other hand, because of the value that experiential offerings provide, they awaken the desire of customers to advocate for that brand.

Experiential offerings don't have to be complex. Low-involvement offerings like corn chips can be designed to be distinctive and sustainable as well. Doritos launched a new product called Doritos Risk in 2015. Each package contains mostly regular nachos, but a few of them are extremely spicy. Customers randomly pick and eat the chips without knowing whether the next chip will be a hot or a regular nacho, thus it creates a new level of excitement for customers. The brand supported its product with a commercial portraying a game that customers can play while eating Doritos Risk. In the ad, a group of friends is sitting in a circle, passing around the bag of chips. Each of them must eat whichever chip he happens to pull from the bag. The one who refuses to eat his chip is laughingly called "chicken." The product became very popular and in 2017 Doritos launched upgrade under the name, Doritos Risk 2.0. This new product had an additional feature—the chips that were hot also dyed the customer's tongue blue. Any player who eats a hot chip can no longer pretend that he didn't get the hot nacho because everyone else can see his blue tongue when he gasps for air after eating it. This elevated the excitement level of this experiential offering even higher than the original version.

The diagram below shows how the innovations added to a vehicle can take a customer through each of the higher offering levels. Notice that there is no "loyalty line" between the basic and expected offering levels. This is because the expected offerings come as standard features in all but the most basic vehicles. Thus, there is no incentive for a customer to be more loyal to those brands than they would to, say, a Tata Nano. The "advocacy line" indicates that the customer has been so impressed with the unique features and relevancy of the experiential offering that they will voluntarily tell others about their experience.

Hierarchy of Offerings

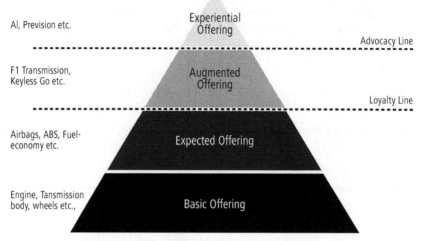

Al, Prevision etc. — Experiential Offering

Advocacy Line

F1 Transmission, Keyless Go etc. — Augmented Offering

Loyalty Line

Airbags, ABS, Fuel-economy etc. — Expected Offering

Engine, Tansmission body, wheels etc., — Basic Offering

Designing Framework for Offerings

When designing their offerings, companies aim to reach at least one of three main goals: Acquisition, Retention and/or Expansion. The "Acquisition Approach" is mainly adopted by companies that operate in relatively lower saturation markets. When a company develops a new product that is relevant to its target customers, it acquires customers. Acquisition, however, is negatively correlated with competition.

As the saturation of the market increases with the participation of new competitors and substitutes, the acquisition-focused period is replaced by an effort to focus on reinforcing and keeping relationships with existing customers. Since there are now more competing products, the "Retention Approach" is used in markets with relatively higher saturation. Businesses in this phase seek to achieve Customer Lifetime Value.

Focusing on customer experiences strengthens relations with customers and gives the company opportunities to compete over a period of time. This enables the company to capture the lifetime value of the customer with a larger face value amount. Companies should understand that customers have needs—they need banks, airlines, cars and so forth—and customers will find a way to satisfy those needs, whether with your brand or with another one. The determinant for the winning brand is the better-designed customer experience.

Design Strategy Ladder

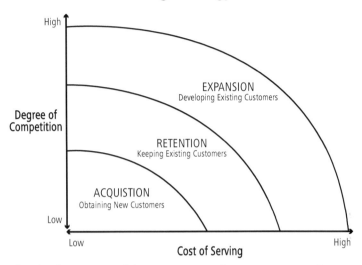

The third purpose of designing a product or service is Expansion. This is how a company develops its existing customers. The "Expansion Approach" works by increasing customer lifetime value and generating cross sell and up-sell operations. Expansion can also be achieved with cost-cutting moves, since expansion reduces the overhead costs as well as the cost to serve each customer.

In order to effectively achieve Acquisition, Retention and Expansion, a company's experiential design needs two critical phases: the first phase is the Conceptual Phase, through which it aims to understand the nature of market. Once the company has a clear picture of the target market, how relevant their experiential offering is to that market and how that all fits with the company's own objectives, the Empirical Phase can begin. This is the application portion of the experiential design. It includes test marketing and the actual launch.

Conceptual Phase

Comprised of three main actions, Idea Generation and Screening, Market Assessment, and Business Analysis, the Conceptual Phase is where the company determines what the experiential offering will be, who will buy it and how it can be implemented in line with the company's objectives.

Stages of the Experiential Design Process

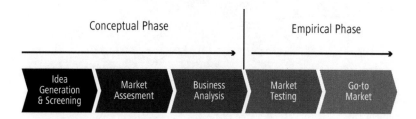

Idea Generation and Screening

Idea Generation is the first step in designing outstanding customer experience. The aim of the idea generation step is to form and solidify the concepts about the experiential offering; hence it is qualitative. When generating ideas for the design, the idea generation process should: 1. Point out customer pains that this offering might solve, 2. Evaluate regulations that might affect the offering, 3. Identify competitors and substitutes in the market and 4. Diagnose possible experiential gaps.

Offerings sometimes overshoot their aim, just as in the case of the motorized cup holders. The company invested a small fortune in the innovation, but it didn't make any sense to customers, so the effort was a colossal failure. A state-of-the-art invention by a brand's R&D team shouldn't cause more trouble than it is worth or dig into profits without sufficient return on investment (ROI). In order prevent this, the first question that should be asked is, "Will this offer deliver relevant value to the customer?" Otherwise, it becomes a pointless novelty instead of relevant innovation. During the Idea Screening process, the focus should be on researching the competition. It is possible that they are already offering an innovation to their customers, but that is not the whole story. Careful research might reveal that the competition has failed to deliver meaningful experiential value—In other words, they have delivered a pointless novelty instead of a true innovation. In that case, the field is wide open for a genuine innovation to fill that experiential gap.

Idea-screening research will equip companies to focus on the unmet experiential needs of their segment, or to find ways to satisfy a need better than their competition. Samsung is great example for demonstrating how to fill this experience gap. When the brand launched their Galaxy model

takeaway!

Every design should have a cause and a goal, so before rolling up your sleeves, it is absolutely necessary to clearly define the customer problem that needs to be solved and how you intend to solve it. The experiential needs and values of your target segment should be your compass for creating and delivering outstanding experiences. Remember that it is these experiences that pave the way to customer loyalty and to a long- term relationship between your brand and the customer. If you are not aware of what they actually need, it is impossible to design any experience to meet it.

into the smartphone market, it was considered by many to be just another smartphone among many smartphones. Samsung, though, knew what it was doing, because studies had shown that customers were demanding larger displays on their phones, and the Galaxy delivered on that feature. Larger screens were the experiential need that other brands like the Apple iPhone had missed. The launch of the big screen Galaxy, supported by heavy ad campaigns, led to inevitable success because Samsung had defined the experiential needs of customers as well as the experiential gap in market from the "get go," and thus designed, produced, communicated and delivered a product that fulfilled those specific needs.

Market Assessment
Once concepts are documented through the Idea Generation/Screening step, any conclusions made by qualitative studies should be backed up with

takeaway!

Diagnose your competitor's missteps with a fine-toothed comb. See where they went wrong and don't repeat their mistakes. Be absolutely sure that your product or service has relevant experiential values for your customers. That way you can trample your competition.

quantitative research through the frontline of market facts. The two major components of market assessment are: 1. Identifying the customer segments that would consider the product relevant, and 2. Determining the size of each segment. This data will guide the company as it maneuvers more toward creating experiences that are meaningful to their customer segments. The growth potential of the market, as well as the growth potential of each segment, needs to be measured when assessing a possible experiential offering. If the market doesn't possess enough growth potential, it is wise to switch gears and re-focus on more promising target markets. Each company should also consider the ability of their suppliers to provide the material and/or services to sustain the experiential product or service, since a low supply of raw materials could cause inconsistency and non-sustainability in its delivery. If such risks exist, it is critical to minimize those risks or abandon the idea early on, while it is still not costly. Regulations are another factor to be evaluated while designing the offering, since, if the product or service doesn't meet legal requirements, it won't be possible to launch it. This stage is also the time to verify customer needs through quantitative experiential research; that way the brand can be sure that their induced ideas have generalizable characteristics.

Business Analysis

Investing in a new design has several financial as well as non-financial effects on companies. To ensure that these effects are positive, a business should consider the cost and the benefits of the new experiential product or service to customers and to the company before investing. The availability of human capital and the potential to recruit capable human capital to sustain a newly-developed offering should be carefully considered. Capital expenditures to make the design a reality should also be evaluated beforehand. Sales forecasts, scenario analysis and profitability of the new experiential product or service are other aspects to put on the desk before going to the next step.

Designing successful experiential offerings requires both a systematic approach and data-driven decision-making. Remember that "data," in this case, means more than just quantities, as we have previously stated several times in this book. Qualities also provide critical data—even if they are in non-parametric form. Qualities enable researchers to formulate the experiential equations that quantitative data is plugged into. They guide the hypotheses that shape the experiential offerings.

The Experiential Design Board

The Experiential Design Board pictured below provides an overview of all the key components needed for designing an effective experiential offering. Each box prompts the company to probe vital information related to the offering while enabling them to take practical steps to achieve each benchmark.

Target Segment

This box should be filled in with the key characteristics of the customer segment being targeting by the offering, for example, "sports fan," "loves to travel," "budget-conscious," etc. Also list bullet points about experiential commonalities and relevant needs of that experiential segment, such as "lives in a close-knit community" and "prefers organic products." These facts will ensure that the offering will appeal to their interests and concerns.

Questions to be asked:

• What are the experiential characteristics of the segment that the offering is designed for?

• What are the needs of the segment?

takeaway!

At the end of the conceptual phase, you should be able to fill in an Experiential Design Board like the one below. This board consists of ten boxes that are vital for making decisions about the direction of your designing efforts. By incorporating this knowledge into your thinking and discussions, you will be better at designing your offering. Encourage employees from different departments and management levels to contribute their ideas as you fill in the board. The more ideas you have from a variety of perspectives and experience levels, the more effective your design will be.

Competition

A general in a battle cannot be effective if he doesn't know who he is fighting. Not only that, but he has to understand why the enemy is fighting, what their strengths and weaknesses are, where they are putting most of their efforts and where they are heading. Without this critical knowledge, the general cannot lead his men to victory. The same holds true when dealing with the competition.

Questions to be asked:
• Who are the competitors?
• What are the substitutes?
• Are there any offerings already on the market that satisfy the need we are trying to meet?

Experiential Design Board

Target Segment	Value Proposition
What are the experiential characteristics of the segment that the offering designed for? What are the needs of the segment?	What are the distinctive key qualities of the offering? Which values of the customers are served?

Competition	Stakeholders
Who are the competitors? What are the substitutes? Is there any offering in market that satisfy the need?	External Who will be the solution partners from supplier side? Who will be the solution partners from buyer side?
Market Trends What is the nature of trends in market? What kind of opportunities do they signal?	Internal Who will contribute to formation of the design internally?

Capabilities & Investments	Communication
May existing suppliers provide the resources to form the experiential value? Does existing channel has possibility to deliver the experiental value? Does existing physical and human capital of organization has ability to form the offering? What kind of human capital investment needed? What kind of physical capital investment needed?	How the offering will be transmitted? What media will be used across decision prism?
	Delivery How the offering will be delivered? Where the offering will be delivered? By whom the offering will be delivered?
Revenue Model What will be the revenue model of the offering? What will be pricing strategy?	**Goal Alignment** What goals will be achived from the side of the company? What goals will be achieved from the side of the customer? What are the metrics to measure the alignment?

takeaway!

You are the general. You must find out everything there is to know about your competition. Who they are and what offerings are already out there that could compete with the offering you are planning. Don't forget to look for substitute products that can distract customers, the way bottled water distracts cola customers from buying Coca Cola or Pepsi.

Market Trends

Understanding the market trends and the cognitive and behavioral tendencies of customers sheds light on the designing phase. Trends indicate momentum. They are a mild version of the "mob mentality." When a group of fans swarms the soccer field because they don't agree with the referee's decision, this is a mob mentality. The fans are not thinking as individuals or making logical decisions. Rather, they are caught up in the emotion and excitement of the moment and they follow the crowd. Fashion and product trends are similar to this, but in a much more subdued way. Customers find out from friends that a particular product has exceeded expectations and they want to try it, too. Emotions in the purchasing process are tempered somewhat by logic, unlike mobs of fans, but the momentum is still there. With social media, this momentum is often intensified and broadened. Hence, businesses that pay close attention to trends and explore how their product or service can connect with that trend will have more effective experiential offerings.

Questions to be asked:
• What is the nature of the trends in the market?
• What kinds of opportunities do they offer?

Value Proposition

The essence of the design lies in this box, since the Value Proposition box highlights how a brand's offering is distinct from those of their competitors and states which customer values will be satisfied by the offering.

Questions to be asked:
- What should the distinctive key qualities of the offering be?
- Which customer values will the offering will serve?

Stakeholders

The stakeholders are the individuals or corporations that help companies achieve their goals. The stakeholders are either external, such as suppliers, buyers, etc., or internal, such as employees, investors, board members, etc. When designing a specific offering, the company should identify which suppliers, which sales channels and which employees, investors, etc., will play a role in the formation of the offering. A successful business is one that makes sure that all the key players are "on board" before going ahead with a new concept or product. By making the effort to involve all the stakeholders to some degree in the designing process, the company will have the commitment of the entire organization and there will be less of a chance that one or more external or internal stakeholders will pull back their support at the last minute.

Questions to be asked:

External:
- Who will the solution partners from the supplier side be?
- Who will the solution partners from the buyer side be?

Internal:
- Which internal partners will be contributing to the creation of the design?

Capabilities & Investments

This box evaluates the capability of the existing value chain partners and elements to provide the newly-designed experiential offering. It can refer to the investment of finances, technology, intellectual property, human capital and so forth.

Questions to be asked:
- Do existing suppliers have the resources needed to create the offering?
- Is it possible for existing channels to provide the experiential value?
- Do the company's existing physical and human capital have the ability to deliver the offering?
- What kind of human capital investment is needed?
- What kind of physical capital investment is needed?

Revenue Model

How the experience is designed affects the amount of income/profit the company receives from it. To determine how much revenue a customer experience design can generate, the company needs to use a Revenue Model and have a Pricing Strategy. Revenue Model is the description of how a business will generate income, produce profits.

A "Pricing Strategy" is more than simply guessing at a good price for the product or service. It is about the value you provide versus your competitors and the value your company receives in return.

Questions to be asked:
- Which Revenue Model will be used for the offering?
- What will the Pricing Strategy be?

Communication

Once the offering is ready to be launched, the approach for communicating the offering to customers needs to be clearly defined. It should dovetail with the "customer decision prism."

Questions to be asked:
- How will the offering will be launched?
- What media will be used throughout the "customer decision prism"?

Delivery

Offerings that are not delivered flawlessly to customers can make it impossible to retain customers and company to foster customer loyalty. Thus, delivery component is essential and should be carefully described on the board to ensure that it is implemented correctly.

takeaway!

How well-equipped is your company for providing what is needed at each touchpoint along the value chain? This could refer, for example, to the ease of navigation on your company's website, so that customers can jump from the sales page to the product description page for more details. Can customers download a digital copy of your product without any issues? Do the downloads work properly once the customer pays for a digital copy of your product? Is your customer helpline congested because you are short-staffed? Are your logistics in place so that physical products can be shipped on time? Think about every micro-stage of your customer experience and make sure that everything is in place so that it flows smoothly.

Questions to be asked:
• How the offering will be delivered?
• Where the offering will be delivered?
• Who will deliver the offering?

Goal Alignment
At the end of the day, the design of the offering must serve the values of both the customer side and the corporate side. Consequently, the value that the exchange provides to corporate and to the customer should be clearly defined and measurable metrics should be assigned to track the efficiency in meeting these goals.

Questions to be asked:
• What goals will be achieved from the side of the company?

- What goals will be achieved from the side of the customer?
- What metrics will be used to measure goal alignment?

After the Experiential Design Board has been filled in and each department knows what it needs to do, it is time to put the concept for the new offering to the test:

Empirical Phase

Once the conceptual design is completed, it has to be tested in several real-life settings. This is the empirical phase of experiential design. Some companies might be in a hurry to construct and launch their offering, thinking, why bother testing it? Isn't that just a waste of time and money?

Again, it comes down to whether the company launching the offer is "ego-centric" or "customer-centric" at heart. Even though the design was formulated from customer experience data, there is still no way to know whether it will really connect with target customers at each critical touchpoint. The only way to find out is to test it.

Market Testing

"Market Testing" has to precede the "Go-to-Market" launch phase because it allows companies to observe real life reactions and responses to their offering on a small scale. The last thing any company wants to do is waste time and money on a failed launch. It makes far more sense to test out the offering on a small sample group first. To accomplish this, a sample value chain needs to be set up for test customers to interact with. This prototype must include each touchpoint, from a customer's very first contact with the offering through the consumption and disposal stages. Once the value chain is set up, the marketing team needs to randomly select a small group of customers from the target segment and have them experience the prototype. Feedback from these customers contains vital information that can enable the offering to succeed on the real market. Any hitches or clogs in the sample value chain need to be immediately fixed. This initial trial also needs to be evaluated by every department that is involved in the offering of the product. This means the operations and production departments must assess both the planned and actual production scenarios, as well as any logistics dimensions that the offering might require. Suppliers must also determine whether they can provide the required inputs as planned. If everything goes well, then launching the experiential product or service in a limited real-market environment is the next step. The reason for testing a limited market is to get a feel for a broader sampling of the segment than the previous test could reveal. Moreover, a limited market test will get answers without incurring too much expense. After this second trial, if all goes smoothly, the offering is ready to "Go to Market"!

One company that rushed the launch was Clairol, a Proctor & Gamble subsidiary. In the 1970s, the "back to nature" movement prompted P&G to successfully create products with all-natural ingredients. Shortly after, it was discovered that cultured dairy products like yogurt had nourishing benefits for hair. Clairol decided to combine the two and introduced a new shampoo called, "Touch of Yogurt" Shampoo. From the company's perspective, this sounded like a perfect product for the mood of the times; but, surprisingly, the product failed miserably.

The fact that the "Touch of Yogurt" Shampoo was rejected by so many customers suggests that Clairol never actually test-marketed this product. Or if they did, they did it wrong. Had they allowed small random groups of their customer segment to try out the shampoo, they would have received some negative feedback long before they spent the money to release the product to the general public. Clairol unfortunately jumped the gun on this one. Yes, there was a new trend emerging with customers wanting natural ingredients in their products, and yes, yogurt had been found to be beneficial for hair. The problem was that Clairol didn't test the connotations of the product's name. "Touch of Yogurt" sounds more like a food than a shampoo. This turned many customers off from the product because it wasn't clear whether this product fit into the hair care or the dairy category convention. It was even confusing enough to make some customers think that the product was actually edible, causing a number of them to become ill after ingesting it. Not properly test-marketing their product robbed the company of profits on top of the costs of advertising, production and delivery. It also tainted the Clairol name for many customers, reducing the number of future sales.[3]

Go-to-Market

Assuming that the small-scale testing of the prototype had positive feedback, and any minor hitches in the touchpoints have been corrected, it is almost time to launch! But before doing so, there are a few things that must be in place first: The entire company should have already studied the marketing plan to know what each employee is responsible for. Any employees who will be in direct contact with customers should have completed their training and should be familiar with the core attributes of the new offering. They should be reminded that each step of the experiential offering is customer-centric and that it is up to them to support the customer experience within the scope of their responsibilities. All along the value chain, what customers feel, think and do takes precedence. The teams need to watch the customers' response to each point of pain and pleasure, note any problems and work to improve them for the next customer.

Despite the excitement of launching an offering, surprisingly, the launch itself is not the goal. The goal is actually adapting, fine-tuning and tailoring the value chain based on how each customer experiences the offering.

takeaway!

Remember that your offering is not set in stone. Rather, it is like clay on a potter's wheel that is continually being reshaped—a little here, a little there—until it is right. So, make it a company policy to continuously re-evaluate each offering that you launch, integrating the feedback that comes in from customers and employees alike. That way you will know that you are providing the best possible customer experience for your segment as they interact with your product or service.

Chapter 10

WHICH EXPERIENTIAL SOURCES SHOULD BE RELIED ON?

B ecause customer experience has so many subjective factors, the qualitative data a company gathers must always be verified quantitatively. The best way to do this is to utilize solid methodologies right from the start. The following experiential cycles, models, approaches and theories have been shown to be extremely reliable. Depending on which aspect of the customer experience a brand is dealing with, one or more of these methodologies can help quantify and reinforce the experiential research.

The Two Camps of Customer Experience Practice

There are several viewpoints on how to deliver ideal customer experience (CE). These diverse perspectives fall into two main camps that CE enthusiasts mostly gather around. The major concern that divides and causes disaccord between them is their approach on how to treat customers.

The first camp is the "Delight Camp": Marketers with this mindset seek to deliver relevant products or services in a way that goes beyond the expectations of the customers. Their goal is to delight customers by surpassing the expectation threshold — in other words, "wowing" them. This fosters loyalty, and increases the chances of creating Customer Lifetime Value (CLV).

The second camp is the "Effortless Camp": Supporters of this viewpoint are staunchly opposed to delighting customers. As surprising as this may seem, their point is logical from an economic perspective. They argue that instead of focusing on delighting customers, and negatively impacting profits by incurring extra cost in the process, the company should make the consumption path as effortless as possible for the customer. According to them, meeting expectations is sufficient because it confirms the offering's value to the customer; they believe there is no need to go beyond that. The "effortless camp" is often criticized for neglecting the bigger picture, saying that customers don't buy something simply because they had an "effortless" experience.

Even though these two camps come at the customer experience concept from different angles and seem to be antagonistic toward each other, they are not conflicting at all; on the contrary, they represent complementary perspectives that, taken together, form the ideal customer experience and pave the way to loyalty.

At the end of the 1950s, Frederick Herzberg suggested a theory known as the "Two Factor Theory of Motivation." According to this theory, satisfaction has two components: hygiene and motivation. Herzberg tested his hypothesis by measuring the satisfaction levels of employees in the workplace. He found that when the elements of hygiene are provided (such as salary, work conditions, job security etc.), they have no effect on increasing the satisfaction of the employees. The existence of hygiene components just keeps employees away from dissatisfaction. Moreover, if these hygiene factors are not provided, employees get dissatisfied and their commitment to the company hits the bottom due to demotivation.

Herzberg's Two Factor Motivation Theory

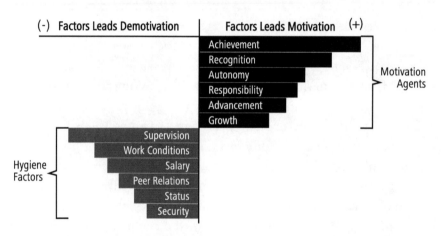

The motivation component affects satisfaction in a reverse direction. When the elements of motivation (such as achievement, recognition, autonomy, etc.) are present, they have the effect of increasing the satisfaction level of employees. When these motivating factors are absent, the satisfaction of employees reduces but not to the extent of being dissatisfied. The inexistence of motivation causes the inexistence of satisfaction, but not the existence of dissatisfaction. In other words, if the motivation factor doesn't rise, the employees are neither motivated nor demotivated. They simply remain in balance. [1]

An examination of the two camps of CE enthusiasts reveals these principles in action. The delight camp aims at delighting customers by providing something beyond the expected, which will motivate them to make repeat purchases. The effortless camp aims to enable customers to consume products without much effort on their part, and thus they flow easily through the value chain. The delight camp harnesses motivation to gain committed customers by making them feel special and by providing pleasant surprises along the way. The effortless camp obtains committed customers by providing hygiene factors, such as a seamless experience across the entire channel and excellent aftersales service.

Two Camps of Customer Experience Practice

(-) Factors Leads Demotivation	Factors Leads Motivation (+)
	Delight Camp: Increase customer delight. Build up motivating, delighting factors that encourage customers to make repeat purchases
Effortless Camp: Reduce customer effort. Suppress demotivating, effort-requiring factors that discourage customers from ma»king repeat purchases.	

Since these two camps act as two sides of the same coin, they are both equally right, which leads to the conclusion that the ideal customer experience is the one that embraces both perspectives. Moreover, given the satisfaction-dissatisfaction motivation dynamic observed by Herzberg decades ago, the ideal customer experience design is the result of a well-balanced, harmonious blend of both camps. The ideas that both camps advance are integral parts of a holistic CE management framework. One part cannot produce effective results without the other. When providing motivating factors, any aspect of the journey that pulls customers towards demotivation should be either corrected or discarded. The only way to know if a touchpoint demotivates a customer is for the company's marketers and CE managers to personally go through those same steps themselves and see exactly where the problems are. By putting themselves in the shoes of the customer, and identifying with the interests of the target segment, they will be able to design, execute and deliver outstanding experiences to their customers.

Means-End Chain Model

On a hot summer afternoon, I was traveling by car to my destination for the summer holiday. The crickets were chirping and the sweet scent of locust flowers was teasing my nose. I rolled down the window the rest of the way and rested my arm on the car door, the warm wind gliding over my hand. No sooner had I done that then I felt thirsty, but there wasn't a store anywhere in sight. After driving around for ten or fifteen minutes, I encountered a small town. I pulled the car into a strip mall to get a cold drink and some snacks. As I entered the store, I heard a conversation between two elderly ladies. Their comments triggered my selective attention. The ladies were standing in front of the detergent shelves and discussing which detergent cleaned better. One recommended a specific brand to the other by telling her that she always has to drive here to get her favorite detergent because the stores near her don't carry it. Also, she told the woman that she pays a premium price here for it, but it is well worth the cost because her neighbors are always admiring how clean all her clothes look. The other detergents just don't do as good a job.

In actuality, the lady who was recommending the detergent wasn't buying the detergent just to have noticeably cleaner and brighter clothes; she was also buying recognition from her friends and neighbors, and the detergent was a means to an end for her. This anecdote demonstrates the fundamentals of the **Means-End Chain Model** offered by Gutman. According to his model, products or services have both concrete and abstract attributes. Moreover, they provide physical and psychosocial benefits and satisfy instrumental and terminal values. [2, 3]

Concrete Attributes are features of a product that don't change. Consider a Ferrari that has a $249,000 price tag and a 3.9 liter engine with 661 hp. It is a concrete concept that the car has a $249,000 price tag and a 3.9 liter engine with 661 hp. Abstract Attributes, on the other hand, are the qualities of an offering that can be adjusted based on customer preference. One individual may prefer a white Ferrari because, to him, white makes the car appear more elegant. Another customer may consider white to be too plain to stand out from other cars. That person might prefer a bright red Ferrari to make an impact wherever he goes. The attributes of the car provide physical benefits to the customer, such as, the powerful engine can take its owner from one place to another faster than the average vehicle. The car provides psychosocial benefits as well. Suppose the owner of a red Ferrari goes to a restaurant and gives the car to the valet. The valet then parks the car right in front of the restaurant in order to attract more customers. The red color allows the owner to immediately spot his car and not have to worry about whether the car is safe or not in the back-parking lot. Hence, these benefits serve specific values for the owner, but the product shouldn't be evaluated strictly on those values. Consider that, due to the car's appeal, the owner becomes the center of attention among his friends and they all want to spend time with him. In this case, the abstract attributes of the car provide the Instrumental Value to the customer of being unique and they provide Terminal Values of being desired and recognized by others.

There are companies in the business world that have successfully implemented Gutman's model. IBM is one of them. The company started out as "International Business Machines," an innovative manufacturer of fast processing, load-taking and thinking machines. It had the iconic slogan, "Think," which summed up the types of products and machines it offered. Around two decades ago, IBM realized that the company wasn't providing machines so much as solutions for business problems, and the slogan of the company evolved to "Solutions for a Small Planet." Today, most tech companies introduce themselves as solution providers or partners; this evolution is the reflection of a means-end chain model.

Returning to the ladies standing at the detergent shelf, what kind of experiential offering should a competitor design to persuade the advocating lady to switch to their brand? Would a detergent with better cleaning performance do it? The market is full of detergents that claim they have better cleaning performance, but most probably they will not be able persuade a loyal customer with such a proposition. She might not even consider trying them. Designing an experiential offering requires out-of-the-box thinking, and the means-end chain model is a perfect tool to achieve it. Now consider a washing machine that operates without detergent and cleans even the most

Gutman's Means-End Chain Model

stubborn stains with only hot pressured steam and water. The lady would no longer need to go to the strip mall and pay a high price for her favorite detergent; with the innovative washing machine, she could gain the Instrumental Value of super clean clothes and the Terminal Value of additional recognition from her friends. She would never again have to spend money on the detergent brand that she had been so loyal to. The washing machine company would have successfully used the means-end chain model to convince a loyal customer to change to their brand.

The Laddering Technique

The Laddering Technique is a method that companies can use to implement Gutman's Means-Chain Model. It identifies consumer choices by linking together product attributes and customer values in a logical order, like climbing the rungs of a ladder. There are four rungs: 1. The product's concrete and abstract attributes, 2. The tangible positive outcomes associated with those attributes (functional consequences or physical benefits), 3. The personal outcomes that pertain to the individual's psychological well-being or relationships with other people (psychosocial consequences), and 4. Ultimately, the values that can be used to identify the means and ends of consumers—i.e., the instrumental and terminal values of the customer toward the offering.

Optimal Experiences Theory

The concept of "optimal experience," also known as "flow," was developed by Mihaly Csikszentmihalyi. He defined it as "the state in which people are so involved in an activity that nothing else seems to matter; the experience itself is so enjoyable that people will do it even at great cost, for the sheer sake

takeaway!

Use this Laddering Technique to identify the means and ends of your customer segment. That way, you can integrate those values in order to design satisfying solution models for your customers, who deserve the pleasure of obtaining both their instrumental and terminal values through your offering.

of doing it." [4] Hence, the perfect customer experience, as defined here in this book, may be a perfect illustration of "optimal experience." According to Csikszentmihalyi, "Concentration is so intense that there is no attention left over to think about anything irrelevant or to worry about problems. Self-consciousness disappears, and the sense of time becomes distorted. An activity that produces such experiences is so gratifying that people are willing to do it for its own sake, with little concern for what they will get out of it, even when it is difficult or dangerous."[5] Activities such as cliff climbing, sky diving and running marathons fall into this category.

Csikszentmihalyi concluded that the dimensions of "flow" are as follows (Applications to the customer experience are in parentheses):

• Attention is focused on a limited stimulus field. There is full concentration and complete involvement. (This is an essential dimension for effective customer experience.)

• Action and awareness merge. (Therefore, the consumer is determined to complete the experience in order to maximize his well-being.)

• There is freedom from worry about failure. (Being free from any kind of worry is a must for the customers to enjoy the shopping adventure.)

• Self-consciousness disappears. This is the symptom of full concentration. (The customer displays resistance to being distracted by other stimuli, including other people.)

• The sense of time becomes distorted. (It is the job of the marketer to create an atmosphere where customers do not feel the pressure of time limits and may even lose track of time when enthusiastically exploring a product.)

• The experience becomes its own reward—it is auto-telic. (This should be the ultimate objective of customer experience designers.)

Many studies conducted in the past twenty years show that "optimal experience" is a positive and complex condition in which cognitive, motivational and emotional components coexist in a coherent and articulated reciprocal integration. As noted in Chapter 2, video games foster high physical and high cognitive involvement. According to the Customer Experience Involvement Matrix, these high levels of involvement trigger a "captive experience." The participant is not easily distracted. We know now that other factors contribute to this mode as well, specifically motivation and emotions, which are built into the game. The player is motivated to conquer each level and to reap the rewards of winning, which triggers another set of powerful emotions. Even losing a level is an emotional motivator to try again and to keep on trying until the player is able to master that level of the game. Every one of the dimensions of "optimal experience" that Csikszentmihalyi describes above occurs when a customer is playing a video game. The reciprocal (auto-telic) nature of the entire video game experience makes the customer loyal to the game, and therefore to the brand. Thus, studying the dynamics involved in playing video games can shed light on how to achieve "optimal experience" along the value chain.

Elaboration Likelihood Model

One of the models that explains the decision-making process of customers is the Elaboration Likelihood Model (ELM). Devised in 1986 by Richard E. Petty and John Cacioppo, ELM claims that there are two major paths to persuasion: the central path and the peripheral path. Several interacting factors determine which path a customer takes during the persuasion process.

According to Petty and Cacioppo, when a person is either involved or motivated to think about the decision, then he usually takes the central path. If he cares about the issue, such as purchasing or using the product and receives the message with minimal distraction, then that person will elaborate on the message. For example, a customer who is profoundly satisfied

takeaway!

Csikszentmihalyi's Dimensions of Flow model provides a practical guide for integrating the necessary conditions so that customers can experience a perfect consumption atmosphere. Let your customers have the fantastic experience of "flow." How? Create an experience that focuses their attention, fosters action on their part, is comfortable enough so that they are free from worry, demands their full concentration, urges deep commitment and is an experience that continues to reward them at each stage of their journey.

with his previous experiences with the brand would most probably rehearse favorable thoughts about the brand's message. Consequently, it is more likely that his persuasion will occur along the central (or main) path and be long-lasting. Petty and Cacioppo go on to say that if the person rehearses unfavorable thoughts about the message, a "boomerang effect" (moving away from the advocated position) is likely to occur. If the message is ambiguous but pro-attitudinal (in line with the person's attitudes), then persuasion is likely. If the message is ambiguous but counter-attitudinal, then a boomerang effect is likely.

On the other hand, if the message is ambiguous but attitudinally neutral (with respect to the person being persuaded), or if the he is unable or not motivated to listen to the message, then he will look for a "peripheral cue" and travel down a peripheral path of persuasion. Peripheral cues include such communication strategies as: 1. Associating the advocated position with things the subject already thinks positively about (e.g., food, money, sex), 2. Consulting an expert on the topic, and 3. Attempting a contrast argument (where the advocated position is presented after several other positions, which the person despises, have been presented). If the peripheral cue association is accepted, then there may be a temporary attitudinal change and possibly future elaboration. If the peripheral cue association is not accepted, or if it is not present, then the person retains the attitude initially held. [6]

Companies can use ELM to guide their persuasion strategies when designing an effective customer experience. If the customer is motivated and able to elaborate on the brand's message, and if there are compelling arguments available, then the central route should be used to persuade the customer. This would work especially well with existing satisfied customers or prospects who have indicated a strong interest or need for the offering. If the customer is unlikely to elaborate the message, or if the available arguments are weak, then the peripheral route to persuasion should be used. Comparing the offering to other things that the customer enjoys or is satisfied with will facilitate a transfer of positive feelings to the product.

Motivational Conflict Theory

When designing a customer experience, it is helpful to understand why people choose one option over another and the process they go through when they have to choose between options that either attract or repulse them. Too many companies forget to consider Motivational Conflict Theory when they put together their customer touchpoints.

Motivational Conflict Theory explores how people handle making decisions when they are faced with two appealing choices, two unappealing choices, or a choice that has both appealing and unappealing aspects. This model lays out three classic dilemmas: Approach-Approach, and Avoidance-Avoidance and Approach-Avoidance.

1. Approach-Approach means that the person is faced with two options that attract him. A toddler may be given the choice of walking to Mommy or to Daddy to get a hug. The child is equally drawn to both of them and has to choose which parent to walk toward first.

2. Avoidance-Avoidance means that there are two goals that are equally distasteful or repulsive to the person, but he or she has to choose one. A college fraternity "pledge" has to choose between cleaning up the frat house after a wild party or studying for his midterms. A similar situation is when a patient who hates taking pills and is embarrassed to get a shot is told by his doctor that in order to get well, he can either take a round of very large oral antibiotic pills or get a shot in his hip. When one is in an avoidance-avoidance situation, people describe it as being "between a rock and a hard place." Since the rock IS a hard place, this idiom accurately describes this kind of dilemma.

3. Approach-Avoidance means that there is only one choice and it simultaneously both attracts and repels the person. This is considered the hardest of the dilemmas because it is not as cut-and-dry as the others. Rather than being an either-or decision, it is more a matter of degrees. "Because of the positive valence of the goal, the [person approaches] it; but as it is approached, the negative valence becomes stronger."[7]

For example, an employee is given a promotion with a raise and significant prestige, but it requires being transferred to a facility in another state. This means uprooting his family and moving them away from all their relatives and friends. He is really excited about the promotion. He has been working hard for it for years, but the move would also take him far from his parents, and he would worry about his mother trying to take care of his father, who has Alzheimer's. This choice has both strong approach and strong avoidance motivators.

Motivational Conflicts Theory fits many situations that people face in their daily lives, but it also is appropriate for marketers who are designing touchpoints along the customer's consumption journey. Each interaction that the customer has with the brand should be either an approach-approach or an approach-avoidance scenario. When the company is trying to convince the customer to choose between two sizes or colors of the same product, or between two service contracts, the approach-approach dilemma works because—either way—the customer is still purchasing the product. If the touchpoint is trying to demonstrate how the brand stands out from its competitors, the approach-avoidance scenario should be used to force the customer to push away the competitor and move toward purchasing the brand.

Equity Theory

Allocation of rewards and resources has been a reality ever since societies were first formed. According to the Equity Theory, proposed in the 1950s, human beings believe that rewards and punishments should be distributed in proportion to the recipients' inputs or contributions.[8, 9] The perception of fairness is a must for social systems to be effective and the members of those systems to be satisfied.[10] Since one of the major exchange relationships in societies is the consumption process, consumer expectations of being treated fairly by sellers and service providers deserve additional attention. Pricing is the main area of concern when consumers are extremely sensitive about fairness.

Unfair pricing seems to be a common complaint of customers who use telecommunications (TELCO) companies. On the whole, loyal customers feel that they are being punished for their loyalty. In order to entice new customers to sign up, the companies offer drastically discounted rates that are much lower than the prices being paid by customers under contract. Usually the low price is only for the first year. After that, the price zooms up and the customer has to pay the higher rate for the length of the contract. Customers know this is not fair, but in order to obtain the services, they reluctantly agree to sign the contract. If at some point before the contract is up, a customer decides to switch companies, he must pay a stiff penalty. Customers either wait out the contract or pay the penalty, at which time they rush to a competing TELCO company. Some savvy customers, though, play the system and, like migratory birds, migrate every year to another TELCO company. They have to decide, though, if the cost of the penalty is worth the savings that the introductory rate at each new company gives them. (A hitch in this strategy is that at some point, they will run out of TELCOs to migrate to.) Equity Theory would point out that the loyal customers, rather than new customers, should receive a discount for staying with the company longer. They should not be punished for their loyalty. From this perspective, the TELCO companies are failing to incentivize contract customers to be loyal beyond the length of their contracts. If the company had a way to give discounts to their loyal customers—for example, offering three-year contracts with the first year discounted on each renewal contract, then customers would sense that this is a fair trade-off and opt to stay with the original company long-term.

takeaway!

The question is: How do you convince the customer to respond positively to your offering? First discover the qualities that are distinctive about your target customer: his tastes, attitudes, weaknesses, priorities and fears. Then customize your persuasion efforts to capture his attention. Finally, let the data about the personality traits of your customer lead you. He may be inner or other-directed, verbal or text-oriented, dogmatic or open-minded, etc. Fine-tune your touchpoints to capitalize on the persuasion method that works best with your customer segment.

Heider's Balance Theory

In 1946, Heider postulated that an individual has relationships with his thoughts and that those thoughts themselves are connected. He pictured the dynamics between the person and two interrelated thoughts as forming a triad. Moreover, he theorized that how the individual and the thoughts relate create balance or imbalance, and that the individual would always seek to balance the triad. In his era, Heider might have thought of WWII in connection with a soldier—the two related thoughts forming a triad with himself. In the late 20th century, a basketball fan might connect Michael Jordan and Nike shoes. Today, a high school student might think about her best friend and automatically link that with a thought about a Facebook post that her friend might enjoy. Heider's schematic for his Balance Theory was a triangle, with the Perceiver (P) at the top, the Other Person (O) on the bottom left, and the Attitude Object (X) on the bottom right. Heider represented the relationships between these three elements with plus or minus signs. He declared that balanced triads have an odd number of plus signs and are more pleasant. Unbalanced triads have an odd number of minus signs and are unpleasant, which encourages the Perceiver to change one of his thoughts to make the triad more balanced. To do this, he may change the Attitude Object (X) or change the Other Person (O) that he associates with the object. [11]

takeaway!

Be cautious! Your customers will likely be overly sensitive about your pricing strategy; they are already wary from experiences with price discrimination tactics used by other companies like the TELCOs. This is because price is the most visible element of nearly every transaction and the parties do have an inherent expectation of fairness, including the payment terms and discounts. The question is: Do you want to reward your loyal customers or your new customers? Are there creative ways to reward both?

For example, if customer Bob didn't like Nike shoes, but he liked Michael Jordan and Bob knew that Jordan has endorsed Nike shoes, those relationships fit into a **Triad**, where Bob is P, Jordan is O, and Nike shoes are the X. The thought or cognition "Bob likes Jordan" is represented by a plus sign between P and O. Jordan's endorsement of Nike shoes is shown by the plus sign between O and X. Bob's current attitude toward Nike shoes ("Bob doesn't like Nike shoes") is represented by a minus sign between Bob (P) and Nike (X). Heider's theory predicts that Bob would feel uncomfortable when he realized the imbalance between these three elements: If Bob admires (likes) Jordan so much (P + O), and Jordan thinks that Nike shoes are great (O + X), then why doesn't Bob like Nike shoes (P - X)? Balance theory predicts that Bob would change one of his attitudes to get rid of the discomfort and restore balance. If Bob changes his attitude toward Nike shoes from a minus (unfavorable attitude: P - X) to a plus (favorable attitude: P + X), then his new set of relations form a balanced Triad, and he feels at peace with himself.

Balance Theory has an advantage over other theories that marketers should be aware of. It recognizes that people sometimes have inconsistent cognitions, and that, once they realize the inconsistency, the uncomfortable imbalance can spur a voluntary change in attitude. People don't compare every thought they have to every other thought, so at times individuals can have several inconsistent cognitions and not realize it. However, once they are aware of an inconsistency, that imbalance can lead to attitudinal change. Heider was the first scholar to spot this and to develop a theory to help explain it.

Heider's Balance Theory

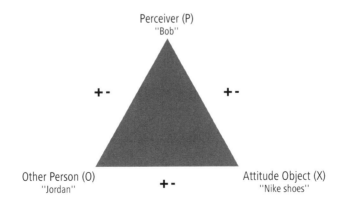

If companies pay attention to the inconsistent cognitions and unbalanced triads of customers in a specific segment, they may be able to portray their offering in such a way as to help restore consistent cognitions along the value chain and spur customers to adjust their attitudes to be balanced in relation to the product or service being offered.

Expectancy Theory

Expectancy theory states that the intensity of a tendency to perform in a particular manner is dependent on the intensity of an expectation that the performance will be followed by a definite outcome and on how appealing that outcome is to the individual.   According to this theory, the individual's behavior is based on self-interest; he or she wants to achieve maximum satisfaction and minimum dissatisfaction.

This theory stresses expectations and perception; what is real and actual is immaterial. Specifically, this theory:

• Stresses expectations and perception; what is real and actual is immaterial.

• Emphasizes rewards or pay-offs.

• Focuses on psychological extravagance, where the final objective of the individual is to attain maximum pleasure while suffering the least amount of pain.

Vroom's Expectancy Theory addresses motivation and management. The theory suggests that an individual's perceived view of an outcome will determine his or her the level of motivation. It assumes that the choices being made maximize pleasure and minimize pain.[12] This is also seen in the Law of Effect: "one of the principles of reinforcement theory, which states that people engage in behaviors that have pleasant outcomes and avoid behaviors that have unpleasant outcomes"[13, 14]   Vroom disputes the long-held belief that the relationship between people's work and their goal is a simple correlation, noting that individual factors, such as skills, knowledge, experience, personality and abilities, can all have an impact on an employee's performance.

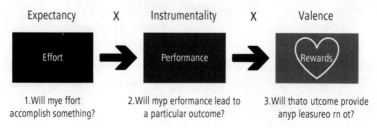

Expectancy   X   Instrumentality   X   Valence

Effort → Performance → Rewards

1.Will mye ffort accomplish something?   2.Will myp erformance lead to a particular outcome?   3.Will thato utcome provide anyp leasureo rn ot?

takeaway!

Combine the Elaboration Likelihood Model and Balance Theory when setting up touchpoints along your customer's journey. If the customer doesn't have sufficient interest in or need of your offering, or a previous positive experience with your brand, use ELM's peripheral cues to persuade the customer to consider your new offering. Peripheral cues are satisfying experiences that the customer has had with things unrelated to your brand. If you link one of these cues positively, like in Balance theory, to your product and to the customer, the customer will feel balanced and will more likely make the purchase.

Vroom theorized that the source of motivation in Expectancy Theory is a "multiplicative function of valence, instrumentality and expectancy."[15] He suggested that "people consciously chose a particular course of action, based upon perceptions, attitudes, and beliefs as a consequence of their desires to enhance pleasure and avoid pain."[16]

Prospect Theory

Prospect Theory describes how people choose between different options (or prospects) and how they estimate (many times in a biased or incorrect way) the perceived likelihood of each of these options. This theory was proposed by psychologists Daniel Kahneman and Amos Tversky in 1979.[17] Later, in 2002, Kahneman was awarded the Nobel Prize in economics for it. (Sadly, Tversky had passed away before the award was given.)

One of the cognitive biases that people rely on when they make decisions is **loss aversion**. People tend to use small probabilities as a hedge against losses. Even though the likelihood of a costly event may be miniscule, most people would rather agree to a smaller, sure loss now—such as paying a monthly insurance premium—than risk a large expense later, like paying out of pocket for major surgery. The perceived likelihood of a major health problem is greater than the actual probability of such an event occurring.

People would all like to believe that they are logical decision-makers. In evaluating the user experience, it is assumed that users would weigh the various alternatives in order to determine which action to take or where to go next. However, when it comes to making decisions about whether to purchase something, make a donation, or select a service contract, people are highly susceptible to cognitive biases, and often don't make the logical choice.

For example, which would most people choose—to be handed $900 or take a 90% chance of winning $1000 (with a 10% chance of winning $0)? Most people would avoid the risk and take the $900 (even though the expected outcome is the same in both cases). However, if they were asked to choose between losing $900 and taking a 90% chance of losing $1000 (with a 10% chance of losing $0), most would probably prefer the second option. They are willing to engage in risk-seeking behavior in the hope of avoiding the loss. The following diagram demonstrates risk-avoidance versus risk-seeking behavior for this scenario:

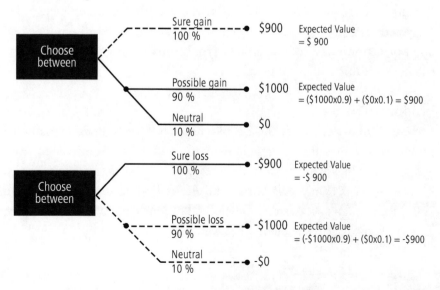

When dealing with gains, people are risk-averse and will choose the sure gain (denoted by the red line) over a riskier prospect, even though with the risk there is a possibility of gaining a larger reward. Note also that the overall expected value (or outcome) of each choice is equal.

Losses are treated in the opposite manner as gains. When aiming to avoid a loss, people become risk-seeking and take the gamble over a sure loss in the hope of paying nothing. Again, both options have equal expected values.

These types of behaviors cannot be easily explained simply by the expected-utility approach. In both of these situations, the expected utility of both choices is the same (+/-$900)—the probability multiplied by the expected win. Yet the preferred option depends on whether the perceived outcome is a win or a loss.

Experiential Life Cycle

Brands need continuous innovation[18], since the experiential value of an offering erodes over time, as we saw earlier with the married couple. Similarly, when a new relevant offering is launched on the market, it creates a "surprise effect," which affects the experiences of customers in positive way. As time passes by and more customers purchase the offering, the experiential value disseminates to a broader frame and it causes a "delight effect." Finally, the experiential value becomes a basic characteristic for the category and it causes a "norm effect." Consider the automobile market. When Tesla first introduced the electric car, it provided a "surprise effect" for most customers. Why? Because it had a noiseless motor and the highest-ever relative torque. Later this technology was disseminated to hybrid cars. Drivers of hybrid cars experienced a "delight effect" because they knew that they were getting the best possible fuel efficiency from the electric/gasoline hybrid engine. In comparison, fossil-fueled cars are still considered "the norm" in today's auto industry because most of the cars on the road still have gas-ethanol or diesel engines. Fossil-fuel engines themselves have gone through the Experiential Life Cycle. When they were first introduced by Ford, they triggered the" surprise effect" because everyone else had to use horse-drawn carriages to travel. As Ford manufactured thousands and then millions of Model-Ts, owning a motorized car was a "delight." Time has reduced that "delight" to the "norm" in today's society.

Experiential Life Cycle

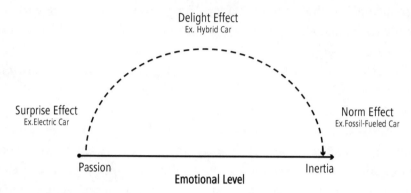

Value Life Cycle

The values of customers are in a constant state of flux and subject to changing moment to moment, context to context and case to case.[19] As a result, the experiential needs of customers change over time, too. For example, when a customer is young, his values may include wanting to feel free from responsibility or to be admired by his peers. He may buy a Ducati motorcycle to express those values. However, as the customer gets older, his values may change. New values, such as family, security and fairness might be added to or even replace the original values. Hence, the customer might prefer the safety of a car instead of the freedom of a motorcycle. Companies promoting their brands need to keep this in mind.

Value Life Cycle

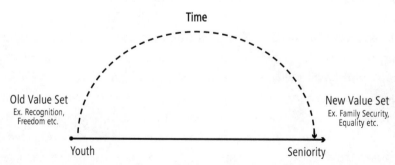

Of course, there will always be older guys who will never give up their motorcycles and younger customers who consider a motorcycle to be dangerous or simply feel safer inside a car. Generally, though, customers follow the Value Life Cycle, and where they are along the cycle directly affects the product choices they make. Recognizing this will prevent brands from making costly errors, such as assuming that a blouse designed to appeal to teenagers would sell just as well in an apparel store that caters to professional women.

Family Life Cycle

Experiential expectancies of customers also evolve as their relational status changes. Companies need to clearly define the customer segment that they are targeting. To assume that a Bachelor would have similar preferences to Newlyweds, or that Empty Nesters would have the same purchasing expectations as Full Nesters with young children, guarantees that the customer experience laid out by the company will fail. Usually the product or service has attributes that appeal more to a particular stage of the Family Life Cycle, so those attributes can provide clues as to how to approach potential customers. Obviously, a swing set with an attached playhouse will catch the attention of Full Nesters with young children. If the product can appeal to two or more stages of the Life Cycle, for example toothpaste, the brand can use several distinct touchpoints that have been fine-tuned to the experiential expectancies of each relational status.[20]

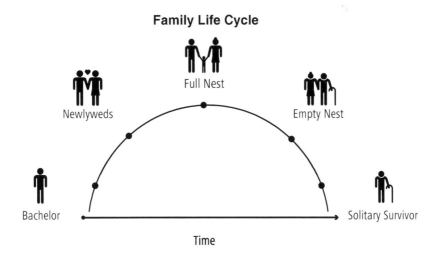

Family Life Cycle

Chapter 11

EXPERIENTIAL MARKETING COMMUNI- CATIONS

Marketing Communication is as old as the beginning of trade on earth. Archaeologists have found ads for candidates etched into the ruins of ancient Pompeii, as well as invitations to travelers to visit a tavern nearby in town. In ancient Rome, a wall painting announced that a residence was available for rent. In Thebes, Egypt, during excavation, a 3000 year-old papyrus ago was discovered that announced a prize for turning in escaped slaves. In Medieval times, merchants used to hire "town criers" to walk through the town and shout announcements about goods offered by merchants or the arrival of a merchant ship at a port nearby. Being a town crier soon became a profession in and of itself. In 1141, King Louis VII granted exclusive rights to twelve town criers in Berry, France, and, under that charter, no one else was permitted to shout announcements in that town.

With the invention of the printing press by Gutenberg in 1445, communications gained effectiveness and efficiency, since a merchant could now print thousands of advertisement flyers and deliver them to the masses inexpensively. The invention of steam powered engines and developments in transportation, such as the railroads, broadened the reach of printed communications as well as goods and commodities. Until the beginning of the 20th century, most of these communication materials belonged to patented medicine manufacturers and merchants who advertised commodities such as coffee, tea, fabrics, etc. to the masses. It didn't take long for consumer brands, like Coca Cola, Jell-O, Ivory, Colgate and Levi's, to steal the communication marketing lead away from local merchants and the national medicine manufacturers.

Advertising continued to evolve as, in the 1920s, public relations and radio joined in the marketing communication mix, followed a few decades later by television. In the 1990s, a new concept emerged, called Integrated Marketing Communication (IMC). IMC sought to introduce coherence and consistency among the various marketing communication avenues. It was first defined by the American Advertising Agencies Association (4A's) in 1989. This concept progressed even further by integrating recent innovations in marketing communication, such as the Internet and social media. By 1991, Don Schultz had developed this definition:

"IMC is the process of managing all sources of information about a product/service to which a customer or prospect is exposed which behaviorally moves the consumer toward a sale and maintains customer loyalty". [1]

More recently, Integrated Marketing Communication, which is widely used and cited both by practitioners and academicians, has come to mean: "A concept of marketing communications planning that recognizes the added value of a comprehensive plan that evaluates the strategic roles of a variety of communication disciplines – general advertising, direct response, sales promotion, and public relations – and combines these disciplines to provide clarity, consistency, and maximum communication impact".[2] Today in textbooks and in leading business schools, these definitions are taught to existing and prospective business people.

The practice of managing communication has evolved quite a bit since the earliest efforts of marketing communication, but the essence still remains— although, the business paradigm has shifted immensely. Traditionally, marketing communication had always viewed its purpose from the perspective of company—not the customer. The aim of the communication effort had always been on selling more, selling again, selling more frequently or selling constantly. Return on integrated marketing communications investments were often measured based on awareness, recognition, consideration, purchase and repeat purchase. KPIs are the reflection of a classical hierarchy of effects models, like AIDA (Awareness-Interest-Desire-Action). Even for measuring ROI in many IMC campaigns, models like DAGMAR (Defining Advertising Goals for Measured Advertising Results) were employed, and the models followed the path of "Unaware, Aware, Comprehension and Image, Attitude and Action." This Era was appropriately named "The Consumer Era."

IMC opened a new chapter, named the "The Relationship Era." In this new Era, "building sustainable relationships" instead of "selling more" became the focus. The goal was to give customers solid reasons to trust the company and the product. The "what the brand does" view changed to "why the brand exists." This new strategy aimed to engage people instead of interrupting or pressuring them to buy. Comprehensive evaluation of the all communication channels, especially the newest ones, led to this major shift to engagement.

As social media began to have even more of an impact on the thinking and mindset of customers, there was a second shift—although smaller, but no less significant: Businesses realized that to be successful in today's digital world, they had to "satisfy the values of their customers." This meant not just engaging them, but serving them as well, and providing what the customers themselves knew they needed. This ushered in "The Experience Era," which emphasizes being proactive and designing brand relevancy.

However, selling still remains the ultimate goal for most companies. This may seem logical, since the purpose of commercial entities is to make profits and increase the value of shareholder stocks. The problem actually runs deeper than that: How a company looks at an issue shapes their attitude toward their customers. That attitude then triggers certain behavioral re-flexes and patterns. What is the issue? The issue is that now there is a new objective: "Satisfying customers." Companies that stubbornly insist that the objective is "selling more" are playing, as one would say in golf, with a hand-icap. It doesn't matter that they were in the top tier yesterday. Today's cus-tomer-centric market has created a whole new set of rules. Thus, not only are these companies several shots behind when they tee off, they are aiming for the wrong hole. In practical terms, starting with the wrong objective causes them to design platforms for their offering from the perspective of selling instead of satisfying. Hence, any campaign they conduct will miss communicating with their customers at an experiential level.

The diagram below shows how Integrated Marketing Communication is still taught today in many business schools. The customers are referred to as the "Marketing Communications Audience." Notice what position the customers have in this model compared to the earlier ego-centric approach. Having the customer in the center of all the channels is a step in the right direction, but IMC is still missing some critical elements, as noted in the next paragraph.

If we examine the mix, we see elements which implicitly focus on selling, like advertising, PR, sales promotion, direct mail and so forth. As you can see, most of these communication efforts are propaganda tools, but building sustainable relationships requires far more than simply applying determin-istic, quantitative CRM systems. Throwing sales messages at the customer and hoping that something will stick does not meet customer experiential needs. The first objective should be to make customers comfortable and satisfied by delivering expected and even augmented experiences in their consumption stages. Remember that those stages are "buy," "use" and "dispose." Please have a look the IMC model again. Are there any components that mention the consumption stage or a disposal stage? IMC is still stuck in the traditional mindset that says, "We sold the offering and that's all we need to do, right?" Hence, Integrated Marketing Communications continues to have selling as its primary focus and is leaking customers as a result.

A Comparison of the 3 Most Recent Marketing Eras

	Consumer Era	Relationship Era	Experience Era
Objective	Sell more	Build relationship	Satisfy values of customers
Strategy	Interrupt and persuade people	Engage people	Please people
Starts With	What the brand does	Why the brand exists	How the customers please
Media	Channel most conductive to influence people	Channel most conductive to engage people	Channel most proactive to serve people
Content	Presents the brand positively	Presents the brand authentically	Presents the brand relevantly
Success Measure	Impact on transactions	Impact on transactions and trust	Impact on satisfaction

On the other hand, if a company consciously and proactively places the customer at the peak of the hierarchy when formulating business models or marketing communication campaigns, sooner or later that company will conquer the mind and heart of their customers.

Thus, what is really needed is **"Experiential Marketing Communications"** (EMC), which discards the sell-only focus and seeks to deliver end-to-end communication with the customer all along the consumption journey. Unlike IMC, in Experiential Marketing Communication the communication doesn't end with the purchase. Instead, it continues to engage the customer through the usage and the disposal of the offering.

Integrated Marketing Communications Audience Contact Tools[3]

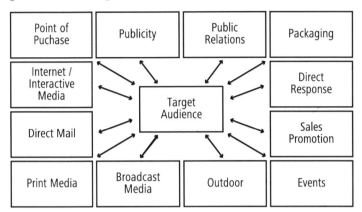

Despite IMC's faults, one positive characteristic of IMC was its consistent channel messages; the same message was repeated again and again throughout the communication mix in order to hammer it into the minds of customers. This gave it a distinct advantage in the traditional sales environment. In fact, this approach was so widely embraced that "advertising gurus" like Ries offered the "Three Rules of Communication": "Repetition, Repetition and Repetition." At first glance this recipe sounds like the perfect solution for getting customer to buy, but in today's Customer Experience Era, this approach falls short, at least for savvy business professionals, because the success of a communication campaign depends on its ability to adapt along the customer journey. As mentioned before, customers may evolve along the value chain. They may even move to a different customer segment, and brands need to be flexible enough to accommodate them. Simple repetition is too static and stagnant to be effective.

Most communication campaigns are run by repeating, repeating and repeating the same message on all channels. A bank designs an ad about loan interest rates. The customer sees it on an Internet banner, a TV spot, on a billboard along the highway, and hears the jingle on the radio. He responds by going to his local bank to check it out. Inside, the customer sees more repetition of the same message with the same slogan, the same tone, the same content, etc. What this communication blast doesn't take into consideration is that the customer has already become aware of the campaign and is ready to pass on to the next stage in decision-making. At this point, the message in the branch should focus on explaining why the customer should take the next step in his consumption journey. But today, most campaigns miss the point by relying on the traditional "repeat" paradigm of the IMC bandwagon.

Marketing campaigns today are widely measured by engagements, such as Facebook likes, tweets and forum mentions, as well as recognition, sales and so on. But in the Customer Experience Age, it is vital to understand the nature of the experiences that customers gather along their journey.

takeaway!

Compared to EMC, IMC is relatively primitive in convincing customers to build sustainable relations with the brand. It still relies too much on repetition, repetition, repetition and focuses on early decision stages of customers as they travel the value chain. In contrast, EMC, engages the experiences of customers into consideration not in early decision stages but through whole consumption journey including using and disposing.

Moreover, the decision characteristics of customers are different than they used to be. Technological advancements have inevitably reshaped the "Customer Decision Funnel" into the shape of a prism. Today people have the tools to gain knowledge faster and more accurately than before and apply their knowledge to almost every purchase. In the past, a customer would be aware of a set of brands, would consider a few of them and would choose to buy one. This is the "Customer Decision Funnel." Today, however, after realizing that he has problem that needs solving, the customer goes online to find a solution. The difference is that the sheer number of options in the set of brands is now much, much larger. The decision funnel no longer

Customer Decision Funnel

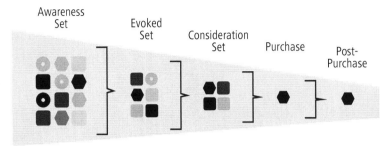

Customer Decision Prism

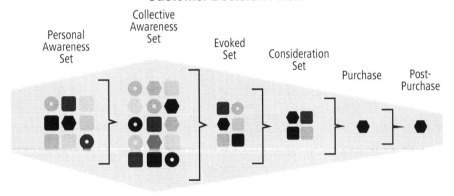

works. Instead, the customer has to rely on a prism approach to narrow his options in order to make a purchase. Compare the two models to see how the ground has shifted dramatically. Companies that are relying on old techniques quickly fall behind the competition that already has realized the new rules and has introduced the "Customer Decision Prism" to their communication strategy.

The Customer Decision Prism is a natural outgrowth of customer behavior in response to digital marketing. This new paradigm has caused the decision-making chain to become longer and faster. Customer can go online and quickly gather an immense amount of knowledge about the products. In order to launch a successful communication campaign, companies should find out what motivates customers to go to the next stage in their purchase decision and what stops them from moving forward. They need to communicate stage-specific messages to potential customers through stage-specific media platforms.

Another characteristic of EMC that distinguishes it from IMC is its perspective on communication itself. IMC sees communication of the brand as a separate from the company itself, while EMC says that communication is part of a holistic approach to marketing. In other words, EMC sees the company as a collocutor a communicator of the brand, with every employee also being a brand ambassador. One time I was traveling by train in Germany, from Hannover to Berlin for a business meeting. On a tight schedule, I had taken the fast train. In the seat next to me was a middle-aged gentleman. After a while, we began to chat. The topic switched to foods, and the man told me that he was working for a particular food brand. He discussed some of the production conditions at the company and surprised me by advising me not to buy the brand. He said that he refused to buy the brand for those same reasons. I began to wonder: If the brand had failed to turn its own employee into an advocate, how likely is it for the brand to foster a loyal customer segment? Most probably that company has little chance to survive in the long run. To overcome objections like this, a company using EMC would take a two-pronged approach: Obviously, fix the production problem to restore customer satisfaction, and then correct any negative feelings about the brand that had resulted from the issues by using all channels to coherently disseminate an ambassador mindset. When customers feel that the company is looking out for them and is responsive to their concerns, they will become loyal customers and ambassadors for that brand.

Comparison Table of IMC and EMC

	Integrated Marketing Communications	Experiential Marketing Communications
Goal	Informing, Reminding, Persuading	Building Bonds
Decision Assumption	Static	Kinetic
Composition	Regardless of Stages	Stage Adapted
Diffusion	Early Decision Stages	Total Decision Stages
Communication Period	Time-bound	Continious
Means	Media Instruments	All About Brand

Chapter 12

MEASURING CUSTOMER EXPERIENCE

Measuring customer experience prevents a brand from becoming the next Yahoo or Nokia, which lost an immense market share, or Kodak and Pan Am, which were swallowed up by their competition. Given how critical this metric is to the success of the brand, companies should seriously involve themselves in customer experience measurement at all levels of the business, from C-suite on down.

The ultimate purpose of the Customer Experience is to foster loyalty in customers. Thus, before rolling up sleeves to develop, manage and lead customer experience initiatives, it would be wise to understand the nature of loyalty itself. If loyalty is not defined in detail for the marketing, it tends to float around as an abstract and rather nebulous concept. As such it is hard to pin down and put into practice. A number of researchers have tried to explain loyalty by describing it: It relies on the sensations of the consumers.[1] It is an affective and positive response toward the outcome of an experience.[2] Experiences that feed positive judgments are the predictor of repeat consumption, an indicator of loyalty.[3, 4] Positive experiences cause the consumer to show less interest in a competing brand,[5] and thus they play a role in the formation of attitudes. One concludes that when consumers experience positive outcomes with their purchases, it is expected that they will show repurchase behavior.[6]

The fact is that the seeds of loyalty can start earlier than most people think. Customers already have some expectations and form a general idea about the offering at the pre-consumption stage. Based on direct and indirect experiences, the level of loyalty is formed or updated continuously as a consequence of learning more about the offering. Each new experience may further cement the customer's loyalty to the brand, lessen it or have a neutral effect. There are two types of loyalty that need to be taken into consideration: "attitudinal loyalty" and "behavioral loyalty." Behaviorally loyal customers repurchase the same brand repetitively, [7] whereas attitudinally loyal customers lean toward making repeat purchases from the same brand,[8] but attitudinal loyalty does not guarantee a behavior, or a repurchase. Thus, a customer might be: just attitudinally loyal, just behaviorally loyal, both attitudinally and behaviorally loyal, or—because of poorly constructed customer experiences—not loyal at all. [9, 10]

The loyalty status of customers explains the nature of their relationship to the brand. Customers develop a state of loyalty or disloyalty as a sum of experiences obtained at the various stages of the consumption process—specifically, buying, using and disposing. This happens through a feedback process. The customer feels a need as the result of an internal or external deficiency. This arousal of need triggers stress. The customer wants to be free from the stress and seeks a solution. From then on, the customer directly or indirectly interacts with the products or services that have the greatest possibility of satisfying that need. Based on previous experiences, the customer may have attitudinal loyalty toward a particular product or service, which may trigger a positive perspective toward repeat purchase of that offering. Behavioral loyalty refers to the actual behavior of customers regardless their attitudes and is verified through observation of their behavior. Attitudinal loyalty, on the other hand, is not as easy to identify, because it has to be inferred. Thus, when a company states that they are measuring loyalty, they should clearly define whether they are attempting to measure attitudinal loyalty, behavioral loyalty or both. This can be rather confusing, so companies should be aware of what they are really measuring in their measurement process. The Matrix below shows how Behavioral and Attitudinal Loyalty can be further broken down to be better understood:

Customer Loyalty Matrix

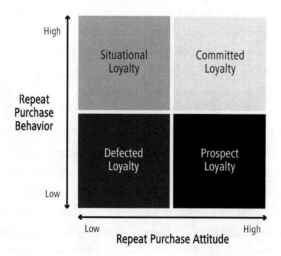

Committed Loyalty is the most sought-after loyalty relationship for brands, since these customers possess both attitudinal loyalty and behavioral loyalty. Apple fans are the perfect example of committed loyalty. It is clear that Apple attracts customers more intensely than most other technology brands. Their innovative products and unique attributes make Apple one of the most desired and valuable brands across the globe. The experiential consistency of the brand has yielded a brand tribe of customers. This tribe has a committed relationship with Apple. Apple customers try to buy each newly launched product the second it is available, and they do not have any intention of buying any other brand. It is obvious that Apple has an immense heart share supporting its market share.

Prospect Loyalty refers to a customer who is attitudinally loyal to a brand but behaviorally disloyal. Several internal and external factors can cause such a scenario: For instance, a customer may be attitudinally loyal to Mercedes SLK, however, due to budget constraints, may not be behaviorally loyal to that make and model vehicle —in other words, he won't purchase the car (demonstrate behavioral loyalty) because he can't afford it. Despite this, attitudinal loyalty will continue to be an internal driver for that customer's behavior. If the opportunity to afford that car were ever to arise, he will pursue what his attitudinal loyalty directs him to do. Suppose he gets a high-paying job or inherits substantial sum of money; he will most likely buy the Mercedes SLK. If, on the other hand, that customer continues to be on a tight budget and still needs a car, he will remain loyal to the Mercedes SLK—may admire it and talk about it—but will purchase a car that fits his budget. He remains attitudinally but not behaviorally loyal.

Defected Loyalty refers to customers who are neither attitudinally nor behaviorally inclined to make a repeat purchase. These customers may have formed the defected loyalty state due to using and being dissatisfied with the product, discovering a better alternative, or being exposed to brand messaging that didn't convince him or generate enough relevancy for him to form loyal attitudes or behaviors. Businesses that realize that their brand is not automatically creating loyalty should rethink their customer experiences. How? First, by determining exactly what kind of "loyalty" they are trying to track. Are they measuring attitudinal loyalty, behavioral loyalty or both? Measuring loyalty and how well the customer experience components are fostering it is not a minor issue. This metric should not be left to generic scales. Instead, it is critical to build an ad-hoc measurement platform that proactively generates a healthy feedback mechanism. That way, companies can measure loyalty as a direct consequence of the customer experience they are providing.

Situational Loyalty refers to a customer **being behaviorally loyal while attitudinally disloyal** towards a brand. A customer may buy a product for any number of reasons without possessing attitudinal loyalty towards that brand. Consider a customer who has his checking and savings accounts with Bank A. Suppose he wants to take out a loan, but Bank A can't give it to him because of his credit score. Bank B has a special loan offer that the customer qualifies for. The customer decides to get a loan from Bank B, which makes him behaviorally loyal to Bank B, but because he is not doing all his banking there, he is attitudinally disloyal to the Bank B brand. The situation changed the customer's behavior but did not change his attitudinal loyalty to the original brand.

According to Freud, the human mind consists of three components that fight for dominance within the self: the "id," the "ego" and the "superego." Ego operates based on reality and id is motivated by pleasure, whereas the superego seeks to stay within the framework of social norms.[11]   Ego plays the role of a moderator between the id and the superego. Id forces the individual to seek self-satisfaction at any cost; Jung and Nietzsche have named this component of the mind "shadow." [12]   On the other hand, the superego finds satisfaction in social conformity. Depending on the circumstances, the ego satisfies either the demands of the superego or the demands of the id. Attitudes occur at the superego or the id level, but before they can turn into behavior, they have to pass through the filter of the ego.[13]   Behavioral loyalty is the most salient and captive status of the ego. In behavioral loyalty, reality (the ego) takes command and behavior emerges despite conflicting attitudes; this is because reality is determinative. The conflicts, however, create variance between attitudinal and behavioral loyalty.

Ajzen (1991), in his influential study of the theory of planned behavior, explored the variance between attitudes and behaviors and postulated "relative control" as a determinant of human behavior. According to Ajzen, the behavior of the individual cannot be explained through social norms or attitudes, because only perceived behavioral control has a significant effect on actual behavior. [14] An example would be a smoker who has been addicted to tobacco for decades. Under pressure from family, friends and his doctor to quit, he may form the attitude to quit smoking, but may lack the fortitude to make it happen. His perceived behavioral control was not strong enough to connect his attitude (the desire to stop smoking) with the desired behavior (actually stopping). In creating effective customer experiences, companies need to pay attention to perceived behavioral control as it relates to customers' purchasing behavior.

Another common mistake when measuring customer experience is not having a clear definition of "needs," "wants" and "demands." Too often, these three terms are used interchangeably, but they are different constructs, each connected to each other. Moreover, they are controlled by mental and emotional filters:

Need is a physiological or psychological internal deficiency that causes an imbalance which leads to stress. Needs, therefore, have great potential for energizing people to act to reduce that stress. Customers often buy things that they don't really need from the perspective of an outsider, if the customer bought something, then it means that the customer felt a deficiency and behaved to fill that void. The onlooker may not understand the behavior. He may even think that it was a foolish or unnecessary purchase. Someone else's opinion, however, doesn't change the customer's belief that he needs that item. In the effort to be competitive, some companies create "pseudo-needs" through their marketing. This may work for a while, but as the consciousness of the target audience increases through the Internet, customers are becoming immune to this tactic. Readily available knowledge about products and services is helping customers recognize the provided value of offerings and are being fooled less often by "pseudo-needs."

Want is internal driver that forces an individual to satisfy a need in a specific way. When a customer feels thirsty, he recognizes that he needs to find liquid food to satisfy his need. The customer may satisfy the need with Guinness beer, Petrus wine or tap water. Customers use their cognitive filters to sort through the possibilities and a "want" for a specific solution arises. When the want arises, it forms an idea in the mind of the customer. This idea may then be converted into a demand that leads to action, or may remain as a want.

Demand refers for the actual purchase behavior of the customer. The customer may want one thing, but may demand (purchase) something else. Consider the thirsty customer again. He needs liquid. He wants Petrus wine (assuming that the customer has discriminating taste). Yet, when the customer goes to the store, he demands Guinness beer—His reason? Insufficient cash on hand. When demands arise, they pass through the filter of "perceived control." Perceived control is a term that refers to the degree of control that an individual has over his own actions. Consider a heavy smoker with health problems. The addict doesn't want to smoke, but the internal deficiency of nicotine forces the smoker to demand cigarettes. Like the aforementioned customer who wanted Petrus, attitude and behavior often conflict. What does that say to companies who are trying to measure customer experience for one of their products or services?

takeaway!

When assessing how target customers might relate to an offering, it is critical to consider their needs, their wants and their demands. These filters pave the way for understanding and engaging target customer segments. When designing and developing your CE measurement platform be sure that you know whether you are measuring their needs, their wants or their demands.

How to Build an Ad-Hoc Customer Experience Measurement Scale

Always remember that a CE Measurement Scale is based on the "voice of the customer." That voice does not only belong to existing customers. Rather, it is also the opinions of every potential customer for the product or service that the brand is offering. Thus, when a company starts to build a customer experience measurement scale, the methodology needs to be adapted to the voice of the brand's existing customers as well as its potential customers. "Ad-hoc" means that it is fine-tuned to the industry, culture and so forth. It will not be exactly the same as the scale designed by a competitor. There may be similarities, but each company should create its own CE Measurement Scale in order to measure how effective its own customer experience is.

Surveys, when conducted properly, have been proven to express the voice of the customer fairly accurately. One would think that annual surveys would do the trick, but in actuality, they are not particular helpful in gathering the data needed for an effective measurement scale. This is because an annual survey can only take a snapshot of what customers are thinking at the time when the survey is conducted. But markets keep changing. They are in continuous evolution—new competitors emerge, new technologies arise, new products are launched, substitutes siphon customers from popular products. As a result, brands are under both symmetrical and asymmetrical attacks from diverse fronts. This means that collecting relevant data in both a timely and continuous manner is the key to success in today's market.

Another vital key is being aware of the nature of the feedback being collected. Today, most companies gather feedback through surveys. With advancements in technology, brands can easily collect survey data through touch points such as mobiles, tablets, online polling, booths in stores and so forth. However, it should always be kept in mind that what a customer says on a survey and does in real life may drastically differ. Thus, it is necessary to also track the customer's behavior to see if their stated behavior matches their actual behavior. Taking time to track stated versus actual behavior increases the reliability of the CE measurement system. Ad-hoc measurements also have the benefit of allowing companies to evaluate customer behavior. For example, if a former customer now seems to prefer a competing product, but still recommends the original brand to his or her friends, it would be wise to investigate and measure the antecedents of this behavior to sort out what happened. This could reveal where the customer experience broke down for that customer and suggest changes for the future.

takeaway!

Don't put the cart before the horse. The "horse" is the step where you uncover the obstacles that are keeping your company from reaching its goals. The "cart" is the step where you form quantitative platforms to measure the degree to which those obstacles are keeping you from your goals. Once you have this information, you can move forward and measure the customer experience.

Defining the Aim of Measurement

Measurement should not be done without a good reason. Behind each decision to measure, there must be a purpose, such as to compare, to combine, to relate one concept with another, and to interpret that relationship. A homeowner may measure the dimensions of a fridge to find out whether or not it will fit through the kitchen doorway, or a grandmother may measure how well her grandson liked the cake that she baked for his birthday to decide whether or not to bake that same kind for another occasion. When a company measures a concept, it aims to understand the current market and the effects of the concept on the target segment as well as on other concepts. The goal is to lay down some guidelines for further activities.

In measurement there are three approaches: "mimetic," "coercive" and "normative."

The mimetic measurement approach simply copies the measurement tools–such as satisfaction surveys, etc.—of the competition. Companies that take this approach are taking the easy route and simply implementing the exact measurement methods that the competition is using. Since their competitor has a legendary brand image, they assume that the successful brand knows what it is doing. If, for example, a company uses NPS only

" takeaway!

Always bear in mind that there might be a metric that is better tailored for your industry and the market you operate in than the one you are currently using. Don't limit yourself or the potential of your company by taking the easy way out when measuring customer experience.

"

because it is commonly used, the company is using this method in a mimetic way. They are not applying rational reason to their decision. They are merely imitating what they think works.

The coercive measurement approach is often taken not by choice, but because the conditions of the marketing ecosystem force all competing brands to utilize the same tools. Hence it is not a real decision; the company feels that there are only certain options, so they take those. A real-life example of this is the ancient inhabitants of America and Africa. Both groups of people built shelters with leaning roofs. This was because they had independently realized that the weight of accumulated rain during a storm would collapse the roof if not drained somehow. They were both equally successful.

The normative measurement approach stands for implementing a measurement practice that is built on scientifically reasoned ratios. In order to adopt this approach, the company should start by asking what their goals are and what can potentially prevent the company from reaching those goals.

Many organizations mimetically measure customer satisfaction or customer recommendation with existing scales. There is nothing wrong with using existing scales—as long as the company knows the pros and cons of using those measurement methods, and determines the degree of their relevancy to the brand's market and industry. Adopting the scales used by other companies should be done wisely. In other words, they should be carefully adapted to the brand so that the satisfaction levels, or NPS, are accurately measured in light of the company's goals.

Once measured, the outcomes should be tested to see whether they can be linked with the established performance metrics of the company. No metric stands alone. It should always be seen in the context of all the other performance measurements being utilized. Aim to see the big picture, which is made up of many smaller pictures.

For example, cultural differences among countries affect the way they respond to surveys. An American company applied an NPS metric in the Dutch market. They were confused by the results, which showed that the number of promoter customers was suspiciously low when compared to American metrics. What they didn't understand was that these numbers were quite normal for the Dutch market because customers in Holland are not as generous with their ratings as USA customers; they rarely rate 9s or 10s. This is also true for customers in Germany. Thus, in order to achieve accurate and robust measurements, companies should use industry and market-specific metrics to properly measure customer experiences.

Measuring the Right Variables

Measuring customer experience is vital for enabling a company to serve better, but numbers are not absolute qualities.[15] This means that any numbers assigned to qualities only provide a relative standing for that measurement. For example, if a student receives a grade of 0 on an exam, does that mean that the student doesn't recall even a single thing from the entire course? Or suppose that it is 0 degrees Celsius outside. Does this mean that a person can feel no heat at all? Is it possible to feel neutral, i.e., neither positive nor negative heat? Obviously, these numbers are relative and have no meaning without the qualitative context. Similarly, when measuring customer experience, customer satisfaction and loyalty, etc., link all numerical outcomes with their qualitative contexts.

Again, it is critical to remember to explicitly define what is being measured. Too often companies measure a concept without properly defining it. As mentioned earlier, they may try to measure customer loyalty without deciding whether they are actually measuring attitudinal or behavioral loyalty. Or they may not distinguish "committed," "prospect," "defected" and "situational" loyalty. By not bothering to use clear definitions, they risk sabotaging their own efforts to build customer loyalty.

Defining Instruments to Measure

Several "voice of customer" (VOC) scales have been offered by both academicians and practitioners for measuring customer experience. Some of these are multi-item scales (these have several questions), whereas others are single-item scales (consisting of just one question). Any company that focuses on customer experience or wants to transition into a customer-centric entity should definitely have a multi-item ad-hoc VOC platform that covers the whole customer journey. This way, they can scrutinize what customers feel, do and think during each stage of consumption, as well as pre-consumption—specifically: awareness, buy, use and dispose—for each experiential segment. If the company regularly runs the scale, it should continuously get feedback across the value stream that it occupies. Developing an ad-hoc scale like this provides businesses with top-notch knowledge to understand both the brand itself and their competition. Moreover, it provides actionable insights for retaining customers as well as acquiring new ones from the competition. When developing a measurement scale, the entire customer experience journey should be considered; it is very easy to get caught up in one or two stages and lose sight of the big picture. The essence and aim of a scale is to understand what customers feel, think and do as they interact with the brand. It measures how they respond as they experience the direction, strength, content and frequency of the offerings. The scale then records their emotions through their resultant behavior. When designing CE measurement scale, start with the essence and aim mentioned above and include both quantitative and qualitative methods. Even though qualitative instruments tend to be more expensive to conduct—and the temptation is to cut back on them to save on cost—they should nevertheless be done at regular intervals during the measurement process.

Generic and traditional measurement methods and even relevant scales may give organizations some feedback about the effectiveness of their customer experience, but they are not enough to build a comprehensive VOC platform that can guide the company forward. They are like the heart beats, blood pressure or pupil size of an organization. By measuring these, a company may understand that something is wrong with the business, however further diagnostics tools are needed to enable that brand to perform better against the competition or to fix problems that are creating barriers for customers.

Generally, traditional generic scales help businesses roughly understand whether they are doing well or not. Knowing oneself is a good thing, but even better is knowing the areas where they can improve and the competition. Hence, companies that also collect VOC related to their competition may have a better chance of understanding the dynamics of the market they operate in. Brands are not evaluated in a vacuum. Rather, they are constantly compared by customers to their competition. So, it is vital that brands know the VOC of their competition in order to foster a significant advantage against their rivals. In order to be competitive, a company must have an ad-hoc VOC platform and should make the results available to C-suite executives and on scorecards to its employees. An outside-in organization may not see what to do without VOC. Today most organization follow competition through single item scales databanks and not surprisingly all they can learn is based on what they are able to conclude with both limited and static data.

We want to underline again that getting volunteer feedback through generic scales is a good tool and definitely helps organizations to roughly understand their performance, but it shouldn't be the whole story for customer-centric companies. Through proper exploration, companies can discover what to do to excel in their business.

On the other hand, we are in the age of technological advancements. By taking advantage of these advancements, brands can explore and reveal causal effects between physical reactions of their customers through sensory devices. A camera system can track a customer's pupil movements and record what they are looking at in real time. Face recognition software may sense a smile or an unhappy face. RFID systems can produce large amounts of data about the experiential patterns of customers by linking them with purchase records. So, a company that wants to deliver ground-breaking experiences, leave the competition behind in the dust, and stay at the top of the minds of customers, shouldn't confine itself to software that only tracks traditional data sources, like online surveys, Internet recommendation tracking, CATI satisfaction polls and so forth.

takeaway!

Don't design your measurement infrastructure according to what is convenient, but design it according to what your company need in order to track the experiences of your customers. Then find the means to support your measurement platform. This way you will be thinking outside the box and be ahead of the competition.

When developing declarative measurement platforms, the following steps should be taken:

1. Specify the content of the measurement platform

It will take comprehensive research to determine specifically which qualities need to be measured so that the scale will elicit the right customer responses. The goal is to see whether the brand's customer experience is meaningful and positive for the customer at each stage. In order to find which qualities to zero in on, start with a literature search. There are numerous studies that have been conducted; however, it is vital to find market and industry-specific literature. If none can be found, then close studies should be reviewed. After review, back up your findings and run exploratory sessions with customers and boundary spanners. Their first-hand views help you to extend your prospect domains.

2. Generate Sample of Items

After you specify what the content of the measurement platform will be, you should provide directions using samples. To do this it, rely on customer feedbacks, expert opinions through meetings, surveys and polls. The aim of this step is to create a list of applicable measurement items that satisfy face validity. (Face validity, also known as logical validity refers to the potential an items has to measure what is expected to be measured.) You should pursue it this step separately for every quality you plan to measure.

3. Distillate the Measure and Scrutinize the Reliability

The items prospected for measuring CE-related qualities should go through a pilot test on participants of the target population. When performing it, a representative sampling is important since the step is like sifting sand and finding both gold and rocks. If the sampling is conducted poorly, then you may potentially lose the gold and keep the rocks, or keep the gold but with a ballast in hand. After collecting the pilot data, the next step is to treat the data, focusing on consistency, randomness and exploratory analysis'. These results will eliminate the ballast and keep the golden items. Following this distillation process, rerun the data on both old samplings and a new sampling from the target audience and measure test-retest reliability as well as parallel forms reliability. Through this step you will get a prospective item list for measuring company-specific CE enhancement metrics;, but please remember, if the previous part of the development process was improperly conducted, the measure won't help you to measure relevant metrics, rather they it will be no more than a mirage.

The measurement construct should be suspiciously questioned as to whether it has generalizability. To do that, reliability analysis should be applied to each component of the CE measurement platform.

4. Assess Predictive Validity

As the components of CE measuring platforms are formed they should be assessed from the perspective of predictive validity. Predictive validity refers to the explanatory power of the developed scale on the relevant company performance metric(s). A well conducted scale development presents you with a great performance measurement prediction tool that explains in detail what to do to increase the company's real life metrics, such as growth, profitability, loyalty rate, churn rate and so forth. It may sound hard to achieve, in fact it is hard to achieve but possible if you pursue the process diligently.

Remember CE scales or other measurement efforts don't help you and your organization as expected unless they have reciprocity in real life.

5. One is Greater than Zero

Now you may wonder, and ask yourself why put so much effort into developing an ad-hoc scale? Especially since there are settled and recognized metrics like NPS, CSAT, etc., which are supposed to measure customer experience? Moreover there are companies who have already witnessed correlation between the score and company performance metrics? As we previously mentioned, generic single item scales do not tell organizations what to do, but rather tell them about the outcomes of what have they done from ambiguous lenses, Plus, they may work for one industry or company and doesn't work for another. Investing in a measure without knowing its real effect is like gambling, if a company has resources why gamble instead of forecasting?

A well-developed ad-hoc customer experience scale measures the performance of the brand, the competition and provides insights about what to do to deliver better experiences. Such a comprehensive scale helps you to scan the entire organization by breaking it into pieces and provides an opportunity to scan it in an actionable manner. Consider a patient who says 'I don't feel well'. The doctor asks 'How would you rate your health from 1 to 10?' The patient tells a number. Does this give the doctor enough clue to start a cure? No, of course not. But if the doctor deepens the examination and asks which part feels worse, and after understanding the exact, backs it up with an x-ray or MRI wouldn't that be better?

On the other hand, this doesn't mean that a company should totally disregard generic single-item VOC scales that are widely used today if they can't put together the kind of comprehensive scanning methods desribed above. The most commonly used single-item VOC scales may not provide a complete, high resolution photograph of the current situation, but it still secures an overall feedback about the performance of the company. If a company lacks human and/or financial resources to have tailor made scales, they shouldn't be discouraged about the customer experience concept, but definitely should use one or a few of these practical, generic VOC measurement tools to at least understand the impact of their offerings on customers. By disseminating the measurement tool across all the functions of the customer journey, it is possible not only to detect the well-performing touchpoints, but to locate the poor performers that are shackling in the value chain. Remember one is greater than zero.

Generic Measurement Scales

There are many one-question scales or easy measurement methods that are widely adopted by many companies. A few of them are listed below. Each of these tools has specific advantages and disadvantages. If a company has not yet put together a company and industry-specific CE measurement tool, these can be used to start diagnosing any clogs in their value stream.

Customer Satisfaction Score (CSAT)

Customer Satisfaction is one of the primary indicators measured by companies. A CSAT score shows the satisfaction level of customers, but it doesn't explain exactly what satisfied or dissatisfied the customers about the brand, the customer experience, the product or the service. Savvy companies take this figure as a guide for further exploration of the reasons for the satisfaction or dissatisfaction.

Most often a CSAT tool will ask the customer a question like, "How would you describe your overall satisfaction with this product/service?" It then gives the customer a scale of five to seven opinions to choose from, starting with "very dissatisfied" and ending with "very satisfied," or vice versa. The question and the answer options of the CSAT scale may vary from one application to another. Typically, the customer would be given the following:

How would you describe your overall satisfaction with this product/service?

Very dissatisfied	1
Somewhat dissatisfied	2
Neither satisfied nor dissatisfied	3
Somewhat satisfied	4
Very satisfied	5

This single-question VOC platform should be supported by additional relevant questions to help brands clarify exactly what satisfied and dissatisfied the customer. The answers in each option are totaled and a percentage score for each, from 0% to 100%, is calculated. Scales like this are mostly used in descriptive analysis, which enables businesses to see what their sample segment thinks of various aspects of the offering. In order to make this generalizable and to make deductive inferences, further analysis is needed. If the company wants to use a bipolar scale like CSAT for predictive analysis, they must use the "squared mean" instead of the "arithmetic mean." Hence, the range of options should be coded as follows:

Very dissatisfied	-2
Somewhat dissatisfied	-1
Neither satisfied nor dissatisfied	0
Somewhat satisfied	1
Very satisfied	2

This way, dissatisfaction yields a negative and satisfaction yields a positive. There are some researchers who code the scale from 1 to 5 (or 1 to 7), but this approach is quite controversial for bipolar scales. As a result, companies—due to the advantage of using the arithmetic mean—may prefer to use the following unipolar itemized rating scale:

Not at all satisfied	1
Slightly satisfied	2
Moderately satisfied	3
Very satisfied	4
Extremely satisfied	5

This modified CSAT tool may include customized survey questions to dig into the reasons lying behind the feelings of customers. There are disadvantages, though to CSAT scores. In most cases, they yield skewed results because people who are extremely happy and extremely unhappy with the offering of a brand are more likely to participate in the VOC platform. Another disadvantage of the instrument is that it is weak for predicting future behavior. The reason for this is that the question covers just one interaction, and it is not reliable to use a single interaction satisfaction score to make inferences about loyalty.

Net Promoter Score (NPS)

NPS is another popular tool for listening to the voice of the customer. This metric was developed by Fred Reichheld and is adopted by practitioners as a predictor of loyalty. The scale consists of a single, unipolar item that asks the question, "How likely is it that you would recommend us to a friend or relative?". Customers are given the option of rating the product or service from 0 to 10. 0 stands for "Not likely at all" and 10 stands for "Extremely likely."

How likely is it that you would recommend us to a friend or relative?

"Not likely at all"   "Extremely likely"
        0   1   2   3   4   5   6   7   8   9   10

Based on the answers they provide, customers fall into one of three categories: "detractors," "passives" and promoters." Detractors are the customers who are not satisfied with the outcomes of the offering that the company provided. It is assumed that they are not likely to make a repeat purchase. Moreover, they are subject to producing negative word-of-mouth. Detractors fall between 0 and 6. Passives are assumed to be customers who are satisfied, but the brand couldn't differentiate itself enough and the offering has fallen into the inertia set in their mind. The attitudinal loyalty or behavioral loyalty of passives is subject to change easily and thus is not very reliable. Passives rate the question as 7 and 8. Promoters are assumed to be strongly loyal customers. They are so highly satisfied with the offering that they will likely advocate for the brand. Promoters rate the question as 9 and 10.

When measuring NPS, the percentage of detractors is subtracted from the percentage of promoters. This yields the Net Promoter Score. The larger the number, the greater the loyalty prediction. NPS is considered such a strong predictor of customer loyalty with just one question that in some articles and books, it is referred to as the "ultimate question." On the other hand, there are some reservations about the Net Promoter Score because, due to its single item approach, it provides a narrow perspective in measuring customer experience. Although some studies show a correlation between NPS and customer satisfaction, company profitability and so forth, it hasn't gained scientific legitimacy yet, there are cases showing that NPS is a weaker predictor against other scales.[16]

Employee Net Promoter Score (eNPS)

Employee NPS is a derivative of NPS that is conducted on employees of a company. When running an eNPS survey, the original question from the NPS is replaced by "How likely is it that you would recommend your employer to a friend or acquaintance?". The rating scale and the calculation system are similar to NPS—the percentage of promoters is subtracted from that of the detractors and the score yields the Employee Net Promoter Score.

How likely is it that you would recommend your employer to a friend or acquaintance?

"Not likely at all"   "Extremely likely"
    0   1   2   3   4   5   6   7   8   9   10

The logic behind using this scale as a referral indicator is the assumption that happy employees have greater motivation and thus the quality of their work is higher. It then follows that higher work quality positively affects the customer experience that the company provides. This scale has some advantages: It is more economical to conduct than other scales, easy to understand and can be quickly completed by employees. However there are also some disadvantages: Recommending a company to work at does not guarantee positive customer experience. Moreover, an employee may recommend a company for several reasons such as higher salary compared to the industry average, pension benefits or perks. Like other metrics, when a company employs a scale, it should definitely link it to the performance metrics of the company.

Net Retention Score (NRS)

Net Retention Score refers to the customers who are most likely to have success with a brand. The score is mostly used by organizations that apply predictive analysis to their data. To obtain the score, a healthy predictive model should be built first. The likelihood of retention of customers is calculated through the model. Then the ratio of customers with high likelihood of success is subtracted from the ratio of customers with low likelihood of success. The yielding result is the Net Retention Score for the company.

Seamless Experience Score (SES)

Seamless Experience refers to delivering consistent experiential stimuli and the ability to trace transactions across an omnichannel experience. While the customer interacts with the brand through various channels, such as mobile apps, websites, or a brick-and-mortar store, he or she expects similar experiences at all touchpoints and should be able to track any transaction such as purchase, complaint case, refunds etc. Suppose a customer starts to fill her virtual cart from her laptop, but has to leave before completing the purchase. If the retailer has an omnichannel setup, she can open the application of that online retailer on her mobile phone at a later time and complete the purchase while she is on her way home. This gives the customer a seamless experience. In other words, seamless experience is experiential consistency across all the contact channels that a customer interacts with. In order to ensure that the experience is seamless, the company has to measure it. There are a number of methods for doing this; one common method is to measure the overall satisfaction level of customers at each channel and compare the results. If one of the channels has a lower score, it needs to be adjusted to align with the other well-performing channels. The Contact Channel Satisfaction (CCS) survey can be used to see where the satisfaction problems are.

Customer Effort Score (CES)

The Customer Effort Score is another metric used in measuring customer experience by practitioners. The logic behind the tool is that if the aftersales problems of customers are solved without much effort, then the customer has the potential to be loyal due to the excellent customer service provided by the company. CES presents a question like, "How much effort did you have to put into handling your issue?" Customers respond on a scale of 1 to 5 or 1 to 7. Another example is:

> How much do you agree with the following statement?
> "The company made it easy for me to handle my issue."

Strongly Disagree	1
Disagree	2
Somewhat Disagree	3
Neither Agree nor Disagree	4
Agree	5
Somewhat Agree	6
Strongly Agree	7

When interpreting this measure, higher numbers indicate better organizational performance, since the customers were able to get their issues resolved without allocating much energy. Another suggestion for interpreting the results is evaluating the distribution of the ratings. Since there are seven options, three negative, three positive and one neutral, the CES approach fundamentally aims to pull customers who have had to put effort into the resolution to the neutral position, which takes them out of the negative realm. The score measures the ease of flow for the customer in the customer service stream of the organization. However, this measurement neither guarantees a repeat purchase nor satisfaction; it only refers to the responsiveness and the barrier-removal capacity of the organization.

Contact Resolution Score (CRS)

The Contact Resolution Score is similar to the Customer Effort Score, but yet different due to the nature of its content. There are two common variations of this indicator: "First Contact Resolution (FCR)" and "Contact Resolution (CR)". FCR, as its name suggests, refers to the number of complaints that are resolved during the first interaction between the customer and the company divided by the total number of complaints. Contact Resolution stands for the ratio of resolved complaints. It is calculated by dividing the total number of resolved complaints by the total number of complaints regardless if resolved or not.

End-to-End Experience Score (EEC)

End-to-End Experience Score stands for the overall satisfaction of customers across the customer journey. It is calculated by multiplying the percentage of satisfied customers at each touchpoint. For example, a customer browsed the company website, then visited the store and bought a product. The customer then called the customer service department to get his product installed. The service personnel arrived at the home of the customer and installed the product. Throughout his journey, the customer interacted at the touchpoints of the company website, store, call center and customer service and at each stage gained experiences and rated them. The ratio of the rate divided by the maximum rating in the scale is calculated for each touch point and the ratios are multiplied to find the EEC score.

Chapter 13

LEADING A CUSTOMER EXPERIENCE INITIATIVE

There are plenty of studies that show that customer experience has a positive effect on loyalty, on revenues and profitability, and on the market share of a company. These studies support the fact that companies that have implemented a Customer Experience program are relatively more profitable than their competitors. Thus, companies that conscientiously manage their customers' experiences have added growth potential in the future. Brands that ignore the importance of this will limp along until one day they realize that "the emperor has no clothes." In a panic, they will try to incorporate a customer experience philosophy into their marketing, but by then, they will be struggling to play "catch-up" to their competitors who have already implemented effective experience initiatives.

Fostering customer experience across an organization requires a transformational leadership effort. This kind of leadership involves building a right-minded team or else transforming an existing team into a right-minded team. In traditional leadership, the leader engages the loyalty or higher performance from employees by offering tangible reinforcement. Traditional leadership is also transactional. In other words, all actions taken are designed to maintain the status quo. It is a self-preservation mindset rather than a growth mindset. In contrast, "transformational" leaders enable their employees be true to their inner selves and perform their jobs to satisfy their own intrinsic values rather than be motivated by external incentives. This new approach results in new, positive attitudes, unwavering commitment to the brand, being motivated by intangible/spiritual values, and being in it for the long haul, rather than just to get a paycheck.

Customer experience programs mostly fail due to a number of reasons; the top seven are critical for company leaders to pay attention to. In descending order from most prominent on down, they are: Employee resistance (fear of change), insufficient legitimate sponsorship (not everyone in the company being on board with the new paradigms), goal uncertainty, technology disintegration, failing to provide quick-wins, resource scarcity, and unrealistic expectations. "An organization that intends to transform requires different leadership strategy," i.e., "Transformational" instead of "Transactional." Transactional leadership is about sustaining status quo; on the other hand, transformational leadership is about creating a vision to guide the evolution of the organization in line with customer centricity.

What are the new paradigms that can guide a brand to become transformational? The chart below shows the key changes that have to be made.

**Major Differences Between Transactional and
Transformational Leadership**

	Transactional Leadership	Transformational Leadership
Aim of Leadership	Fostering Behavior	Fostering Attitude
Leadership Focus	Controlling Employee	Developing Employee
Intendance	Directive	Delegative
Employee Attitude	Acquiescence	Commitment
Source of Authority	Legitimate Position of Leader	Character of Leader
Reinforcement Motive	Tangible, Monetary	Intangible, Spritual
Effect Period	Short Run	Long Run

Transformational leadership requires more than simply changing individual behaviors within the organization. A few forced behavioral changes won't help the company sustain new behavior patterns in the long run, since old attitudes still lie behind the behaviors. If the conditions are right, they will wield their non-productive heads again and the company will revert back to what it was before. This means that when a leader is trying to transform the company, he or she should start by changing the attitudes of all the employees across the entire organization—which is why, at the very beginning of this book, the authors defined "customer experience" as an "organizational attitude." In order to disseminate this new attitude to every employee, leaders should focus on creating a committed team of employees instead of attempting to control their actions with external rules. This new approach needs to be a dynamic blend of delegation and autonomy so that each employee is recognized for what he does well and inspired to do his best. In contrast, leaders who rely on the authority of their position to impose order cannot produce this kind of commitment; under an authoritarian leadership, the employees will only change their behavior in the short run to obtain specific tangible rewards. Thus, it is obvious that a transformational leadership style is much more effective in leading the customer experience initiative of a company and has the potential to result in long term success.

The Role of the Customer Experience Department

In order to deliver outstanding customer experience, a dedicated team is needed to align the entire organization towards the customer experience vision. A team is needed because each department in the company tends to focus on its own goals and objectives. Plus, some departments may not have the chance to interact with certain other departments in their daily routines, so the company ends up operating in a disjointed way unless there is a concerted effort to get all departments on the same page, so to speak. This is why it is so critical to set up a Customer Experience Department that can oversee the beginning-to-end journey of the customer and to make sure that the entire company sustains a customer-centric position in an ever-changing marketing environment. The CE department is responsible for working with HR to set up customer experience employee training, finding ways to optimize customer service departments, interacting with the marketing department to develop offerings and so forth. Companies can take a lesson from nature: the strongest and the smartest are not always the ones that survive. Rather it is the ones who are able to adapt to a changing environment that survive. Hence, a customer experience department that creates an integrated and flexible atmosphere becomes the compass of company to know what direction it should go.

Naming a department "Customer Experience" doesn't mean that the company really possesses a customer experience department. It is common mistake that some companies simply rebrand their customer service department, operations department, call-center operations or a part of their CRM as a quote unquote "Customer Experience Department"—yet, the departments kept doing what they've always done. Nothing has changed, and there still isn't anyone overseeing or developing the Customer Experience.

takeaway!

Having a CE department is about having a "Customer Experience" attitude; it is not about keeping up with business buzz words. Therefore, forming a customer experience department should be a reflection of having customer-centric experiential mindset, rather than struggling to generate the perception of a customer-centric approach for the sake of stakeholders.

A company's Customer Experience Department is the department that is responsible for tracking and optimizing interactions between the brand and customers throughout the entire customer journey. Another key responsibility of the CE department is developing relevant initiatives to disseminate the CE mindset across the organization through training sessions, workshops and events. The customer experience department also acts as a revenue insurance policy because it seeks to capture lifetime customer value. It tracks the outcomes of fostering attitudinal and behavioral loyalty between customers and the brand. The CE department keeps an eye on all the other departments and how well they interact with each other, as well as how effective they are at integrating outputs to provide a seamless customer experience. Moreover, the department satisfies the requirements of a well-performing customer experience initiative in that every interaction or touchpoint between the customer and the brand has been assigned to a specific employee to take care of and develop further. The CE department knows who in what department is responsible for what stages and micro-stages of the value chain. This kind of proactive monitoring prevents the common problem of departments operating as separate silos while customers and potential sales fall through the cracks.

Dissemination of the Customer Experience Mindset

As noted earlier in this book, some companies are able deliver incredible experiences to their customers. The customer experience mindset has been disseminated effectively throughout the entire organization. Employees at the Disney theme parks play their roles with the enthusiasm and professionalism of actors and actresses, getting into the character and convincing their audiences to join in the fun. Similarly, the guards at Caesar Casinos are dressed in togas, creating the illusion for customers that they are experiencing ancient Greece. Themed hotels start their performances at the front door—with every employee consciously working together to elevate the customer experience.

Companies in the entertainment business invest time and money in training employees to deliver outstanding customer experience. This same mindset can be activated in any kind of business, from retail to finance to TELCOs. Effective customer experience is about adopting an attitude. Customer experience is about being one single body that serves a community without ulterior motives.

Unfortunately, many ordinary businesses fail to see the importance of disseminating the customer experience attitude throughout the company. A number of large entities in the banking, telecom, energy and other industries, have set up "customer experience departments," but they haven't done much to disseminate specific knowledge about what customer experience is, why the organization founded the department or what the organization is trying to achieve through delivering customer experience. In most, employees learn about the CE initiative of their company through the rumors they hear during lunch breaks. Since the employees are not aware of the customer experience concept, they will not be able to deliver the level of customer experience that the company expects of its employees. Had the CE concept been disseminated, each department would have coordinated with the others; each employee would have worked harder to make sure that the customers gain positive experiences. Instead, the staff had never been trained on customer experience.

Companies develop strategies for their various departments. They have their sales people receive training on how to sell, their distributors on how to treat customers, their HR teams on how to recruit or retain talent. These trainings are quite effective and help to keep the company functioning. But, in order for a company to excel in today's highly competitive business world, the entire company has to have a "customer experience perspective." This means that just as they teach their sales team and other departments specific critical skills, they must train all their employees to understand what customer experience is and why it is so critical to the success of the company. It boils down to employee motivation, which relies on their understanding how what they do fits into the bigger picture of what the company is trying to accomplish. Victor Vroom's research, as referenced in Chapter 10, suggests that when employees are able to see the big picture and feel that they are a valuable part of the company, they are more likely to put their best effort into the goals of the company. This is because being a part of something—having a purpose and value—in this case, to the company—triggers pleasure. Vroom found that people would choose a course of action, "based upon their perceptions, attitudes and beliefs," that brought them pleasure. What does this say to businesses? That if a company is serious about delivering outstanding customer experience, then its entire staff must be trained so that they understand what the company is trying to deliver, how, why, and to whom—in other words, customer experience. When everyone and every department in the company are aligned, then, the whole company will benefit—profitability, customer retention, and more. This is the key to outperforming the competition.

Launching a Customer Experience Program

Some professionals consider a "customer experience program" to be merely a fad or a buzzword, but several academic and practical findings point out that the companies who realize the importance of customer experience management have already started enjoying growth and differentiation as a result. In order to succeed in disseminating the CE attitude and maneuvering the organization toward a whole-hearted customer-centric approach, the support of top management is vital. A CE initiative without the conscious and full support of C-suite executives will eventually flounder—just as surely as it will without the committed support of the rest of the employees.

Here are several steps to take when launching a Customer Experience Program:

1. Set up an announcement campaign, consisting of preliminary posting of an announcement from the CEO and other top executives on the company website, emails to employees, posters on bulletin boards and fliers sent to each department to build excitement for this new company initiative—the Customer Experience Program. This will give employees a brief glimpse into the new direction the company is taking and let them get used to the idea. Also promote the date and time for the Customer Experience Program Launch.

2. The Customer Experience Program Launch. This event can be a celebration, complete with refreshments. Remember that the goal of the event is to inspire an eagerness to be part of the company transformation. The CE program leaders can use a short power point to illustrate some of the Customer Experience concepts and give employees a brief overview of what the program is trying to accomplish and a general idea of the kind of training that they will be required to take. Include some of the benchmarks that the company is planning to achieve as well. Pass out a packet to each employee that has been fine-tuned for each department or position. It should provide details about the training sessions with the times and places where the workshops will be held.

3. The Training Workshops. These can be somewhat informal so that employees feel relaxed and not stressed. The goal of the workshops is to provide specific training that prepares employees to translate the Customer Experience objectives into action as they perform their jobs. Role playing, videos and group interactions are all effective ways to get employees to be able to integrate a customer-centric approach when they interact with customers and, moreover, to feel that they are a vital and active part of the company's transformation rather than passive prey.

4. Follow-up Evaluations. This initiative shouldn't be launched and then left to destiny. On the contrary, C-suite needs to meet regularly with the CE program leaders and department heads to discuss how the CE program is unfolding and to review benchmarks and other relevant metrics to see how well each department and touchpoint is doing. Each department needs to pass this information down to their people so that they will be able to make changes, etc. Remember, the company is in this for the long haul. By keeping the employees in the loop, they will continue to be motivated and know that they are contributing meaningfully to the ongoing transformation. Also create quarterly brochures and reports for the stockholders, delineating the benchmarks that were achieved and how that was accomplished. Where appropriate, print off reports for suppliers, etc., so that they can see how their efforts are making a difference.

5. Awards Ceremonies. Positive reinforcement is far more effective than so-called "constructive" criticism, which tends to be judgmental. Periodically reward your employees who have demonstrated that they are applying the new Customer Experience concepts to their jobs. Hold events, recognize them in front of the whole group. Give awards, bonuses, free tickets, etc., to departments that have made a difference or whose metrics have improved. Continually emphasize that the company is successful because each employee is a living example of how to provide effective customer experience. Invite the stockholders, suppliers and sales channel partners to the ceremonies and recognize them for their dedication, support and investments that helped to make all this possible.

Chapter 14

COLLECTING, ANALYZING AND REPORTING OUTCOMES

CEM is a holistic initiative that, although it is authorized from the top down, will only successfully transform a company if all people in the company are aware of their role and responsibility to manage customer experience. By being aware of the importance of their roles, everyone in the company—C-suite, department heads, division managers, frontline employees and even behind-the-scene employees—should conscientiously contribute to the experience delivery process. However, in order for them to know whether they are delivering effective customer experience or not, their performance has to be measured. More specifically, they need to realize exactly what they are doing right and which of their actions or inactions have resulted in negative customer experiences.

Company executives and CE leaders need to remember that each employee sees the current experiential position of the company from a different angle, thus picking up on details that someone else might miss. In order to capture all these details, each department should develop role-specific scorecards so that employees can help record and track key variables. A Chief Marketing Officer may prefer a scorecard that covers a broader scope while a division head of frontline employees should track a more specific KPI. For example, that CMO may want to track the experience score of the brand, retention rate, etc. One of the team leaders might need details like: Product Reviews, Upsells, Poll or Survey Results etc. If the scorecard has great numbers, the company may want to share some of these results at a follow-up evaluation or even at an awards ceremony to build enthusiasm.

Defining Key Metrics through an Integrated CE Approach

As mentioned before, in most companies, departments work separately as silos. Each department has its own metrics to meet. The Finance Department might trace accounts payable turnover, cycle time to resolve an invoice error, employee work-center loading, payables turnover and so forth. The Marketing Department will aim to meet the KPIs of brand awareness percentage, total cost of customer acquisition, leads generation, growth sustainability rate of the brand and so on. Human Resources has to deal with compensation cost as a percentage of revenue, time to fill a position, cost per hire, etc. Customer Service seeks to satisfy metrics for cost per minute of handling time, inbound calls processed per agent hour, field service technician utilization, number of complaints and so on. In short, in the traditional business world, each department works to satisfy their own KPIs and the result is that most often the company delivers awful customer experience. For example, an HR department has a tight deadline to fill a customer service position with a qualified person. HR manages to find a new hire on time, but was not able to recruit the best talent in the market because of the time crunch. So, they settled for someone who met the lowest standard for that position. Say that the customer service department has a key metric to meet, such as inbound average wrap-up time, but the time taken to "wrap up" a customer's case after the call has ended is frequently delayed because the finance department takes its time getting back to the customer service rep (CSR). This means that the CSR can't take another call yet. This delay causes deficits in customer service's target numbers, since an increase in inbound wrap-up time causes an increase in the inbound non-availability rate. This forces waiting customers to have wait longer and consequently negatively affects the customer experience. Each department needs to be in sync as much as possible with the departments it works with so that the customer experience is as seamless as possible. Thus, when assigning KPIs, objectives and timetables to departments, the goal should be a more integrated approach.

Allowing for CE Metrics on Scorecards at Every Level

When tracking customer experience metrics, implement a method that gathers data from each and every touchpoint of the brand. Every function needs to be traced from top to toe in order to ensure the delivery of outstanding customer experience. C-suite, mid-level management and frontline employees should be assigned certain CE goals and objectives. The employees should: 1. know what their position's CE goals and objectives are, and 2. be trained to know how to reach those goals and achieve those objectives. By doing this, companies will be able to support the emersion of a healthy and fertile Customer Experience Program that produces outcomes of loyalty, growth and profitability. In order to accomplish this, companies should revise their scorecards and upgrade them with the new CE metrics, and then disseminate them to every employee.

This way, employees will be able to trace relevant metrics for self-evaluation. For self-performance evaluations like this, every employee doesn't have to see all the CE metrics for the entire organization; rather, the scorecards should be designed to be role-specific for the employee who has that position.

Linking the CE Initiative to Performance Appraisal Metrics

Linking the CE Initiative to Performance Appraisal Metrics (also called CE Metrics) increases the contribution and motivation of employees. For example, some companies set a certain score, such as a specific customer satisfaction level, as a requisite for an employee to be eligible for promotion. In similar manner, CE Metrics should link performance appraisal to bonus packages, fringe benefits and other financial or non-financial compensation. These incentives should be delivered on both a personal level and organizational level as an expression of the success of the customer experience program. This further motivates employees to meet CE Metrics to the best of their ability.

On the other hand, the KPIs that are linked to the success of a CE program should continuously be matched with the overall performance of company. In other words, the CE Metric should be linked to ratio level metrics, such as growth, profitability, customer retention and so forth, to ensure that the antecedent metrics that are to be followed by the entire organization are sound. For example, an organization shouldn't try to apply an NPS measure blindly if it has no relation to the overall performance of the company.

takeaway!

Always remember that CE is about exploring new ways of engaging, satisfying and pleasing customers; it is not about following standardized clichés. So, ask questions like, Is NPS the best way to measure CE or loyalty in our industry and market? Does it fit the cultural background of our target audience? Is there a better metric that we can use? Consider it. Attempt it. Be bold. Be curious and courageous enough to do more.

Chapter 15

SUMMARY AND IMPLEMENTATION GUIDE

In this book we have explored the history of marketing which paved the way for the emergence of Customer Experience. We have shared how numerous companies have approached their customers during that evolution and shown how today's customers are vastly different from previous generations. Through multiple studies, theories and models, we have demonstrated why companies must understand their customers' perspectives and respond accordingly in order to build a marketing strategy that works in today's world. We have even developed a powerful CEM model that incorporates the key factors that businesses need to be aware of. Based on all this, we can definitely say the following about Customer Experience Management:

• In order to be effective in today's market, CEM must be customer-focused, not brand or company-focused. The customer must be at the center of all marketing efforts—not only in the formulation stages, but also in the implementation stage. In other words, every Customer Experience Management program should be a holistic and company-wide system, where the perspectives, needs and wants of the customer are explored and then integrated into every facet of the CEM process, from start to finish.

• We also now know what CEM is *NOT*. CEM is not the job of either the Sales or Marketing Department. That would be putting the cart before the horse. Only CEM can isolate exactly what the customer is looking for. CEM cannot be dumped onto the shoulders of the Customer Service Department with the hope that somehow Customer Service personnel can manage the Customer Experience for the entire company. Unfortunately this job is too large and involves aspects outside the scope of Customer Service. Similarly, CEM cannot be considered an IT project. IT ensures that computers and software work properly and support the functioning of the company. Although CEM requires numerous reports and analyses enabled by IT, CEM engages numerous departments, including marketing and operations, in ways that IT cannot. Also, despite the fact that social media is a powerful way to connect with customers, it cannot be used to implement CEM in its entirety. Social media, however, can be an effective tool for advancing the priorities of CEM.

• What we discovered in Chapter 13 was that Customer Experience Management must have its own department within the company. Although no other department within a company is equipped to implement CEM, every other department connects with the CEM Department to some degree and needs to be coordinated with it. Having a separate CEM Department enables the brand to disseminate its Customer Experience Management philosophy throughout the entire organization, so that every employee can embrace it and become excited about meeting customer expectations within his or her own job parameters. Once a company has set up its CEM Department, it will be able to utilize many of the models and tools that have been described in this book. One particularly vital tool is the Customer Journey Map (CJM). Companies that still hold on to an egocentric approach to marketing may undervalue the CJM because they keep stubbornly imposing their brand-first hard sell onto their customers. As a result, they completely miss the mark of meeting the expectations and needs of customers in today's market.

takeaway!

Please make sure that your company is fostering a holistic, "customer-first" attitude throughout every aspect of the Customer Experience—from conception to operations to delivery and beyond. Complete a Customer Journey Map for each of your customer segments to plan out and track how customer are responding to each stage in your value chain.

• Even more, Customer Experience Management is not static. Once it is in place, it cannot be checked off as completed and then left to collect dust. Rather, it needs to be continually updated because customers and the market are constantly changing. Hence, CEM evolves with the times. This is another reason why every company should have a separate CEM Department so that it can implement, track, revaluate and fine-tune CEM so that it is always creating the absolutely best experience for customers.

As you have noticed, this book connects with multiple audiences who are each sekking applications tailored to their own field or business:

If you are a researcher in the business, management or marketing field, you may be called on to evaluate how various customer segments respond to specific types of product or service offerings. This book has provided you with a wealth of models and studies to work with; and yet, these are actually just a starting point for you because CEM is still evolving. Moreover, CEM has urged all of us to think beyond simple Customer Satisfaction and has even overpowered Customer Relations Management (CRM) as the standard measurement of where the customer stands in relation to a brand. Meanwhile, on the other end of the spectrum, customers themselves are also evolving in response both to new technologies and more persuasive and pervasive social media. The Erdem-Tavsan CEM Model (Chapter 4) has accomplished a major step toward crystallizing the Customer Experience perspective. It zeroes in on the critical aspects that need to be considered and provides targeted questions for businesses to ask as they apply this model to their own products and services. Using this as a springboard, researchers like yourself can examine CEM as it continues to develop and as various companies implement it. Moreover, you can project where this approach to CEM can take businesses in the future.

If you are an academician or professor whose responsibility it is to inspire tomorrow's business, management and marketing leaders, this book is a goldmine for class discussions and critical thinking. It is already the basis for an MBA course and is in use at universities. The numerous real-life examples of companies that have capitalized on the marketing ideas of their day provide a solid context against which students can explore both the theoretical and practical sides of Customer Experience. The experiments, models and theories in this book can challenge students to try to duplicate them or to integrate facets of CE and take them to the next level. By mastering both the Customer Experience concept and the Customer Experience Management system that we have developed, your students may become the business leaders and thinkers of the next generation.

If you are a business owner, top manager, customer experience execu-

tive or marketing executive, you can use this book to increase your company's customer loyalty, profitability, growth and sustainability.

Today's customers are definitely a challenge. They no longer consider the brand to be the expert. They do intensive comparative shopping. This forces companies to find ways to prove that they are better than their competitors. Are you currently doing that? If you set up a CEM Department and follow the guidelines in this book, you will have the tools to demonstrate to your customers how you outshine other brands. More importantly, you will be able to know what your customers are really looking for and meet those expectations.

Experiential segmentation, customer journey mapping and other critical analytic and tracking tools described in this book will allow you to see market expectations through the eyes of the customer segments you are targeting. This way, you can pinpoint which customer expectations you might be missing (and that your competitors are meeting). Effective Customer Experience Management can provide solutions for attracting new customers, upselling current customers and even getting a specific customer segment away from the competition.

The CEM model that we have designed **enables businesses and managers to see inside their customers' hearts and minds**—and consequently allows you to better predict your customers' behavior in response to the customer experiences you offer.

How to Set Up a CEM Program for Your Own Company

As a business owner, top manager or decision maker, your first priority is to the success of your business, which, as you have seen, means that you have to find a way to consistently satisfy your customers by creating engaging customer experiences. You have discovered that in today's "Customer Experience Era," a company cannot rely on traditional metrics to understand how to connect with customers. Customers do their homework long before they see a salesperson in your store or purchase online, so the old "tried-and-true" tactics for selling and creating loyal customers no longer work.

The GOOD NEWS is that what you also discovered in this book were exciting strategies to use to convert and retain customers for your business! You found out that the way to make your company successful is by changing your perspective from an ego-centric to a customer-centric (or "outside-in") mindset. By putting your customers at the center of all your marketing efforts, you can transform your entire company and enable it to be more than competitive in a tough, saturated market.

This transformation will not occur, however, if you merely put your customers in the center and surround them with your touch points. You know now that the key to getting loyal customers is not to assault them with your brand, but rather to get to know what they are genuinely thinking and feeling about your offering. Getting inside the mind and heart of your customer is the key to convincing them to buy. Understanding the shared accumulation of each customer segment is the only way to anticipate and begin to predict how they will respond when they come into contact with your brand's value chain.

You may recall some comments we made in our Introduction: "…in today's digital environment, customers themselves now have a heavy hand in redefining what it takes to make them happy enough with a product or service to buy it, and then to keep coming back to the same brand and company." Moreover, "too many businesses flounder because they either didn't know how to give their customers a satisfying customer experience, or else they hang onto the mistaken assumption that seeing things from the customer's viewpoint isn't all that critical to the future of their company." But you understand that because customers experience the world subjectively, they will also experience your brand through the filters of their own age, gender, ethnic background, life events and personal motivators. This means that they will have a lot of questions and your brand touch points need to answer them.

Although putting together a customer experience journey that accomplishes this sounds daunting, with this book you are now equipped to design customer experiences for your product or service that will more than satisfy your customers and prompt them to buy.

You have also learned that it is vital that you proactively manage every stage of the customer experience journey in relation to your brand. This calls for a Customer Experience Management Program. A CEM Program will enable your CE leaders to inspire, enact, track and measure each micro-stage along the customer journey to see which touchpoints are effective and which ones might be forcing customers to turn to a competitor.

Setting up a Customer Experience Program does not mean suddenly dropping it onto your employees and expecting them to understand it well enough to implement it for you. Rather, this has to be an initiative that—although a top-down decision—is all inclusive, educating and motivating each and every employee to implement it within the scope of his or her position.

In Chapter 13, we outlined five basic steps for implementing a Customer Experience Management Program. Let's see how you can adapt this for your own business:

Steps for Launching your Customer Experience Management Program:
Pre-Launch

• Establish a Customer Experience Management Department – **See Chapter 13**

• Have company execs and department heads read this book and meet to:

• Share the points in the book that they feel are most important about CEM

• Make a list of the points that are applicable to your company and this new dept.

• Define the purpose and scope of your CEM Department.

• Create your Customer Experience Vision Statement– **Introduction and Chapter 8**

• Suggest personnel from the company to be in this dept.

• Decide on accountability—who is accountable to whom within the dept. and the dept. to whom in the company

• Make a schematic of how your CEM Department will connect with all the other departments in your company

• Decide which metrics, models, and scales this dept. will use to measure Customer Experience— **Chapters 10, 11 & 12**

• Decide on the first product or service the dept. will apply the CEM initiative to

• Plan out the Announcement Campaign and the Launch—**Chapter 13**

• Outline and start planning the training Workshops

The Launch – See Chapter 13
  • Set up an Announcement Campaign to build enthusiasm throughout the company
    • The "Customer Experience Program" Launch & Celebration Event
    • Departmental Training Workshops
    • Follow-up Evaluations
    • Periodic Awards Ceremonies

Post-Launch
  • Evaluate effectiveness of the Launch and the Workshops in building enthusiasm for the CEM initiative and for equipping employees with the tools they need to implement Customer Experience within the scope of their own positions
  • Your CEM Department needs to:
    - Implement the research that will be used to identify the shared accumulations of each customer segment — **Chapter 7**
    - Create personas to fit each customer experiential segment.   **Chapter 6**
    - Plan out touchpoints for the first product/service to be transitioned into the CEM initiative
    - Integrate them into a complete customer journey; create customer journey maps— **Chapters 5 & 6**
    - Launch and apply the metrics, models and scales for measuring CE selected earlier
    - Evaluate the effectiveness of the touchpoints over the entire customer journey
  • Set up a touchpoint guide for the dept. drawn from what worked well in the first offering. This way you will not be re-inventing the wheel each time you set up a value chain for another product. You can adapt some of the methods and language to fit the new product and the customer segment for that product.
  • Set up the schedule for integrating future products/services into this protocol
  • Schedule quarterly and annual evaluations
  Now that you understand how to design, integrate, measure and lead the

Customer Experience, it is just a matter of being committed to doing it. **ARE YOU COMMITTED?!** Are you committed to transforming your company into a customer-centric organization that honestly wants to know what your customers are thinking and feeling? Do you want your customers excited about what you are offering? Are you willing to tailor your touchpoints to answer their questions, accommodate their perspectives and opinions, and enable them to see how your product or service is what they are looking for?

If so, then, armed with this book, you will be able to connect with them, create true loyalty, and surpass your competition.

For more resources, visit **www.theCEMbook.com**

References

Introduction
[1] Oracle (2012), "Customer Experience Impact Report", p.4, goo.gl/MFQZiE.

Chapter 1: How Did the Customer Experience Concept Emerge?
[1] Schlich, B., (2014), "Winning through customer experience: EY Global Consumer Banking Survey", Ernst and Young, goo.gl/M4Voeh.
[2] Derksen, J. R. (2015) "Improving Customer Experience is Top Business Priority for Companies Pursuing Digital Transformation", Accenture, October 27, goo.gl/YZuH29.
[3] Rose, K.; Walker, K.; Allen, C.; Valenti, J.; Rotatori, D., (2014), "Reshaping the Retail Banking Experience for the Customer of Tomorrow", Deloitte, December 14, goo.gl/jAz37A.
[4] Marketing Science Institute (2011), "Research Priorities 2011-2013", goo.gl/UdnKaT.
[5] Marketing Science Institute (2014), "Research Priorities 2014-2016", goo.gl/Wctbkb.
[6] Kurylko, D. T. (2003), "Model T had many shades; black dried fastest", Automotive News, goo.gl/XVMoTz.
[7] Collins, T. (2007), "The Legendary Model-T Ford: The Ultimate History. of America's First Great Automobile", Iola, Krause Publications.
[8] Self, D. (2018), "Father Knows Best", ImdB, goo.gl/qdtp5c.
[9] Adage (2003), "History:1940s", September 15, goo.gl/ngBtvM.

Chapter 2: What Exactly is Customer Experience?
[1] Harley Davidson (2018), "Get the Rest of the Story", goo.gl/cxuTwU.
[2] Laverie, D. A.; Kleine, I. E.; Kleine, S. S. (1993), "Linking emotions and values in consumption experiences: An exploratory study", Advances in Consumer Research, 20 (1), 70-75.
[3] Roove-Collier, C.; Hayne, H.; Colombo, M. (2000), "The Development of Implicit and Explicit Memory" Amsterdam, Netherlands: John Benjamins Publishing.
[4] Squire, L. R. (1992) "Declarative and Non-Declarative Memory: Multiple Brain Systems Supporting Learning and Memory", Journal of Cognitive Neuroscience, Vol.3 (4), 232-246.

[5] Tulving, E. (1972), "Episodic and Semantic Memory ", Organization of Memory, 381–403, New York, Academic Press.

[6] Renoult, L.; Davidson, P. S. R.; Palombo, D. J.; Moscovitch, M.; Levine, B. (2012), "Personal semantics: At the crossroads of semantic and episodic memory", Trends in Cognitive Sciences, Vol.16, 550–558.

[7] Ullman, M. T. (2004), "Contributions of memory circuits to language: The declarative-procedural model", Cognition, 92, 231–270.

[8] Moscovitch, M.; Rosenbaum, R. S.; Gilboa, A.; Addis, D. R.; Westmacott, R.; Grady, C. (2005), "Functional neuroanatomy of remote episodic, semantic and spatial memory: A unified account based on multiple trace theory", Journal of Anatomy, 207, 35–66.

[9] Tulving, E. (2002) "Episodic memory: From mind to brain", Annual Review of Psychology, Vol.53, p.1–25.

[10] Schacter, D. (2011), "Psychology", New York, Worth Publishers.

[11] Yonelinas, A. P. (2002) "The nature of recollection and familiarity: A review of 30 years of research", Journal of Memory and Language, 46, 441–517.

[12] Conway, M. A.; Pleydell-Pearce, C. W. (2000) "The construction of autobiographical memories in the self-memory system", Psychological Review, 107 (2), 261–288.

[13] Baker-Ward, L., Hess, M. H. & Flannagan, D. A., (1990). The effects of involvement on children's memory for events. Cognitive Development, 5, 55-69.

[14] Greenberg, D. L.; Verfaellie, M. (2010) "Interdependence of episodic and semantic memory: Evidence from neuropsychology", Journal of the International Neuropsychological Society, 16, 748–753.

[15] Hanslmayr, S.; Spitzer, B.; Bauml, K. H. (2009) "Brain oscillations dissociate between semantic and nonsemantic encoding of episodic memories", Cerebral Cortex, 19, 1631–1640.

[16] Greve, A.; van Rossum, M. C.; Donaldson, D. I. (2007) "Investigating the functional interaction between semantic and episodic memory: Convergent behavioral and electrophysiological evidence for the role of familiarity", Neuroimage, 34, 801–814.

[17] Klimesch, W.; Schimke, H.; Schwaiger, J. (1994) "Episodic and semantic memory: An analysis in the EEG theta and alpha band", Electroencephalography and Clinical Neurophysiology, 91, 428–441.

[18] Clayton, N. S., Salwiczek, L. H.; Dickinson, A. (2007) "Episodic Memory. Current Biology", 17 (6), 189-191.

[19] Renoult, L.; Davidson, P.; Schmitz, E.; Park, L.; Campbell, K.; Moscovitch, M.; Levine, B. (2015), "Autobiographically significant concepts: More episodic than semantic in nature? An electrophysiological investigation of overlapping types of memory", Journal of Cognitive Neuroscience, 27(1), 57-72.

[20] Clayton, N. S.; Salwiczek, L. H.; Dickinson, A. (2007), "Episodic memory", Current Biology, 17(6), 189-191.

[21] Kumar, A.; Meenakshi, N. (2011) "Marketing Management" , New Delhi, Vikas Publishing.

[22] Clayton, N. S.; Salwiczek, L. H.; Dickinson, A. (2007) "Episodic memory", Current Biology, 17(6), 189-191.

[23] Williams, H. L.; Conway, M. A.; Cohen, G. (2008) "Autobiographical memory", Memory in the Real World (3rd ed., 21-90). Hove, UK: Psychology Press.

[24] Conway, M. A. (2005) "Memory and the Self", Journal of Memory and Language, 53, 594–628.

[25] Conway, M. A.; Pleydell-Pearce, C. W. (2000) "The construction of autobiographical memories in the self-memory system", Psychological Review, 107 (2), 261–288.

[26] Johnson, M. K.; Foley, M. A.; Suengas, A. G.; Raye, C. L. (1988) "Phenomenal characteristics of memories for perceived and imagined autobiographical events", Journal of Experimental Psychology, 117, 371–376.

[27] Pillemer, D. B. (2001) "Momentous events and the life story", Review of General Psychology, 5 (2), 123–134.

[28] Conway, M. A.; Pleydell-Pearce, C. W. (2000) "The construction of autobiographical memories in the self-memory system", Psychological Review, 107 (2), 261–288.

[29] Conway, M. A. (2005) "Memory and the Self. Journal of Memory and Language", 53, 594–628.

[30] Einstein, A.; Lawson, R. W. (1921) "Relativity: The special and general theory", New York, Holt.

[31] Diogenes, L.; Yonge, C. D. (1853). The lives and opinions of eminent philosophers. (Book IX, Vol. 2). London, Bohn.

[32] Palmer, A. (2005) "Principles of services marketing. London, McGraw Hill.

[33] Berry, L.L. (1981) "The employee as customer", Journal of Retail Banking, 3, 33-40.

[34] Donnelly, J. H. (1976) "Marketing intermediaries in channels of distribution for services", Journal of Marketing, 40, p.55-70.

[35] Pine II, B. J. & Gilmore, J. H. (1999) "The experience economy: Work is theatre and every business a stage", Boston, Harvard Business School Press.

[36] Suddendorf, T.; Corballis, M. C. (1997) "Mental time travel and the evolution of the human mind", Genetic, Social & General Psychology Monographs, 123(2), 133.

[37] Bower, G. H. (1981) "Mood and memory", American Psychologist, 36(2), 129-148.

[38] Murray, B. (2003) "What makes mental time travel possible?", Monitor on Psychology, 34(9), 62.

[39] Tulving, E. (2002) "Chronesthesia: Conscious Awareness of Subjective Time", Oxford, Oxford University Press.

[40] Ingham, M. (2005) "Afterimages: Photographs as an external autobiographical memory System and a contemporary art practice (Ph.D. Dissertation Thesis)", Goldsmiths College, London.

[41]Murray, B. (2003) "What makes mental time travel possible?" Monitor on Psychology, 34(9), 62.

[42] Tulving, E. (2002) "Chronesthesia: Conscious Awareness of Subjective Time", Oxford, Oxford University Press.

[43] Tulving, E. (1993) "What Is Episodic Memory?", Current Directions in Psychological Science, Vol 2, Issue 3, 67–70.

[44] Saint-Exupery, A. (1943), "The little prince", New York, Brace & World.

[45] Aristotle, (1936) "On the Soul (De Anima) with W. S. Hett Translation" Volume 8, London, Loeb Classical Library.

[46] Hallock, (2003) "Color Preferences Based on Gender As a New Approach In Marketing", Advanced Social Humanities and Management 2(1), 35-44.

[47] Statista (2018), "Number of Mobile (cellular) Subscriptions Worldwide from 1993 to 2017", goo.gl/2Nk3uz.

[48] Holbrook, M. B.; Hirschman, E. C. (1982), "The Experiential Aspects of Consumption: Consumer Fantasies, Feelings, and Fun," Journal of Con-

sumer Research, Vol.9, p. 132–140.

[49] Apostle, H. G. (1975), "Aristotle's Nicomachean Ethics", The Peripatetic Press.

[50] Perloff, J., M. (2012), "Microeconomics", p. 278, Pearson Education, Boston.

[51] Strohmetz, D., B.; Rind, B.; Fisher, R.; Lynn, M. (2002), Sweetening the Till: The Use of Candy to Increase Restaurant Tipping", Journal of Applied Social Psychology, Vol.32(2), pp. 300-309.

[52] Rind, B.; Strohmetz, D., B. (1999), "Effect on Restaurant Tipping of a Helpful Message Written on the Back of Customers' Checks", Journal of Applied Social Psychology, Vol.29(1), pp. 139-144.

[53] Seiter, J. S. (2007), "Ingratiation and Gratuity: The Effect of Complimenting Customers on Tipping Behavior in Restaurants", Journal of Applied Social Psychology, 37(3), 478–485.

Chapter 3: Facets of Customer Experience

[1] Brakus, J. J.; Schmitt, D. H., Zarantonello, L.. (2009), "Brand Experience: What Is It? How Is It Measured? Does It Affect Loyalty?" Journal of Marketing, 73 (3), 52-68.

[2] Schmitt, B. H., (2003), "Customer Experience Management", Hoboken, Wiley and Sons.

[3] MacDonald, J. (2008) "You think your credit smells? Cards with aromas issued", September 22, goo.gl/tKyyvD.

[4] Christensen, W. (2012) "Torches of Freedom: Women and Smoking Propaganda", February 27, goo.gl/SdHTLu.

[5] Adage (1999) "The Marlboro Man", March 29, goo.gl/tGE6wm.

[6] Seth, R. (2010) "Four Flavored Butter Spoon", Yanko Design, October 29, goo.gl/vGfTYn.

[7] Horatiu Boeriu, H. (2014) "How the Perfect Car Door Sound Is Made For BMW", December 22, goo.gl/5tr7LW.

[8] Cya (2018) "These soap bar shaped game controllers are ridiculously realistic and I want them all", goo.gl/F3QtbK.

[9] Vitaly Air (2018), "Bottling Lake Louise air", goo.gl/rb1kFU.

[10] Vitaly Air (2018) "Now this is just crazy. Flavoured oxygen?", goo.gl/CygQBs.

[11] McCarthy, E. J. (1960) "Basic marketing: A managerial approach", Homewood, Irwin.

[12] Bitner, M.J.; Booms, B.H. (1981) "Marketing Strategies and Organization Structure for Service Firms. In Donnelly JH, George WR. (Eds) Marketing of Services", Conference Proceedings: American Marketing Association, Chicago, IL, 47- 52.

[13] Eisert, P.; Rurainsky, J.; Fechteler, P. (2007) "Virtual Mirror: Real-Time Tracking of Shoes in Augmented Reality Environments", International Conference on Image Processing, Proceedings, 2, 557 - 560.

[14] Rodriguez, Y. (2015), "Tesco Virtual shop for South Korea", November 30, goo.gl/cy9Co6.

[15] (2012) "Emart: Shadow QR Code", April 3, goo.gl/vPxteq.

[16] Amazon (2016) "Introducing Amazon Go and the world's most advanced shopping technology", December 5, goo.gl/mmt6kH.

[17] Creative Business Futures (2015) "Management by Inspiration - Seattle's World-Famous Pike Place Fish Market", June 2, goo.gl/ZEGFKL.

[18] Shedroff, N. (2001) "Experience Design I", Indianapolis, New Riders.

[19] Garrett, J.J. (2003) "The Elements of User Experience. User-Centered Design for the Web", Aiga and Pearson, New York.

[20] Davis, F. D. (1989), "Perceived Usefulness, Perceived Ease of Use, and User Acceptance of Information Technology", MIS Quarterly, Vol. 13 (3): 319–340.

[21] Bird, M. (2015) "A stock exchange-themed bar is opening in the City of London — with prices that dip and surge with demand", June 12, Business Insider UK.

[22] Norum, B. (2015) "Stock Exchange theme bar with fluctuating drinks prices is coming to the City", Go London, June 12, goo.gl/E2VTsa.

[23] Bird, M. (2015) "A stock exchange-themed bar is opening in the City of London — with prices that dip and surge with demand", June 12, Business Insider UK.

[24] Amazon (2016), "Amazon Prime Air's First Customer Delivery", December 14, goo.gl/QBwzpj.

[25] Amazon (2015), "Amazon Prime Air", November 29, goo.gl/RX2Q8E.

[26] Wingfield, N.; Scott, M., (2016), "In Major Step for Drone Delivery, Amazon Flies Package to Customer in England", December 14, New York

Times.

[27] The Planet D (2016), "Teppanyaki Show with Chef Johnny on Grand Cayman", September 15, goo.gl/rRaAkC.

[28] Lin, D. (2009), "Hangerpak", April 27, goo.gl/s2tpGX.

[29] Tamer, M. (1997), "Önce Hüpletip Sonra Gümletelim mi?, Milliyet, August 5.

[30] Nalewajek, M. & Macek, R., (2012), "Product package second life: Exploratory research of secondary use of product package", Management Knowledge and Learning International Conference Proceedings, 731-739).

[31] Seo, D.; Lévy, J. (2011), "Upcycling: Create beautiful things with the stuff you already have", Philadelphia, Running Press.

Chapter 4: The Customer Experience Management Model

[1] Tavşan, A. N. (2017). "Customer Experience and its Consequences on Attitudinal and Behavioral Loyalty", İstanbul : Yeditepe University.

[2] Angga Pandu, W. (2017), "Role of Experience in Customer Self-Congruity to Maintaining Loyalty: A Study on Fashion Store", Entrepreneurial Business and Economics Review, 5 (3), 189-198.

[3] Gurski, D. (2014), "Customer Experiences Affect Customer Loyalty: An Empirical Investigation of the Starbucks Experience Using Structural Equation Modelling", Hamburg, Anchor.

[4] Tavşan, A. N. (2017). "Customer Experience and its Consequences on Attitudinal and Behavioral Loyalty", İstanbul : Yeditepe University.

[5] Ibid.

[6] Spielberger, C. D. (1966), "Anxiety and Behavior" New York: Academic Press.

[7] Ibid.

Chapter 5: Experiential Research

[1] Vaillancourt, R. (2009), "I Hear and I Forget, I See and I Remember, I Do and I Understand", The Canadian Journal of Hospital Pharmacy, 62(4), 272–273.

[2] Poynter, J. (2002) Mystery Shopping: Get Paid to Shop, Leromi Publishing, Denver.

[3] Wagoner, B. (2010), "Symbolic transformation: The mind in movement

through culture and society", London, Routledge.

[4] Carr, H. A. (1931), "The laws of association. Psychological Review", 38(3), 212-228.

[5] Heraclitus; Robinson, T. M. (1991), "Heraclitus: Fragments: a text and translation with a commentary", Toronto, University of Toronto Press.

[6] Boer, K. (2010), "On Hegel: The sway of the negative", Basingstoke: Palgrave Macmillan.

[7] Buckingham, H. W.; Finger, S. (1997), "David Hartley's Psychobiological Associationism and the Legacy of Aristotle", Journal Of The History Of The Neurosciences, 6(1), 21-37.

[8] Kallich, M. (1945), "Association of ideas and critical theory: Hobbes, Locke, and Addison", Elh, 12290-315.

[9] Valdes-Dapena, P. (2016), "Volvo promises deathproof cars by 2020", January 21, goo.gl/w2YSoM.

[10] Obias, R. (2016), "12 Discontinued Products From Coca-Cola and Pepsi", February 11, goo.gl/rHmL3N.

[11] Morse, J. M.; Barrett, M.; Mayan, M.; Olson, K.; Spiers, J. (2002), "Verification Strategies for Establishing Reliability and Validity in Qualitative Research", International Journal of Qualitative Methods, 1(2), 13-22.

[12] Stamp, J. (2013), "The Fisher Space Pen Boldly Writes Where No Man Has Written Before", January 11, goo.gl/6wpUcH.

Chapter 6: Customer Experience Journey Mapping

[1] Lecinski, J. (2014), "ZMOT: Why It Matters Now More Than Ever", August, goo.gl/9xkx7v.

[2] Revella, A. (2015), "Buyer personas: How to gain insight into your customer's expectations, align your marketing strategies, and win more business", New Jersey, Wiley.

[3] Ibid.

[4] Whitehorn, M. (2006), "The parable of the beer and diapers", August 15, goo.gl/iT7eAX.

[5] Sullon, N. (2002), "Behind the 'beer and diapers' data mining legend", July 31, goo.gl/WMVXSh.

Chapter 7: Experiential Segmentation and Targeting

[1] Smith, W. R. (1956), "Product differentiation and market segmentation as alternative marketing Strategies.", Journal of Marketing, 21, (1), 3-8.

[2] Rubinstein, S. (2016), "Lessons Ad Agencies Can Learn From The 'Mad Men' Era", August 8, goo.gl/L96Ky8.

[3] Esquire, (n.a.), "Lucky Tiger Gets the Gals", September, goo.gl/5DU1Xz.

[4] Yankelovich, D. (1964), "New criteria for market segmentation", Harvard Business Review, March, 83-90.

[5] Ziff, R. (1971), "Psychographics for market segmentation", Journal of Advertising Research, 11(2), 3-9.

[6] Demby, E. (1974), "Psychographics and from whence it came", Life Style and Psychographics, Vol. 9-30. Chicago, American Marketing Association.

[7] Mitchell, A. (1978), "Consumer values, a typology", Menlo Park, SRI International.

[8] Yankelovich, D.; Meer, D. (2006), "Rediscovering Market Segmentation", Harvard Business Review, 84(2), 122-131.

[9] Ibid.

[10] Comte, A. (1957), "A general view of positivism", New York, R. Speller.

[11] Kaku, K. (1975), "Increased induced abortion rate in 1966, an aspect of a Japanese folk superstition", Annals Of Human Biology, 2(2), 111.

[12] Gladwell, M.(2011), "Outliers, The Story Of Success", New York, Back Bay Books.

Chapter 8: Experiential Positioning

[1] Reeves, R. (1961), "Reality in advertising", New York, Knopf.

[2] Ogilvy, D. (1963), "Confessions of an Advertising Man", New York, Atheneum.

[3] Trout, J. (2012), "Positioning Myopia", Marketing News, 46(3), 34.

[4] Trout, J.; Ries, A. (1972), "Positioning era cometh", Advertising Age, 4335.

[5] Ries, A.; Trout, J. (1986), "Positioning: The Battle for Your Mind", New York, McGraw-Hill.

[6] Trout, J. (2012), "Positioning Myopia.", Marketing News, 46(3), .34.

[7] Miller, G. (1956), "The magical number seven, plus or minus two: some limits on our capacity for processing information", The Psychological Review, 63, 81-97.

Chapter 9: Designing Experiences

[1] Consumer Reports (2016), "Guide to Car Safety Features: These features can help make driving safer", June, goo.gl/xMxYLn.

[2] Ibid.

[3] Frohlich, T. C. (2014), "The 10 worst product fails of all time", March 3, goo.gl/mvFJXw.

Chapter 10: Which Experiential Sources Should be Relied On?

[1] Herzberg, F.; Mausner, B.; Snyderman, B. B. (1959), "The Motivation to Work", New York, John Wiley & Sons.

[2] Gutman, J. (1981), "A means-end model for facilitating analysis of product markets based on consumer judgement", Advances in Consumer Research, 8, 116-121.

[3] Gutman, J. (1982), "A means-end-chain model based on consumer categorization processes", Journal of Marketing, 46(2), 60-72.

[4] Csikszentmihalyi, M. (1991), "Flow: The psychology of Optimal Experiences", New York, Harper & Row Publishers.

[5] Wong, M. M.; Csikszentmihalyi, M. (1991), "Motivation and academic achievement: The effects of personality traits and the duality of experience", Journal of Personality, 59, 539–574.

[6] Petty, R.E.; Cacioppo, J.T. (1986), "The Elaboration Likelihood Model of Persuasion", Communication and Persuasion, Springer Series in Social Psychology, New York, Springer.

[7] Lewin, K. (1935), "A Dynamic Theory of Personality", New York, McGraw-Hill.

[8] Adams, J.S. (1963), "Towards an Understanding of Inequality", Journal of Abnormal and Normal Social Psychology, (67), 422-436.

[9] Adams, J. S. (1965), "Inequality in Social Exchange in Advances in Experimental Psychology, L. Berkowitz (ed.)", Academic Press, New York, 267-299.

[10] Homans, G.C. (1961), "Social Behavior: Its Elementary Forms", New York, Harcourt.

[11] Heider, F. (1958), "The Psychology of Interpersonal Relations", New York, John Wiley & Sons.

[12] Vroom, V. (1964), "Work and motivation", New York, Wiley.

[13] Thorndike, E.L. (1927), "The Law of Effect", The American Journal of Psychology, 39, 212-222.

[14] Thorndike, E. L., (1921), "Educated psychology: The psychology of learning", New York: Teachers College, Columbia University.

[15] Vroom, V. (1964), "Work and motivation", New York, Wiley.

[16] Ibid.

[17] Kahneman, D.; Tversky, A. (1979), "Prospect theory: An analysis of decision under risk", Econometrica, 47, 263–291.

[18] Gruber, W. H.; Niles, J. S. (1972), "Put Innovation in the Organization Structure", California Management Review, 14(4), 29-35.

[19] Rokeach, M.; Regan, J. F. (1980), "Role of values in the counseling situation", Personnel & Guidance Journal, 58, 576-582.

[20] Murphy, P. E. ; Staples, W.A. (1979), "A Modernized Family Life Cycle", Journal of Consumer Research, 6(1) 12–22.

Chapter 11: Experiential Marketing Communications

[1] Duncan, T.; Caywood, C. (1996), "The concept, process, and evolution of integrated marketing communication", Integrated communication: Synergy of persuasive voices, 13-34.

[2] Belch, G. E.; Belch, M. A.; Kerr, G. F.; Powell, I. (2014), "Advertising: An integrated marketing communication perspective", New York, McGraw-Hill Education.

[3] Belch, G. E.; Belch, M. A. (2004), "Advertising and promotion: An integrated marketing communications perspective", Boston, McGraw-Hill.

Chapter 12: Measuring Customer Experience

[1] Jafari, S. M.; Forouzandeh, M.; Ghazvini, S. A.; Safahani, N.; Moslehi, M. (2016), "The impact of online brand experience on customer's satisfaction and loyalty", International Business Management, 10 (5), 599-603.

[2] Ganesan, S. (1994), "Determinants of long-term orientation in buyer-seller relationships", Journal of Marketing, 58, 1-19.

[3] Reynolds, K.E.; Arnold, M. (2000), "Customer Loyalty to the Salesperson and the Store: Examining Relationship Customers in an Upscale Retail Context", Journal of Personal Selling & Sales Management, 20 (2), 89-98.

[4] Reynolds, K.E., Beatty, S.E. (1999). Customer benefits and company consequences of customer-salesperson relationships in retailing. Journal of Retailing, 75(1), 11–32.

[5] Fitzell, P. (1998), "The Explosive Growth of Private Labels in North America", New York, Global Books.

[6] Zeithaml, V. A.; Berry, L. L.; Parasuraman, A. (1996), "The behavioral consequences of service quality", Journal of Marketing, 60 (2), 31-46.

[7] Odin, Y.; Odin, N.; Valette-Florence, P. (2001), "Conceptual and operational aspects of brand loyalty: An empirical investigation", Journal of Business Research, 53(2), 75-84.

[8] Kim, J.; Morris, J.D.; Swait, J. (2013), "Antecedents of True Brand Loyalty", Journal of Advertising, 37 (2), 99-117.

[9] Santouridis, I.; Trivellas, P. (2010), "Investigating the impact of service quality and customer satisfaction on customer loyalty in mobile telephony in Greece", The Total Quality Management Journal, 22(3), 330-343.

[10] Kumar, V.; Reinartz, W.J. (2006), "Customer relationship management" Hoboken, Wiley.

[11] Freud, S.; Strachey, J. (1962), "The ego and the id", New York, Norton.

[12] Huskinson, L. (2004), "Nietzsche and Jung: The whole self in the union of opposites", New York, Routledge.

[13] Rummel, R. J. (1975), "Understanding Conflict and War", Beverly Hills, Sage.

[14] Ajzen, I. (1991), "The theory of planned behavior", Organizational Behavior and Human Decision Processes, 50(2), 179-211.

[15] Blackmore, J. T. (1978), "Three Autobiographical Manuscripts by Ernst Mach" Annals of Science, 35(4), 401–419.

[16] Keiningham, T. L.; Cooil, B.; Andreassen, T. W.; Aksoy, L. (2007), "A Longitudinal Examination of Net Promoter and Firm Revenue Growth", Journal of Marketing, 71(3), 39-51.